OXFORD MONOGRAPHS IN
INTERNATIONAL LAW

General Editor: Professor Ian Brownlie QC, DCL, FBA
Chichele Professor of Public International Law in the University of Oxford and Fellow of All Souls College, Oxford.

JUDICIAL REMEDIES IN INTERNATIONAL LAW

OXFORD MONOGRAPHS IN INTERNATIONAL LAW

This new series of monographs will publish important and original pieces of research on all aspects of public international law. Topics which will be given particular prominence are those which, while of interest to the academic lawyer, also have important bearing on issues which touch the actual conduct of international relations. None the less the series is intended to be wide in scope and thus will include the history and philosophical foundations of international law.

ALSO IN THIS SERIES

The Juridical Bay
GAYL WESTERMAN

The Exclusive Economic Zone
DAVID ATTARD

State Responsibility and the Marine Environment
BRIAN D. SMITH

The Legality of Non-Forcible Countermeasures in International Law
OMER ELAGAB

The Shatt-al-Arab Boundary Question
A Legal Re-Appraisal
KAIYAN KAIKOBAO

Relevant Circumstances and Maritime Delimitation
MALCOLM D. EVANS

JUDICIAL REMEDIES IN INTERNATIONAL LAW

CHRISTINE D. GRAY

CLARENDON PRESS · OXFORD
1990

Oxford University Press, Walton Street, Oxford OX2 6DP
Oxford New York Toronto
Delhi Bombay Calcutta Madras Karachi
Petaling Jaya Singapore Hong Kong Tokyo
Nairobi Dar es Salaam Cape Town
Melbourne Auckland
and associated companies in
Berlin Ibadan

Oxford is a trade mark of Oxford University Press

Published in the United States
by Oxford University Press, New York

First issued as a paperback (with revisions) 1990

British Library Cataloguing in Publication Data
Gray, Christine D.
Judicial remedies in international law.—
(Oxford monographs in international law).
1. Remedies (Law) 2. International law
I. Title
341.7'8 K2315
ISBN 0-19-825432-6

Library of Congress Cataloging in Publication Data
Gray, Christine D.
Judicial remedies in international law.
(Oxford monographs in international Law)
Bibliography: p
Includes index.
1. International courts. 2. Remedies (Law)
3. Arbitration, International. 4. Arbitration and award, International. I. Title. II. Series
JX1990.A2G73 1987 341.5'52 87-5816
ISBN 0-19-825432-6

Printed and bound in
Great Britain by Biddles Ltd,
Guildford and King's Lynn

Editor's Preface

THIS book is impressive in combining the characteristics of boldness of theme, rigour of treatment of the material, and a mature style. Dr. Gray has produced a classical study of problems which are persistent in the international system and which, whilst having a highly practical nature, relate to important questions affecting the essence of the judicial function in international relations. International lawyers always pay tribute to the principle of judicial settlement of disputes, but in recent times most writers have tended to avoid touching on the particular questions falling under the fairly loose headings of the 'judicial function' or 'State responsibility'. The present study subjects many of these particular questions to careful examination and can be expected to occupy a prominent place in the literature.

All Souls College,
Oxford
7th January 1987

IAN BROWNLIE

Acknowledgements

THE argument of the present monograph was originally formulated in a Ph.D. thesis submitted at Cambridge University in 1980. I thank there the governing body of Selwyn College, which elected me to its fellowship, and the staff of the Squire Law Library. My supervisor was the late Professor Clive Parry, whose kind and expert aid I recall with much gratitude.

At Oxford my thanks are due to St Hilda's College, the staff of the Law Library, and the typists of the Faculty of Law. Professor Ian Brownlie QC, of All Souls College, encouraged me to develop the thesis into a book, and I am indebted to him for his authoritative comments.

C.D.G.

St Hilda's College, Oxford
Michaelmas Term, 1986

Contents

Abbreviations

ACHR	American Convention on Human Rights
AD	*Annual Digest of Public International Law Cases*
AFDI	*Annuaire Français de droit international*
AIDI	*Annuaire de l'Institut de Droit International*
AJ	*American Journal of International Law*
AJCL	*American Journal of Comparative Law*
ASIL	*Proceedings of the American Society of International Law*
BYBIL	*British Yearbook of International Law*
CLJ	*Cambridge Law Journal*
CLP	*Current Legal Problems*
CMLR	Common Market Law Reports
CML Rev.	*Common Market Law Review*
Col. JTL	*Columbia Journal of Transnational Law*
Col. LR	*Columbia Law Review*
ECHR	European Convention on Human Rights
ELR	*European Law Review*
GYBIL	*German Yearbook of International Law*
Harvard LR	*Harvard Law Review*
HR	*Recueil des cours—académie de droit international*
ICJ	International Court of Justice
ICLQ	*International and Comparative Law Quarterly*
IECL	*International Encyclopaedia of Comparative Law*
ILC	International Law Commission
ILM	International Legal Materials
ILR	International Law Reports
Int. Lawyer	*International Lawyer*
Int. Rel.	International Relations
Iran–US CTR	Iran–United States Claims Tribunal Reports
Jap. AIL	*Japanese Annual of International Law*
JMLC	*Journal of Maritime Law and Commerce*
J World TL	*Journal of World Trade Law*
La Fontaine	H. La Fontaine, *Pasicrisie internationale* (Berne, 1902)
Lapradelle and Politis	A. de la Pradelle and N. Politis, *Recueil des arbitrages internationaux* (Paris, 1954–7)
LNTS	League of Nations Treaty Series
Moore	J. B. Moore, *History and Digest of the International Arbitrations to which the United States has been a party* (Washington, 1898)
Moore *Int. Adj.*	J. B. Moore, *International Adjudications Ancient and Modern* (NY, 1929–33)

NYJILP	*New York University Journal of International Law and Politics*
Oregon LR	*Oregon Law Review*
Parry	The Consolidated Treaty Series, ed. C. Parry
PCIJ	Permanent Court of International Justice
Rev. belge DI	*Revue belge de droit international*
Rev. hell. DI	*Revue hellénique de droit international*
RGDIP	*Revue générale de droit international public*
RIAA	Reports of International Arbitral Awards
TAM	Tribunaux arbitraux mixtes
Texas ILJ	*Texas International Law Journal*
UNTS	United Nations Treaty Series
US For. Rel.	Foreign Relations of the United States
Virg. JIL	*Virginia Journal of International Law*
Virg. LR	*Virginia Law Review*
Whiteman	M. M. Whiteman, *Damages in International Law* (Washington 1937, 43)
Whiteman *Digest*	M. M. Whiteman, *Digest of International Law* (Washington, 1963–73)
Yale LJ	*Yale Law Journal*

Table of Cases

PERMANENT COURT OF INTERNATIONAL JUSTICE AND INTERNATIONAL COURT OF JUSTICE

INTERNATIONAL ARBITRAL CASES

EUROPEAN COURT OF JUSTICE

EUROPEAN COURT OF HUMAN RIGHTS

INTERNATIONAL ADMINISTRATIVE TRIBUNALS

Introduction

THE question of judicial remedies has generally been regarded as peripheral to the main study of international law; attention has been centred on the substantive rules with little consideration of the consequences of their violation in general or judicial remedies in particular.[1] This reflects the lack of any compulsory jurisdiction in the international legal system, the low incidence of modern judicial and arbitral settlement, the decentralized nature of the international legal system, and the resulting predominant role of self-help.[2]

The political limitations on the role of judicial settlement of disputes in international relations have been much discussed. Writers argue against over-optimism as regards the results to be expected from judicial settlement,[3] they discuss the reasons why states do not make greater use of this means of settling disputes,[4] they consider the conditions necessary for judicial settlement and the types of dispute most suitable for this.[5] Much less attention has been paid to the question of the nature and role of judicial remedies in international law. Obviously the questions of how judicial remedies have been used in the past and may be used in the future and of the inherent limits on their role in international law are part of the larger question of the role of judicial settlement, but they have not yet received the separate consideration they deserve. The possible judicial remedies and the appropriateness of their award in various different types of disputes and for different types of injury should influence any argument for or against a greater use of judicial settlement of disputes in international law and, more immediately, any consideration of what results may be expected from current resort to this method of settlement.

The recent examination by the International Law Commission of the highly controversial topics international liability for injurious consequences arising out of acts not prohibited by international law[6] and international criminal responsibility[7] demands consideration of the role, if any, envisaged for judicial remedies in these new areas and of the relationship between judicial remedies for international crimes and for lawful acts and judicial remedies in the traditional areas of state responsibility. But the International Law Commission has not been much concerned with judicial remedies either in its work on liability for injurious consequences of lawful acts or in its protracted struggles with state responsibility.[8] As regards the latter there is an interesting contrast between the approach of textbooks and that of the Commission: the former generally give a perhaps distorting emphasis to judicial remedies in that when dealing with the consequences of state responsibility they concentrate, often exclusively, on judicial remedies, whereas the latter has corrected (even perhaps over-corrected) this emphasis, for it has been more occupied with the consequences of breaches of international law than with remedies in general and judicial remedies in particular.

The International Law Commission has been working on State Responsibility for over thirty years. Its first attempt at codification with García-Amador as Special Rapporteur[9] failed largely as a result of disagreements on the substantive law on treatment of aliens. In response to this the Commission radically altered its approach in its second attempt with Ago as Special Rapporteur.[10] It decided not to restrict its work to state responsibility for injury to aliens but to deal with the whole of state responsibility. But it would not attempt to cover all the substantive rules breach of which would lead to state responsibility. Rather it would try to separate general principles of state responsibility from the particular substantive rules.[11] The first part of its draft, on the origin of responsibility,[12] is rather unimpressive; perhaps it was inevitable that an attempt to set out the general principles of liability under international law would result in painstaking statements of long accepted principles, for the most part uncontroversial[13] and unilluminating. As far as remedies are concerned, Article 17 of Part I confirms the irrelevance of the origin of the international obligations breached. Remedies, including judicial remedies, are not affected by the origin, whether customary, conventional, or other, of that obligation, although the content of a particular substantive rule may affect the regime of responsibility.[14] And the Commission in its discussions accepts another traditional rule, that damage is not necessary for there to be a breach of international law. But it does not at this stage, nor even when it later considers Part II of its draft on the Content, Forms and Degree of responsibility, make clear the implications of this as far as remedies are concerned.[15] For the Commission has now produced its first draft of Part II of its work on state responsibility. Here, as with Part I, the main cause for concern is whether the draft articles are so abstract and general as to be incapable of providing any real guidance to states. It remains to be seen whether Part III on Implementation can possibly transform the whole draft.

In its work on Part II on the Content, Forms, and Degree of state responsibility the Commission has not been much concerned with judicial remedies. Riphagen, the Special Rapporteur for Part II, began his task by saying that his aim was not only to state the rights and responsibilities of states, but to establish guidelines for international courts and tribunals.[16] But his subsequent consideration of the special role of courts and tribunals led him to reject the possibility of relying on their decisions as a source of general rules on the consequences of state responsibility.[17] Because the powers of tribunals vary according to their constituent instruments, and they are involved in a special task rather than in the application of general rules, because they are limited by their judicial function, because they may be deciding the case a long time after the alleged breach, and in judicial reparation the obligation to stop a breach may be submerged, because they generally do not pronounce on the most serious wrongs and have been mainly concerned with injury to aliens, and because they are not always explicit about the way the amount of damages is assessed—for all these reasons the Special Rapporteur concludes,

> In short for the purposes of drafting articles dealing with the content, forms and degree of international responsibility in general and independent of the existence of a machinery for implementation, they [sc. judicial and arbitral decisions] are of limited value.[18]

And, conversely, it follows that the general rules evolved by the Special Rapporteur and the Commission will have only limited significance for courts and tribunals; the Commission has not taken this opportunity to regulate judicial remedies.

This is in fact an area of considerable uncertainty. This book will examine the decisions of international arbitral tribunals, the Permanent Court of International Justice and its successor, human rights courts, administrative tribunals, and international commercial tribunals; it will consider the approach of these tribunals to the question of judicial remedies, the remedies they employ, and the common rules, if any, that they evolve.

NOTES

1. On the consequences of a breach of international law see F. A. Mann (1976–7) *BYBIL* 1; C. Oliver in R. B. Lillich (ed.), *International Law of State Responsibility for Injury to Aliens* (1983), at 61; B. Graefath (1984) 2 *HR* 9. There are detailed studies of judicial remedies in international arbitral practice (see works listed in Ch. 1 n. 2), and brief discussions of judicial remedies by Mann (op. cit. above) and I. Brownlie (*System of the Law of Nations: State Responsibility*, Part I (1983)). See also the American Law Institute Restatement of the Law—Foreign Relations Law of the United States (revised) Tentative Draft no. 5 (1984), at §901, 902.
2. The effect of all these factors is in practice modified by the functioning of international organizations.
3. See, for example, C. de Visscher, *Theory and Reality in Public International Law* (1957), iv. 327; H. Lauterpacht, *The Development of International Law by the International Court* (1958), 3; F. S. Northedge and M. D. Donelan, *International Disputes: The Political Aspects* (1971).
4. Although it is advisable to bear in mind the warning of R. Y. Jennings in Max Planck Institute for Comparative Public and International Law, *The Judicial Settlement of International Disputes* (1974), at 35, that as long as few

governments in practice resort to the International Court almost any suggested explanation for this will seem to be borne out by the facts.

5. See, for example, M. Katz, *The Relevance of International Adjudication* (1968); I. Brownlie (1967) *BYBIL* 123; R. Higgins in J. E. S. Fawcett and R. Higgins (eds.), *International Organization* (1974), 37; L. Fuller in R. A. Falk and S. H. Mendlovitz (eds.), *The Strategy of World Order* (1966), iii. 440.
6. *ILC Yearbook* from 1980.
7. *ILC Yearbook* from 1976.
8. *ILC Yearbook* from 1956.
9. Ibid.
10. *ILC Yearbook* from 1969. See particularly 1973 *ILC Yearbook*, Vol. i. 5.
11. See C. Gray (1985) *BYBIL* 25.
12. 1980 *ILC Yearbook*, Vol. ii, Part II, 30.
13. Apart from its proposals on international criminal responsibility, loc. cit. in n. 7. See discussion by Q. Wright (1974–5) *Virg. JIL* 561; P. M. Dupuy (1980) *RGDIP* 449; I. Brownlie, op. cit. in n. 1, at 32.
14. According to draft Article 3 of Part II.
15. See 1971 *ILC Yearbook*, Vol. ii, Part I, 3rd Report of the Special Rapporteur, 199.
16. 1981 *ILC Yearbook*, Vol. i. 126.
17. 1981 *ILC Yearbook*, Vol. ii, Part I, 83–4, 92–3; 1981 *ILC Yearbook*, i. 126; and see Reuter, ibid., at 126, Ushakov at 134.
18. 1981 *ILC Yearbook*, Vol. ii, Part I, 92.

I

International Arbitral Practice

THE award of judicial remedies goes back to the start of modern arbitral practice and the Jay Treaty of 1794.[1] Then for the first time a mixed commission was established and a judicial element was introduced into arbitration through the involvement of an independent umpire. A study of the large arbitral practice that followed is still vital for a proper understanding of judicial remedies and their award by more recent tribunals. Since there are already long and detailed surveys of the large mass of arbitral practice[2] this chapter is intended to provide a historical background to the rest of the book, a brief description that is nevertheless full enough to show clearly the problems involved in any attempt to derive coherent rules on judicial remedies from arbitral practice.

The approach of the tribunal established under Article 7 of the Jay Treaty to settle claims arising from violations of the laws of neutrality is in certain ways typical of what was to follow. Although the opinions of Pinkney in the *Betsey*[3] and Gore in the *Neptune*[4] give more detailed consideration to the question of assessment of damages than many later decisions, its other awards of damages are brief and not fully reasoned. There is disagreement between arbitrators over the proper method of assessing lost profits.[5] Most significantly the tribunal apparently assumed that, just as there were substantive rules of international law (or, strictly, of the law of nations) on the question of neutrality, so were there also rules on judicial remedies. Pinkney and Gore referred to Grotius, Pufendorf and Vattel to justify the award of compensation for lost profits. This invocation of the authority of these early writers on international law was not followed by later tribunals, but arbitral tribunals since 1794 have assumed without question that international law governs judicial remedies and that it allows remedies analogous to those of municipal law. They do not discuss the source of the rules they apply on the availability of remedies and the assessment of damages.[6]

There is general agreement among writers that customary international law could not in 1794 and cannot today provide 'any principles, criteria or methods for determining a priori how reparation is to be made for the injury caused by a wrongful act or omission'.[7] First, because the availability of remedies such as *restitutio in integrum* and specific performance in state practice depends on the agreement of the states concerned; this cannot determine the scope of the jurisdiction of an arbitral tribunal to award these remedies. Second, as far as methods of assessing damages are concerned, it is clear from Whiteman's collection of diplomatic practice that there are no uniform rules governing reparations. The determination of the consequences of a breach of international law is left initially to the discretion of the injured state; there are many examples of claims completely out of proportion with the injury suffered being met and also of similar breaches of international law being followed by different means and amounts of reparation. The result may well depend not so much on the extent of the injury suffered but rather on various political considerations including the relative power of the two states.[8] Nor did tribunals refer to state practice for guidance on the methods of assessing damages except in the most general terms.

Nor did international arbitral tribunals turn in any systematic or considered way to particular systems of municipal law or to general principles of law. In those exceptional cases where remedies other than damages or declaratory judgments were awarded this was done without any mention of their availability and use in municipal legal systems.[9] The borrowing of remedies from municipal law was carried out unquestioningly by tribunals and has not been much questioned since by writers. In their awards of damages tribunals clearly applied techniques of assessment similar to those of municipal courts. This is a natural result of the fact that in cases of injuries to foreign nationals the interests they were evaluating and the problems they encountered were the same. Certain writers have been encouraged by this to speak of general principles of municipal law as a source used,[10] or to be used,[11] by international tribunals; others are more sceptical.[12]

This scepticism seems justified. In international arbitral practice there are few express references, even in general terms, to general principles of law. References to particular legal systems are even less common and there is very little detailed consideration of specific municipal law rules.

Such references are most common on questions of interest. In the *Russian Indemnity* case[13] the Permanent Court of Arbitration said,

> All the private legislation of the states forming the European concert admits, as did formerly the Roman law, the obligation to pay at least interest for delayed payments as legal indemnity when it is a question of the non-fulfilment of an obligation consisting in the payment of a sum of money fixed by convention, clear and exigible, such interest to be paid at least from the date of the demand made upon the debtor in due form of law.

But this reasoning was rejected in the *Georges Pinson* case,[14] where it was held that the rules of civil law governing interest on private pecuniary debts had no direct relevance to the question of interest under international law, since the rules regarding the latter had developed independently and in entirely different spheres from those prevailing with reference to moratory interest in private law. Both these cases refer in general terms to 'civil law' and 'private legislation'. However, in some cases specific rules of particular legal systems are referred to in order to fix the rate of interest appropriate. For example, in the *Delagoa Bay Railway Company* case,[15] the *Orinoco Steamship Company* case,[16] and the *Religious Properties* case[17] the rate chosen was that of the responsible state.

Tribunals have also referred to municipal law to justify the award of lost profits. This can be seen in the *Cape Horn Pigeon*,[18] where the tribunal said,

> Considering that the general principles of civil law, according to which the damages should include an indemnity not only for the loss suffered but also for the profit of which one has been deprived, is equally applicable to international litigation.

Similarly in *Delagoa Bay Railway Company* the tribunal referred to Portuguese law, saying that on this question there was nothing in it different from the general principles of the common law of modern nations, to support the award of lost profits. Apart from *Fabiani*,[19] such references by tribunals to municipal law have been brief, no more than a passing reference to Mexican or Guatemalan law in *Baldwin*[20] and *May*,[21] or the simple adoption of municipal law rules on heads of damage[22] or distribution of damage in collision cases.[23]

These cases in which the tribunal refers to municipal law, whether in general or in specific terms, are very much the exception. International arbitral tribunals have not borrowed systematically from municipal law, they have not attempted to develop a coherent theory of the relationship between the rules of international law and those of municipal law on damages or other remedies. When they do refer to municipal law these references are brief. Tribunals do not undertake thorough comparative surveys, nor do they usually discuss their choice of a particular legal system.[24]

Indeed there would in the nineteenth century have been substantial problems, and there are today even greater problems, in any attempt to derive general principles on judicial remedies from municipal law. The danger is that any general principle that can be derived from municipal legal systems may be so general as to be no guide at all; regarded in isolation from those rules that give it substance it may lack all content. It is significant that Bin Cheng in his search for general principles, not borrowed by international law from municipal law but common to both, finds inherent in the concept of responsibility the principle of integral reparation.[25] He goes on to make certain controversial deductions from this principle—and here again we see writers filling in the meaning of full reparation on the basis of their own policy preferences—on the inadmissibility of punitive damages. But he concludes by saying

While the juridical principle of integral reparation is well established and quite simple in conception, its practical application to life may present problems of infinite complexity and international judicial decisions bear witness to a certain amount of flexibility in its application. Conjecture . . . and compromise . . . cannot be entirely excluded.[26]

For the problem of reparation is complex. The basic principle of full reparation that can be derived from the various municipal legal systems—in civil law and communist countries expressed in terms of *damnum emergens* and *lucrum cessans*, in common law countries in terms of putting the claimant in the position he would have been in if there had been no injury to him—represents very little advance on the determination that an obligation to make reparation has arisen. Clearly this basic principle cannot be a practical guide to the assessment of damages, as can be seen from the fact that although all legal systems share this aim, their methods of assessment and the results arrived at vary considerably. Moreover the basic principle is subject to important qualifications and exceptions in every legal system.

This is not the place for a detailed comparative study of municipal law on judicial remedies. The International Encyclopaedia of Comparative Law[27] makes very clear the differences not only of methods of assessment but also of result between the various systems. Thus in Germany under BGB 249 and in the communist countries specific performance is the primary remedy for breach of contract. In France, Italy, and Switzerland the judge has the power to order either damages or specific performance as he thinks appropriate. Specific performance is an exceptional remedy in common law systems. It is an equitable remedy and therefore will only be awarded where this would not lead to injustice and where the common law remedies are inadequate. Similarly in delict, *restitutio in integrum* is the primary remedy in German law, optional in French law, and exceptional in common law systems. But in fact the difference between the results produced by common law and civil law systems is not very great because the restrictions on specific performance and *restitutio in integrum* in the latter ensure that they are rarely allowed where they would not be allowed in common law countries.

On the assessment of damages the differences between municipal systems are not only theoretical. Questions of the date of valuation of property, the role of fault in the assessment of damages, tests to limit the extent of compensation, the treatment of non-pecuniary loss, the evaluation of personal injury, and the compensation of purely economic loss show wide variations between legal systems. The practice of forum shopping is a rational response to this variety. After the Bhopal disaster it was a matter of considerable consequence for the victims whether they would be allowed to claim in India or in the United States, for the amount of damages available to them in the United States could be up to ten times as much as that in India.[28]

So the pursuit of general principles more specific than that of full compensation is beset with difficulties. International arbitral tribunals have not in the past embarked on this enterprise in any rigorous way nor, as will be seen, have more recent tribunals taken this approach to the discovery of rules on judicial remedies. Perhaps a more practical approach would be for the international tribunal to turn not to municipal legal systems in general but rather to a particular legal system for guidance on judicial remedies. Those few tribunals which adopted this approach did so without discussion but they turned to the law of the respondent state, that is, the law that would have been applied in any exhaustion of local remedies.[29] There are, however, certain problems with this approach. First, it might be argued that certain legal systems do not live up to the international standard in their assessment of damages. This brings us back to the problems of the uncertainty of the international standards to be derived from international arbitral practice and of differences between municipal legal systems. In practice this question of municipal remedies being inadequate in their assessment of damages has not generally arisen before international arbitral tribunals in their consideration of the exhaustion of local remedies. And Trindade in his very thorough study of the exhaustion of local remedies refers only very briefly to this question.[30] So the practical advantages of greater certainty and the intuitive fairness of turning to the law of the respondent state might outweigh this problem. Alternatively, another approach—that of taking the rules, if any, common to the claimant and respondent states on the assessment of damages—might avoid this difficulty.

But a more serious objection remains to turning to the law of a particular state or states. This involves the separation of questions of liability, to be governed by international law, from questions of remedies, to be governed by municipal law. Although it is common practice among writers to separate the question of the assessment of damages from the question of liability,[31] even those who advocate this approach admit that such a separation cannot be absolutely clear cut and often breaks down. For example, the measure of damages is often affected by the degree of fault of the tortfeasor, by statutory limits on liability, and by special rules of assessment for the different areas of liability. The distinction between the question of which injuries the defendant should compensate and the question of the extent of compensation is often blurred. Indeed in the event of purely economic loss no such distinction is possible. But in the English conflict of laws rules the latter question is treated as procedural, to be governed by the *lex fori*, and the former as substantive, to be governed by the *lex causae*.[32] This has been strongly criticized by Rabel who argues that the distinction is artificial and not followed by any other system in its conflict rules.[33] He says that the restrictions imposed by the public policy of the forum on the remedies available should be kept to a minimum so that as far as possible the extent of the compensation and the nature of the remedy should be governed by the *lex causae*. For the question of the remedy is not purely procedural. Consideration of the rules of the law of damages in isolation from issues of liability is not simple; the question of damages concerns the extent and measurement of liability.

Thus in international arbitral practice the question of the remedies available and the more common question of the methods of quantification of damage were left to the discretion of the arbitrator. And the immediate impression made by an examination of international arbitral decisions is of a chaos of conflicting decisions. It is notorious that at the 1930 Hague Codification Conference on State Responsibility the subcommittee which considered the question of damages decided that it would be best to leave this for development by the jurisprudence of arbitral tribunals as there had not been a sufficient crystallization of principles to warrant codification.[34]

Perhaps the main reason for this impression of a remarkable collection of conflicting decisions is the fact that international arbitral tribunals rarely referred to, or considered, the decisions of earlier tribunals on the question of remedies in general and the assessment of damages in particular. Of course before the twentieth century the reports of arbitral awards were not often widely available and this helps to explain the tribunals' apparently wilful blindness to what had gone before. This situation improved in the twentieth century and there are occasional examples of references by tribunals to the discussions and decisions of earlier tribunals.[35] But such references remained exceptional and so it seems that Moore is misleading when he says,

> I venture to assert that the decisions of those international tribunals are characterized by about as much consistency, by about as close an application of principles of law and perhaps as marked a tendency on the part of one tribunal to quote the authority of tribunals that preceded it as you will find in the proceedings of ordinary judicial tribunals.[36]

At least as far as judicial remedies are concerned most arbitral tribunals appear to work in isolation. Decisions are supported, if at all, only by reference to 'generally recognized principles', and even such references are exceptional.

Moreover it is not common for the agreement under which a tribunal is set up to contain any specific provision on the question of remedies[37] or any detailed guidance on the assessment of damages. This is true not only of those *compromis* that provide for the settlement of just one or two claims, but also of those establishing a commission to decide a large number of claims. Treaties such as that of 1829 between Brazil and Great Britain,[38] which contains precise rules for the adjustment of claims for indemnities, and the 1923 agreements between Mexico and various European states,[39] which give some guidance on the appropriate measure of damages, are extremely rare. This lack of clear instructions in the agreements setting up the tribunals is compounded by the fact that arbitrators do not generally, or even in the majority of cases, discuss the general principles governing their decisions on the award of damages, neither do they give detailed explanations of their decisions.[40]

Thus for the most part it is possible to draw conclusions only on the basis of the actual awards. It is perhaps not surprising then that those awards based on 'equity' as provided for in the *compromis* do not differ noticeably or consistently from those based on law. There is no norm from which the equitable assessment could deviate, no need for a mitigation of the results of a particular legal rule. Rather the express permission to assess damages on the basis of equity rather than law seems to represent a recognition of the absence of clear rules of law in this area. In the context of awards of interest, Subilia[41] exhaustively catalogues the decisions of international arbitral tribunals according to the nature of the tribunal's jurisdiction, whether it is to decide according to international law, equity, or a combination of the two, and finally concludes that this makes no difference to the decisions reached by the tribunals. Again, the admission of responsibility by a state, so that the only decisions for a tribunal are whether the particular claim is covered by the admission and on the assessment of damages, apparently makes no difference to the rules applied in the calculation of compensation: the standards applied are no different from those in the other cases.

(i) REMEDIES AVAILABLE UNDER INTERNATIONAL LAW

A high proportion of the international arbitral tribunals were established to deal with claims for damages for injury to foreign nationals. Indeed this formed the largest single class of claims. Of the 435 arbitral tribunals between 1794 and 1972 listed by Stuyt,[42] at least 261 were dealing with claims for damages. (45 of these concerned claims arising from wars and a further 36 concerned claims from civil wars.) The remaining tribunals were, almost exclusively, charged with giving their interpretations of international law rather than awarding remedies for its violation. They gave declaratory judgments stating the law. Of these, 85 tribunals handled boundary disputes or questions of title to territory. Remedies other than damages for breaches of international law are rare.

The power of tribunals to award particular remedies depends on the agreements under which they are established, but in general states parties have not made express provision on this. Some arbitral tribunals were expressly given the power to decide on 'claims for pecuniary satisfaction', but many more were authorized simply to settle 'all claims' and not surprisingly they saw nothing to prevent their fulfilling what were obviously the intentions of the parties and making awards of damages.[43] Nor are there jurisdictional problems when the tribunal is asked to interpret a treaty or otherwise declare the state of international law. But in the absence of express provision the power to give other remedies familiar in municipal law—injunctions, specific performance, and *restitutio in integrum*—is less certain. Their availability must depend on the practice of the tribunals themselves and on arguments on the basis of principle. It is the relation between these two that produces controversy, especially over the primacy or availability of *restitutio in integrum* as a remedy in international law. For the award of remedies other than damages by international arbitral tribunals is extremely unusual.

(*a*) *Negative Injunctions*

The *Trail Smelter* arbitration[44] is exceptional in its order of an injunction, but express provision had been made for such an order in the *compromis*. This stated that the tribunal should decide

> (1) Whether damage caused by the Trail Smelter in the State of Washington has occurred since 1 January 1932 and if so what indemnity should be paid therefor.
> (2) In the event of the answer to the first part of the preceding question being in the affirmative, whether the Trail Smelter should be required to refrain from causing damage in the State of Washington in the future and, if so, to what extent?

There is apparently no instance of the award of a negative injunction by an international arbitral tribunal where no such provision was included in the *compromis*. In *El Salvador* v. *Nicaragua*[45] the Central American Court of Justice was asked to issue an order enjoining the defendant state from carrying out its obligations under the Bryan–Chamorro Treaty because these were incompatible with the requirements of a prior treaty made with the claimant state. It appears that the Court did not regard such an order as necessarily beyond its jurisdiction, but refused to give an injunction in this case, since one of the parties to the Bryan–Chamorro Treaty was not subject to the jurisdiction of the Court.

(*b*) *Restitutio in integrum*

There is some uncertainty among writers and tribunals as to the exact scope of this remedy. It has even been treated as conterminous with specific performance.[46] But the most common view is that adopted by the Permanent Court of International Justice in the *Chorzów Factory* case,[47] that *restitutio in integrum* demands the re-establishment of the situation which would in all probability have existed if the illegal act had not been committed. That is, it does not expressly involve an order for specific performance, and it goes further than specific performance in that it may involve the rectification of harm already caused by the illegal act. *Restitutio in integrum* is often divided into two categories, legal and material.[48] The former involves an order by a tribunal for the repeal or alteration of a measure of the defendant state's legislature, executive or judiciary, the latter typically involves an order for the restoration or repair of property unlawfully seized. There is rarely any specific provision for either type of *restitutio in integrum* in arbitration agreements.

It is controversial whether arbitral practice supports the primacy (or even the possibility) in international law of the remedy of *restitutio in integrum*. There are those like Reitzer who argue that this is the primary remedy: 'Depuis plus d'un siècle les commissions et tribunaux internationaux appliquent la règle qui prescrit une restitution en nature au profit du lésé et seulement en cas d'impossibilité une indemnité pécuniaire.'[49] But the actual awards of *restitutio in integrum* in international arbitral practice are few and well known. Those who support the primacy of *restitutio in integrum* say that this primacy is not undermined by the rarity of its award in practice. But their position is open to attack not only because the gap between their suggested principle and practice is so wide that the principle is misleading, but also because the principle itself is doubtful in so far as it is based on a distorted picture of municipal law. For those who invoke the municipal law remedy of *restitutio in integrum* to support its availability in international law do not take the analogy very far; they tend to play down the diversity of municipal legal systems on this question and to discount the exceptional character of *restitutio in integrum* in the common law.[50]

There is little, if anything, to support the primacy of *restitutio in integrum* in international arbitral practice. In any consideration of those few cases where *restitutio in integrum* was awarded it is important to distinguish between those cases where express provision for the award of *restitutio in integrum* was made in the *compromis* and those where no such provision existed. The former are not numerous enough to create a general rule of international law establishing the primacy of *restitutio in integrum*,[51] so that it is only the latter which are significant as evidence of the existence or otherwise of the suggested general rule.

The *Martini*[52] case is often quoted as an example of legal restitution. In this and in the following two examples no specific power to award *restitutio in integrum* was given in the *compromis*. In this case the tribunal held that a Venezuelan court had acted unlawfully in demanding certain payments from Martini.

Bien que ce paiement n'ait jamais été effectué, les obligations existent en droit. Ces obligations doivent être annullées, à titre de réparation. En prononçant leur annulation le Tribunal Arbitral souligne qu'un acte illicite a été commis et applique le principe que les conséquences de l'acte illicite doivent être effacées.[53]

Again in the case of *El Salvador* v. *Nicaragua* the Central American Court of Justice held that

The Government of Nicaragua, by availing itself of measures possible under the authority of international law, is under the obligation to re-establish and to maintain the legal status that existed prior to the Bryan–Chamorro Treaty between the litigant republics in so far as relates to matters considered in this action.[54]

Finally, in *L'Affaire de la Société Radio-Orient*[55] the Permanent Court of Arbitration directed the revocation of an order which they held had been made in violation of Egypt's treaty obligations. There do not appear to be any further instances of this kind of award in international arbitral practice.[56]

Nor are orders for material restitution much more common. The most often quoted example is one of the cases concerning the rights of Britons in Spanish Morocco.[57] The tribunal ordered the Spanish Government to provide premises for use by the British Consul at Tetuan to replace those for whose unlawful destruction it was responsible. Eulate provides a long list of instances of material restitution.[58] However, the examples of restitution of persons, documents, and ships[59] that he refers to are all the result of diplomatic not arbitral settlement. Similarly in the cases where restitution of property was allowed this was either the result of diplomatic proceedings or else had been expressly provided for in the treaty that established the arbitration tribunal concerned. Finally there are some arbitral awards that order the return of sums of money unlawfully seized.[60] But these may be regarded as a special case in that it is clear that in these cases it is not the actual coins or notes that were seized whose return is demanded but rather their monetary equivalent. In fact in these cases reference is made to the sum seized as the basis for the award of damages. This sum, often augmented by an award of interest, represents the loss of the claimant.

The disadvantages of *restitutio in integrum* as a remedy in international law are considerable and explain the rarity of its award, its refusal in certain cases, and the preference of claimants for the remedy of damages. Legal restitution raises the problem of the relationship between international and municipal law, and the effect of the judgment of an international arbitral tribunal in a municipal legal system. More specifically a defendant state may because of its constitution have difficulty in annulling or amending legislation or other measures. This was recognized in a series of arbitration and conciliation treaties made in the 1920s; all such treaties to which Germany was a party contained a clause providing that if, according to the constitutional law of the offending state, the effects of an act or decision found in violation of international law could not be obviated by administrative measures, the injured state should get appropriate relief in another form. The 1928 General Act includes this type of provision. Article 32 says,

> If, in a judicial sentence or arbitral award it is declared that a judgment, or a measure enjoined by a court of law or other authority of one of the parties to the dispute, is wholly or in part contrary to international law, and if the constitutional law of that party does not permit or only partially permits the consequences of the judgment or measure in question to be annulled, the parties agree that the judicial sentence or arbitral award shall grant the injured party equitable satisfaction.[61]

There are also considerable difficulties with material restitution in international law: the length of time that has elapsed since the original unlawful act may make restitution difficult or impossible; restitution may not constitute an adequate remedy for all the damage involved; certainly it cannot repair moral or personal injury.

Restitutio in integrum was refused by the tribunal in several cases. Thus in the *Rhodope Forests* case,[62] Bulgaria had unlawfully confiscated forests belonging to Greek nationals. The choice whether to order *restitutio in integrum* or damages was left to the arbitrator who decided against the former on the ground that it would be unacceptable to compel Bulgaria to restore integrally the disputed forests as only some of the dispossessed owners had made claims and it was not likely that the forests were in the same position as they had been in 1918. Again, in the *Walter Fletcher Smith* case[63] the claimant United States requested either restoration of the property illegally seized and damaged by Cuba or pecuniary compensation. The arbitrator held simply that it was 'for the best interests of the parties and of the public' that the remedy be damages. In two cases decided by the Permanent Court of Arbitration where it was held that there had been a breach of international law and where it might have seemed at first sight that restitution would be the appropriate remedy this was refused. Thus in *Savarkar's* case[64] the Court held that while an irregularity had been committed in the arrest of Savarkar and his delivery to the British police by a French police officer there was no rule of international law which imposed under the circumstances of the case any obligation on the Power which had the custody of the prisoner to restore him because of a mistake made by the foreign agent who delivered him up. In the *Casablanca* case[65] the secretary of the German consulate was held guilty of a grave violation of his duties for obtaining the protection of the Consul for deserters not of German nationality. The tribunal further held that the French military authorities should have respected the authority of the German Consul by leaving the deserters in his possession until the question of jurisdiction could be decided. The use of force by the French soldiers to seize the deserters was declared to be unwarranted, but the tribunal declined to direct the surrender of the deserters. These two cases make it difficult to argue that for the Permanent Court of Arbitration at least *restitutio in integrum* is the primary remedy in international law.

The few cases in which arbitration tribunals have awarded *restitutio in integrum* seem a weak foundation on which to build the primacy of *restitutio in integrum* in international law. Nor have any of the tribunals said that this is the primary remedy. But the fact that there are a few cases where *restitutio in integrum* has been awarded without express provision for this in the *compromis* is sufficient to undermine the argument that not only is *restitutio in integrum* not the primary remedy in international law, but that a tribunal may not give this remedy without specific provision in the *compromis*.[66] However there is not sufficient arbitral practice to provide clear guidance to a tribunal as to when *restitutio in integrum* would be a suitable remedy and when not.

(c) *Specific Performance*

There is no clear instance in international arbitral practice of a tribunal ordering the specific performance of a treaty or of a contractual obligation.[67] The issue arose in two Postal Treaty cases[68] where the claimant states requested the tribunal to order the payment of interest on payments by Venezuela that were overdue, as required by the Postal Treaty. However, the question whether it could order specific performance of the treaty obligation was not decided by the tribunal in either of these cases for it held that it was not able to award interest to run beyond the termination of its labours. In the *George W. Hopkins* case[69] the Mexican Government had refused payment of six postal money orders issued by a revolutionary regime. As regards three of these orders, the tribunal ordered that

> The Government of the United Mexican States shall pay to the Government of the United States of America on behalf of George W. Hopkins the total amount of the orders . . . with interest at the rate of 6% p.a. to the date on which the last award is rendered by the Commission.[70]

This could be interpreted as an order for the specific performance of Mexico's obligation to honour the postal order, but here again the substance of the award is the payment of money by Mexico to the United States; it is probable that this is just another award of damages.

Therefore it is not clear from international arbitral practice whether this is a remedy that is available in the absence of express provision. According to Mann,[71] 'There is no reason in logic or justice why such an order should not be made', but for Ralston it is not a suitable remedy for an international tribunal. 'A tribunal . . . would have no right to decree specific performance of a contract, something which requires action of a more positive character than the direction of the payment of debt. The same would be true with regard to enforcing a duty by way of mandamus.'[72] And he goes on to cite examples of United States courts refusing to issue orders against States. This disagreement clearly results more from differences on policy than from interpretations of the existing law. Here, as with *restitutio in integrum*, some writers want to attribute an extensive jurisdiction to international tribunals whereas others prefer to emphasize state sovereignty. And as with *restitutio in integrum* those who support the power of international tribunals to award specific performance tend to emphasize the possibility of this remedy in municipal legal systems. But at the same time they play down both the significant differences between systems, in particular between the Anglo-American and German systems, and also the restrictions on the award of specific performance against governments.[73]

(*d*) *Declaratory Judgments*

Have international arbitral tribunals used the declaratory judgment as a remedy for breaches of international law? Tribunals were often called upon to give declaratory judgments on the interpretation of a treaty or contract, or on the position of a boundary, or on sovereignty over a particular area. Obviously no strict distinction between such judgments and a declaration that a state has acted in violation of international law is possible: the second may be implicit in the first. Also a declaratory judgment may be construed as requiring a certain course of behaviour from the states involved. For example, according to Brownlie[74] declaratory judgments on sovereignty over territory may be interpreted as orders for specific performance. However, international arbitral tribunals certainly did not give judgments in this form. Nor did they commonly make declaratory judgments that there had been a breach of international law; that is, the declaratory judgment as a preliminary to a possible agreement by the parties or later decision by the tribunal, or as a substitute for other remedies, was unknown. However, the few awards of nominal damages that were made[75] may perhaps be regarded as a form of declaratory judgment to the effect that there had been a breach of international law. But the declaratory judgment as a remedy for violation of international law did not, in the awards of international arbitral tribunals, approach the importance that it was later to attain in the judgments of the International Court of Justice.[76] It is not discussed by early writers on remedies in international law.

The *Sanchez* case[77] decided by the 1903 Spanish–Venezuelan Claims Commission shows that international arbitral tribunals did not then regard the declaratory judgment as an available substitute for other awards. Here the Commission was asked for an award of damages, but no adequate evidence of harm was produced. The umpire held that

The Umpire does not take up this question of responsibility, because, in the supposition that it might be determined abstractly or in principle against Venezuela it would not be possible to fix these terms concretely in order to make it effective, because the claimant has not proved even one of the facts necessary to estimate and determine any indemnity.[78]

The *Cayuga Indians* case[79] also reflects a restrictive view of the tribunal's powers to allow declaratory judgments. The tribunal said that its powers were limited to making a monetary award and that it could not make a declaration, 'That the Cayuga Indians are entitled to the annuity for the future', but could only award a lump sum representing the present value of such an annuity. Later the International Court of Justice relied not on this ground of lack of jurisdiction but on considerations of propriety to justify its refusal to allow declaratory judgments.[80] International arbitral decisions, therefore, do not provide any examples of the declaratory judgment being used as a remedy for breaches of international law other than the two famous cases decided by the Permanent Court of Arbitration, the *Carthage*[81] and the *Manouba*.[82] In these cases the tribunal considered that a declaration constituted satisfaction for breach of an obligation: 'Considering that in case a power should fail to fulfil its obligations whether general or special, to another power, the establishment of this fact especially in an arbitral award, constitutes in itself a serious penalty', the tribunal refused pecuniary compensation for insults to the French flag.

(*e*) *Damages*

Damages have been accepted without question by international arbitral tribunals as a remedy in international law and are by far the commonest remedy in arbitral practice. These tribunals built up a fairly consistent set of rules on state responsibility for injury to foreign nations; today the status of these rules is controversial.[83] Did they develop a comparably coherent set of rules governing the award of damages, and can they provide any guidance for the assessment of damages today?

As was said above, most awards of damages by arbitral tribunals were not fully reasoned and it is difficult to draw conclusions as to their methods of assessment. It was not often that a tribunal's discussions on the assessment of damages were held in secret—perhaps the *Alabama* claims[84] are the only example of this—but often they might as well have been for all the explanation that is given in the award. But one reasonable inference from the collection of arbitral awards is that the basic aim of almost all the tribunals was to give full compensation to each injured individual for his loss. This intention is made express in a few cases such as the *Norwegian Shipowners* case, where it was said: 'Just compensation implies a complete restitution of the status quo ante based upon the loss of profits of the Norwegian owners as compared with other owners of similar property'.[85]

The authors of the draft codifications on the law of state responsibility for injury to aliens also accept this as the proper function of damages.[86] But the question of what is involved in the award of full compensation is a complex one. It raises the issues which consequences of an unlawful act should be compensated, on whose injury is the amount of damages based, and for whose act are damages given. 'Full compensation' must be given content by particular detailed rules: it has no single, logically determined, fixed meaning. This rather obvious point needs to be made only because there is a temptation facing writers in this area to choose between cases on the basis of their preconceptions as to what is meant by full compensation.

One of the problems facing tribunals, and perhaps the most important factor determining their choice of method of assessment, is that of evidence. It is well known that international tribunals are not bound by municipal law rules of evidence and it is clear from Sandifer's exhaustive study of this topic[87] that international tribunals are not bound to adhere to strict judicial rules of evidence. Sandifer attributes this to the special character of international proceedings: 'International tribunals, as compared with municipal tribunals are preoccupied with getting at the facts of the question presented for their decision.' Furthermore he argues that international proceedings derive a distinctive character from the fact that the parties are sovereign states. From this it follows that 'The consequences of error or failure to ascertain the facts in reaching a decision are in many instances more far-reaching in their effect than in litigation between ordinary private parties in municipal tribunals'.[88] Lauterpacht also subscribes to this view, arguing that the importance of the interests at stake in international proceedings precludes excessive or decisive reliance upon formal and technical rules.[89]

These arguments may have some validity as far as direct interstate claims are concerned, but as regards claims for injury to aliens they are less convincing. The picture of municipal tribunals as less concerned with the truth than are international tribunals seems unrealistic, and the interests at stake in international claims for injury to aliens are precisely similar to those involved in much municipal law litigation between governments and individuals. A better explanation for the less exacting rules of evidence applied by international tribunals is probably the practical one that the problems involved in finding evidence are greater in international claims than in municipal law litigation. Sandifer lists some of the factors which contribute to these difficulties:[90] the fact that there is often a considerable lapse of time between the injury and the arbitration, the fact that the events which form the subject matter of the dispute may have taken place far from the seat of the tribunal and the current residence of the claimant, the often bad conditions of written records, and even the negligence of claimants in furnishing evidence to substantiate their claims. Tribunals frequently complained about the inadequacy of the evidence presented to them. For example, in the *Hudson Bay* case[91] the United States commissioner said,

> Coming then to the question of the adequate money consideration spoken of in the Treaty for the transfer to the United States of all the rights and claims of the Hudson's Bay Company, I encounter serious embarrassments. From a mere trifle on the one side, all the way to the enormous sum demanded in the Claimants' memorial, on the other, almost any sum could be supported by testimony free from criticism affecting either the fidelity or intelligence of the witnesses.

Similar remarks were made by the umpire in the *Colonel Lloyd Aspinwall*.[92] In such circumstances international tribunals make rough estimates of the loss involved. They do not refuse damages altogether because there is uncertainty about their extent. Thus in the *Compagnie Générale of the Orinoco*,[93] although many elements in the claim were uncertain, an award was made. The arbitrator held that 'Approximate equity is all that can be required and all that can be gained from a case so indefinite in many of its important facts'. In certain cases the assessment of damages was made *ex aequo et bono*.[94]

As regards the problem of whose injury should be assessed and for whose act damages should be calculated, the traditional theory of international claims is that, as only a state may be the subject of international law, only a state may possess a claim in international law. That is, although it may be an individual who is the immediate victim of an unlawful act, the state is injured through injury to its national and it is the state's claim that is presented to the international tribunal.[95] And damages are to be awarded only for injuries caused by a state's own unlawful acts. In theory this means that damages should be assessed on the basis of the injury to the state itself and only for the harm caused by the defendant state's own acts. But in practice arbitral tribunals have modified these strict theoretical requirements as to the assessment of damages by the employment of convenient fictions. Compensation is in fact assessed on the basis of the injury of the individual national; this is rationalized as a suitable means of measuring the injury to the state.[96]

Again, the problems created by the theory that damages are to be awarded only for injuries caused by the state's own unlawful acts are well known. For although the state is identified with its national for the purposes of making an international claim—that is, an injury to a national is said to constitute an injury to the state—this identification is not made for the purposes of state responsibility. The acts of an individual are not necessarily attributable to the state so as to involve state responsibility. So in those cases where the state's unlawful act consists only of the non-pursuit or non-punishment of those responsible for a crime, the exact calculation of damages raises problems if it is to be based on injury caused by the state's act or failure to act, rather than on the original injury to the alien. *Janes's* case,[97] where the arbitrator purported to base the measure of damages on the injury caused by the state's failure to punish the murderer of an American citizen, is one of the most discussed cases in the whole of the law of state responsibility.[98] Here $12,000 were awarded to compensate for the individual grief, the lack of opportunity of subjecting the murderer to a civil suit, and also as a 'reasonable and substantial redress for the mistrust and lack of safety resulting from the government's attitude'. The majority of the Commission added

> One among the advantages of severing the government's dereliction of duty from the individual's crime is that it grants an opportunity to take into account several shades of denial of justice, more serious and lighter ones, whereas the old system operates automatically and allows for the numerous forms of such a denial one amount only, that of full and total reparation.[99]

It is generally agreed that the purpose of this award was at least in part to impose a penalty on Mexico, to express disapproval of the actions of the Mexican government. As Dunn said, the explanation in the award was 'just a convenient peg on which to hang the award after the decision to make it had been reached on other grounds'. The consequences of following the theory expressed in this case to its logical conclusion may be seen in *Mecham's* case.[100] Here the Mexican Government did not attempt to capture and punish the robbers of property belonging to an American citizen. It was held that they were liable to pay damages only for that part of the property which might have been recovered if the robbers had been caught.

However, later tribunals did not adopt this method of assessing damages, and even the United States–Mexican General Claims Commission did not apply it in all its decisions.[101] In general, arbitral tribunals have calculated damages on the basis of the loss caused by the original injury even though strictly the state is not responsible for this.

Any attempt to establish on the basis of international arbitral practice the existence of rules for the assessment of damages that are specific and capable of guiding other tribunals involves difficulties. It is striking that all the writers who have made detailed studies of international arbitral practice on the assessment of damages in general or of some particular aspect of this question find uncertainty and conflict rather than clear rules.[102] Thus, even on the basic question of the extent of compensation, of limits on the award of damages, there are inconsistencies between tribunals.

(ii) LIMITS ON THE AWARD OF DAMAGES

As in municipal law, the award of damages in international law raises the problem of setting a limit to the extent of the loss for which damages will be given. In international arbitral practice the most common test is that of indirect damage; tribunals agree in not allowing damages for this. But exactly what constitutes 'indirect damage' is not clear. The decisions of tribunals have not given this rule a uniform content. Whiteman's examination of the cases on this question led her to conclude that 'The decisions and holdings are not uniform. However, it may be stated that damages allowed on account of the commission or omission of an act giving rise to responsibility generally are those which it is reasonable to allow',[103] and in arbitral practice the phrase 'indirect damage' covers various different means of restricting the award of damages. According to Personnaz,[104] what is treated as a question of fact in municipal law is wrongly regarded as a question of law by international tribunals. That is, the problem whether or not to compensate indirect damage is treated as a question of the competence of the judge. He argues that this was the approach adopted in the *Alabama* claims, and that this influenced subsequent tribunals. However, this supposed contrast does not stand up to examination. While it is true that in civil law systems this problem of indirect damage is regarded as one of fact, this is not always so in the common law. Here certain types of injury, however direct, are not compensated in certain areas of the law of torts. This is particularly true of purely economic injury. Moreover in international practice the question is not usually treated as one of competence. It is doubtful whether considerations of competence were in fact of major importance in influencing the commissioners' decision in the *Alabama* claims to decline jurisdiction over certain claims; political considerations seem to have been decisive on this question. Also the influence of this tribunal on subsequent tribunals as regards the question of indirect damage has not been very great.[105] Often damage is rejected as indirect because the tribunal regards it as too remote or uncertain. Thus in the *Trail Smelter* arbitration the tribunal held that 'Damage of this nature due to the reduced economic status of residents in this area is too indirect, remote and uncertain to be appraised and not such for which an indemnity can be awarded'.[106] And in the nineteenth century indirect damage was sometimes identified with lost profits.[107]

But writers show an unusual degree of agreement in rejecting the indirect damage test so commonly employed by tribunals.[108] They argue that the proper approach is for the tribunal to refuse to compensate a particular loss if there is no adequate causal link between it and the wrongful act, and they invoke the decision of the 1923 United States–German Commission as a model. In Administrative Decision no. II the umpire said,

> The proximate cause of the loss must have been in legal contemplation the act of Germany. The proximate result or consequence of that act must have been the loss, damage or injury suffered. It matters not whether the loss be directly or indirectly

sustained so long as there is a clear, unbroken connection between Germany's act and the loss complained of. It matters not how many links there may be in the chain of causation connecting Germany's act with the loss sustained, provided there is no break in the chain and the loss can be clearly, unmistakably, and definitely traced link by link to Germany's act.[109]

This chain of causation metaphor is a commonplace in the writings of lawyers. However unsatisfactory as a philosophical concept,[110] it provides a useful policy instrument for the exclusion of whatever damage the arbitrator does not wish to compensate. And causation was certainly an important factor in many international arbitral decisions in determining for what consequences of an illegal act damages could be given. Various tribunals applied the test of normality to decide this question: the defendant state was held responsible for the normal consequences of its unlawful act. This approach was adopted in the *Naulilaa* cases,[111] for example, and also in the *Heirs of Jean Maninat*.[112] Alternatively, the test of foreseeability may be applied as in the *Samoan* claims,[113] where the commissioners agreed that

The effect of these rules is that the damages for which a wrongdoer is liable are the damages which are both, in fact, caused by his action, and cannot be attributed to any other causes, and which a reasonable man in the position of the wrongdoer at the time would have foreseen as likely to ensue from his action.

If a state is liable only for the direct consequences of its own unlawful act it should not have to pay full compensation for injuries partly caused by external factors. This was accepted by the tribunals in the *Costa Rica Packet*[114] and *Cowper's* case.[115] In the former, the Netherlands Government was held responsible for the arrest of the captain of a British ship. The arbitrator said,

Whereas the unjustifiable detention of Captain Carpenter caused him to miss the best part of the whale fishing season; Whereas on the other hand Mr. Carpenter, on being set free, was in a position to have returned on board the ship Costa Rica Packet in January 1892 at the latest, and whereas no conclusive proof has been produced by him to show that he was obliged to leave his ship until April 1892 in the port of Ternate without a master, or, still less, to sell her at a reduced price; Whereas the owners or the captain of the ship being under an obligation, as a precaution against the occurrence of some accident to the captain, to make provision for his being replaced, the mate of the Costa Rica Packet ought to have been fit to take the command and to carry on the whale fishing industry; and whereas thus the losses sustained by the proprietors of the vessel, Costa Rica Packet, the officers, and the crew, in consequence of the detention of Mr. Carpenter, are not entirely the necessary consequences of this precautionary detention,[116]

a reduced amount of damages should accordingly be allowed. The arbitrator gave no exact explanation of the calculations involved in his award.

Cowper's case is similar in that Cowper's negligence in not replacing the work-force illegally seized contributed to the loss of future crops. It is well established in international jurisprudence that the claimant should not act unreasonably and unnecessarily increase the extent of his loss. If the claimant is in some way negligent and contributes to his own loss he will not receive full compensation.[117]

The question of the fault of the respondent state is more difficult.[118] Quite apart from the problems raised by the personification of the state involved here, it is hard to see whether or not the fault of the respondent state has influenced the extent of the arbitrator's award of damages. Strictly, if the aim of the award is to compensate the loss of the injured alien then the fault of the respondent state should be irrelevant. This was the line taken by Judge Ehrlich in his Dissenting Opinion in the *Chorzów Factory* case,[119] but this seems slightly unrealistic. In *Fabiani's* case it was said that, 'La preuve est d'ailleurs soumise à des questions moins strictes en cas de faute lourde ou de dol'. Also it is clear that in the series of cases that adopted the theory of damages first expressed in *Janes's* case not only the gravity of the original injury but also the degree of the denial of justice were taken into account. Probably it is not possible to make any statement more precise than that the degree of fault of the respondent state will influence the arbitrator in his calculations.

There are many other cases where the arbitrator has reduced the amount of damages, not because of the fault of the claimant, but because other, extraneous factors have contributed to the loss suffered. However, it is often difficult to determine the proportion of responsibility that should be borne by the defendant state. Thus in *Metzger's* case,[120] the arbitrator simply stated that, 'Le réclamant alléguant des dommages ne résultant pas entièrement de la rupture de l'engagement, les dommages qu'il était juste de prendre en considération seraient compensés par le paiement de la somme de $15,000'. The cases of *Yuille, Shortridge and Company*[121] and *Lacaze*[122] are similar in that although the award is reduced to take into account causes other than the unlawful act, no precise explanation is given of the amount finally awarded. In other cases, the arbitrator decided that the defendant state should be held responsible for a certain percentage of the loss. In the *British Claims in Spanish Morocco*, the *compromis* provided that Spain was not responsible for an uprising nor for acts of brigandage. Accordingly, the arbitrator, Huber, held that for acts in certain areas Spain was liable for only 25 per cent of the injury, in others for 50 per cent. Similarly in the *Martini* case,[123] Venezuela had to pay only one third of the total damage as it was held that the rest was caused by the existence of war. Hauriou[124] welcomes such decisions, for, in discussing the question of what damage should be compensated, he makes a distinction between *dommages éloignés*, which have an indirect causal link with the unlawful act however remote, and *dommages étrangers* which have none. He says that no compensation should be given for the latter, but that some compensation is necessary for the former. However, this is not necessarily full compensation: 'Indemniser les dommages éloignés jusque dans leurs plus lointaines conséquences serait donner aux hommes l'impression que les faits sont irrévocablement déterminés et que leur liberté et leur volonté ne peuvent à aucun moment s'interposer pour détourner le cours des événements.' A strange argument, apparently based on an opposition to determinism, but acceptable as a plea for the necessity for the claimant to mitigate his loss. Hauriou suggests that partial compensation is desirable; he realizes that this will involve difficulties in the determination of the proportion of responsibility that the state should bear, but argues that these are not insuperable. However, he recognizes that tribunals did not in fact uniformly accept his distinction and allow compensation for *dommages éloignés* and gives a list of cases where damages for such injury were refused. In practice arbitrators differ on what amounts to indirect damage. There are famous examples of pairs of cases with apparently similar fact situations where the judges came to directly opposite results. For instance, the cases of the *William Lee*[125] and the *Canada*,[126] both claims from sealships illegally prevented from fishing. The former was allowed damages for the loss of the season's catch, in the latter these were rejected. Again there are the contrasting cases of *Yuille*, *Shortridge* and *Lacaze*, both claims for the interruption of business. Compensation for lost profits was allowed in the former, but rejected as indirect in the latter. There are many such contradictory decisions; a final example is to be found in the decisions of the French–Mexican Claims Commission on compensation for the loss of crops.[127] The original tribunal allowed such claims but its successor refused these as being for indirect damage.

It is generally accepted by international tribunals that compensation includes both *damnum emergens* and *lucrum cessans*. There are many statements like that in the *Cape Horn Pigeon*:

> Considering that the general principle of civil law, according to which the damages should include an indemnity, not only for the loss suffered, but also for the profit of which one has been deprived, is equally applicable to international litigation, and that in order to apply it, it is not necessary that the amount of the profit of which one is deprived should be exactly determined, but that it suffices to show that in the natural order of things one would be able to realise a profit of which one is deprived by the act which gives rise to the claim.[128]

Lauterpacht lists those cases where compensation for lost profits was refused,[129] and shows convincingly that in almost every case the refusal can be explained by the uncertainty of the profits claimed rather than as a rejection in principle of damages for lost profits.

Although there is general agreement that an award for loss of profits is permissible in cases both of injury to property and of breach of contract, there is no uniform practice on the methods of assessment. Sometimes tribunals just allow interest on the amount representing the principal injury and this is held to constitute compensation for lost profits. This method was used in the *Canada*, *Bronner*,[130] *Mora and Arango*,[131] and *Compagnie Générale des Asphaltes*.[132] Alternatively, the tribunal may make an evaluation *in abstracto*, a calculation based on the earnings of the enterprise concerned in a previous period, or of similar enterprises over the period in question. This was done in the *William Lee* where lost profits were based on those from previous catches. Finally, there is the concrete method of assessment; an estimate based on the facts of the particular case, on the profits which the injured enterprise or property would have made in the period in question. For example in *Cheek's*[133] case a complicated calculation was made by the arbitrator to enable him to arrive at a probable figure for lost profits. Again, in the *Betsey*, damages for lost profits were based on the actual price obtainable for the ship's cargo at its probable time of arrival in port. This was allowed, against the strong protests of one of the Commission, although the price had been inflated by the existence of the war. The rule that compensation should be based on 'the net value of the cargo at its port of destination at such time as the vessel would probably have arrived there', was followed in subsequent decisions of the Commission set up under Article 7 of the Jay Treaty. It is clear that the content of 'full compensation' is variable; the choice of method of assessment will be determined or influenced by the evidence available.

(iii) PUNITIVE DAMAGES

There are at least two possible exceptions to the general rule of full compensation assessed on the basis of the injury to an injured national. First, it is a controversial question whether punitive damages are permissible under international law. Punitive damages are an institution of the common law used to mark disapproval of the wrongdoer's acts and their award may result in a victim receiving more than compensation for his injury. Certain writers have denied that punitive damages have any place in international law,[134] and today this is just part of the wider debate over the possibility or desirability of international criminal responsibility.[135]

Those who argue against punitive damages base their rejection partly on arguments from principle and partly on the practice of tribunals. First, they say that to give punitive damages is not a suitable award against a sovereign state. Secondly, they rely on the explicit refusal by certain tribunals of the award of punitive damages. The most famous of these is perhaps Umpire Parker's lengthy discussion of the problem in the 1923 United States–

Germany Commission.[136] Eagleton attempts to dismiss all these cases by arguing that they refuse punitive damages merely because to award them would have been beyond the jurisdiction of the tribunal under the *compromis*.[137] This is convincing as regards those decisions where the tribunal expressly bases its refusal on its powers under the *compromis* or on the intention of the parties, as Umpire Parker did. He said,

> But it is not necessary for this Commission to go to the length of holding that exemplary damages cannot be awarded in any case by any international tribunal. A sufficient reason why such damages cannot be awarded by this Commission is that it is without the power to make such awards under the terms of its Charter, the Treaty of Berlin.[138]

Eagleton's argument is slightly weaker when applied to cases such as *Aaron Brooks*[139] and *Manasse*,[140] where Umpire Lieber rejected punitive damages. He held simply that the tribunal had no punitive mission and there was no offence to be punished. But it is just possible to include this under Eagleton's theory by interpreting it as a reference to the intention of the parties. Admittedly there are few arbitral decisions that expressly allow punitive damages; perhaps the only examples are *Moke's* case,[141] where the tribunal said that it wished to condemn the practice of forcing loans, and, possibly, the *I'm Alone*,[142] if this is to be regarded as an award of punitive damages rather than as satisfacton.[143] However, there are several examples of punitive damages in diplomatic practice.[144] Also in certain cases punitive damages were refused on the facts of the case, but the possibility of such an award was admitted in principle. Thus in the *Delagoa Bay Railway Company* case it was held that there were extenuating circumstances that alleviated the government's liability, warranted a reduction of the amount allowable, and excluded the allowance of exemplary and punitive damages. Similarly, the tribunal in *Cheek's* case decided that 'In this case there are circumstances which would render it quite unjust that anything in the nature of a fine should be inflicted on the Siamese government'.[145] Other such cases are *Metzger* and *Torrey*.[146]

In personal injury and death cases it sometimes appears that the award represents more than mere compensation although, in the absence of explanation by the tribunal, and because of the impossibility of an exact relation between physical injury and pecuniary compensation, it is not possible to be quite sure about this. But where the award of damages takes into account the gravity of the defendant state's behaviour, as in the *Janes's* case, or where damages are awarded when there is no evidence of pecuniary loss, as in claims for the loss of a relative who did not make pecuniary contributions to the claimant's support, such cases 'may be considered punitive in their nature, although not so denominated'.[147] Therefore the possibility of punitive damages in international law cannot be decided purely on the basis of the decisions of international arbitral tribunals; policy considerations will be crucial. On this question as on that of the availability of remedies other than damages and declaratory judgments much depends on one's conception of the role of an international tribunal. In particular the strength of the municipal law analogy is important: does the mere existence of remedies in some systems of municipal law in itself make them acceptable also in international law? Or would it not be preferable to require widespread acceptance of a remedy in municipal law, and also to accept that the restrictions on the remedy in municipal law would govern its analogous application on the international level? These considerations and the extreme rarity of clear awards of punitive damages in arbitral practice suggest that it is not a suitable remedy in international law. It is difficult to imagine the International Court of Justice being prepared to order this remedy.

(iv) NOMINAL DAMAGES

The second exception to the general rule that damages should compensate injury is nominal damages. These are very rarely awarded in international arbitral decisions, but there are a few instances where damages are given for a breach of international law that did not cause any loss. Thus in *Brower's* case,[148] one of the Fiji Islands claims, it was held that Great Britain had violated its international obligations by its failure to recognize the claimant's title to land which was, however, worthless. The owner was awarded the nominal sum of one shilling. Whiteman also cites the *Compagnie Générale des Asphaltes*[149] as an example of nominal damages, but it is not clear that any actual payment was envisaged and other writers have categorized this decision as one of the rare examples of legal *restitutio in integrum*. For the duties wrongfully imposed by Venezuela had not actually been paid by the claimant company. The arbitrator nevertheless said,

> An unjustifiable act is not made just because, perchance, there are not evil results which might well have followed. The claimant government has a right to insist that its sovereignty over its own soil shall be respected, and that its subject shall be restored to his original rights before consequent results shall be discussed,[150]

and accordingly ordered that the amount of the duties should be restored. In these cases nominal damages apparently perform a function similar to that of satisfaction, and pecuniary compensation unrelated to actual loss is awarded in order to declare the legal right involved. For this purpose, and indeed also where it is desired to punish the respondent state, a large sum is not necessary; a nominal amount would be equally satisfactory. This was the argument of the Mexican commissioner in 1868 Mexican–United States Mixed Claims Commission.[151] He urged that an indemnity for 'moral purposes' could be expressed as well by a small as by a large sum and that it was the act of expressing guilt or indicating a wrongful act on the part of the respondent state that was important. And now the development of the declaratory judgment as itself a remedy for the violation of international law makes nominal damages redundant. This was certainly the view of the Permanent Court of Arbitration in the *Carthage* and the *Manouba*; here it rejected claims for nominal damages of one franc for injury to French sovereignty on the ground that 'In case a power should fail to fulfil its obligations, whether general or special, to another power, the establishment of this fact, especially in an arbitral award, constitutes in itself a serious penalty'. But the tribunal in the *Lighthouses* arbitration[152] subsequently made an award of nominal damages.

Devant l'inconsistance de la réclamation française qui, apres avoir fixé à 1,000 Fr. le montant du préjudice a ensuite déclaré ne plus pouvoir le chiffrer, le Tribunal, tout en reconnaissant en principe le bien-fondé de la demande, ne peut qu'accorder une indemnité symbolique de 1 Fr.

(v) INTEREST

The award of interest is a significant element in full compensation because there is often a considerable lapse of time between the original injury and the arbitration and again between the arbitral award and payment of damages. Factors contributing to these delays include the rule that an alien must exhaust local remedies before an international claim may be brought, the fact that it is for the state to choose when to bring a claim, and also the fact that claims may be settled only after a lengthy period of civil war, interstate war, or domestic unrest.

Most often the *compromis* makes no express provision on the award of interest. A few exceptional agreements explicitly allow interest, either on the award, as in the 1860 Treaty between the United States and Costa Rica,[153] which provides that 6 per cent interest shall be paid from the day on which the indemnity is due, or in the event of a delay in payment of the award as in the 1863 Convention between the United States and Peru,[154] under which interest of 6 per cent is to be paid if the awards are not made within a month of the decision, or, finally, certain agreements explicitly allow interest as part of the award. Examples of this last type of provision may be found in the 1829 Treaty between Great Britain and Brazil,[155] and the 1885 Convention between the United States and Venezuela.[156] But in general no such express power to award interest is conferred by the *compromis*. In its absence tribunals have assumed this power; they have shown themselves very willing to award interest. Often they do so without giving any justification for this, as in the awards of the 1903 United States–Venezuelan Commission,[157] or else they support their decision to allow interest only by saying that this is just or equitable.[158] In contrast, decisions refusing interest are usually explained by the tribunal. However, here too sometimes the only explanation given is that it would not be equitable to allow interest, as in the *Canadienne* case,[159] and the British–Mexican and Spanish–Mexican Claims Commissions refused interest without any explanation at all.[160] Apparently the only case where interest was refused partly as a matter of principle is the *Montijo*.[161] The umpire said,

> As regards the opinion of the arbitrator of the United States that interest at the rate of 5% per annum should be allowed from the 1st January 1872 to the date of payment of the claim, the undersigned is not prepared to say that such an allowance would not be strictly justifiable. He nevertheless decides against it for the following reasons:–
>
> First, because there is no settled rule as to the payment of interest on claims of countries or governments;
>
> Secondly, because it seems open to question whether interest should accrue during the progress of diplomatic negotiations which are often protracted in their character;
>
> Thirdly, that this reason applies with special force to negotiations which result in an arbitration or friendly arrangement;
>
> Fourthly, that, whilst doing what he considers strict justice to the claimants by giving to them the full value of the use of their vessel during her detention, he wishes to avoid any appearance of punishing the Colombian people at large for an act with which very few of them had anything to do and which affected no Colombian interests beyond those of a few speculators in revolutions in Panama.

The last reason for the refusal of interest is the most typical of general practice in that it is based on the particular circumstances of the case. Thus refusal to allow interest may be justified by a delay in making the claim,[162] by fault on the part of the victim,[163] by implied waiver of the right to interest,[164] or by the method of calculating the injury that is used.[165] In *Pinson's* case the French–Mexican Claims Commission held that where the award was based on an *ex gratia* agreement to pay as opposed to state responsibility no interest would be awarded.

Whereas tribunals are in agreement on their power to give interest even when there is no explicit conferment of such power, practice as regards the method of assessment is not uniform. There are diverse decisions on the date from which interest should be calculated. The most common solutions chosen are, first, the date of the injury. The 1922 United States–German Mixed Claims Commission[166] made a distinction between liquidated and unliquidated claims; in the former interest would be allowed from the date of the injury, in the latter from the date of the award. The French–Mexican Claims Commission also accepted this approach.[167] But the distinction between liquidated and unliquidated damages in the award of interest was not generally accepted. For example, in the *Costa Rica Packet*, interest on unliquidated damages was allowed from the date of the injury. It has been argued that full compensation requires that this date be adopted as the starting-point for the award of interest. Subilia[168] suggests that as the aim of compensation should be to re-establish the situation that would have existed if the unlawful act had not taken place, then it is necessary to take account of all the loss that has occurred since the injury, and that this involves the payment of interest from the date of the injury. However, this would not always lead to a just result where the delay in settling the claim was caused by the claimant state.

Subilia's ideal of payment of interest from the date of injury is not always attained in the decisions of tribunals. In many cases interest is allowed only from the date of the claim. In the *Macedonian*[169] this principle was followed even though the claim was for a liquidated sum. Sometimes the date is taken to be that of the local rather than the international claim, as for example, in the decisions of the French–Mexican Claims Commission[170] on forced loans and contractual debts, and in the decisions of the German–Venezuelan commission.[171] However, in *Cervetti's* case,[172] the arbitrator held that the appropriate date was that of the international claim as it was not just to make the defendant state responsible for any delay by the claimant state in its presentation of the claim. Certain tribunals have even adopted the date of decision as the date from which interest is allowed. Thus Verzijl in the French–Mexican Claims Commission held that in claims for delicts and requisitions interest should run from the date of the tribunal's decision as it was at this moment that the claim turned into the right to demand a fixed sum.

In their choice of the date until which interest is allowed tribunals again come to different conclusions. Most common is the date of the decision or of the final award of the commission. This is sometimes based on the erroneous impression of the tribunal that it has no jurisdiction to make an order for the payment of interest after its functions have terminated. This was the reasoning apparently accepted by the various Venezuelan commissions of 1903, and the 1868 and 1923 United States–Mexican commissions.[173] Interest is allowed until the date of payment of the award more often in individual arbitrations than by claims commissions.[174] This was the date accepted in the *Portendick* claims,[175] the *Delagoa Bay Railway Company* case, the *Rhodope Forests* case, and the *Cape Horn Pigeon*.

Nor is there any greater uniformity among the decisions on the rate of interest. Here again in many cases the tribunal gives no explanation for the rate it chooses. In some cases, however, the rate applied is that of the respondent state. This practice was adopted by the Italy–Venezuelan Commission and the Great Britain–Venezuelan Commission of 1903.[176] In one of the cases decided by the former, *Cervetti*, Umpire Ralston said,

The practice among prior mixed commissions has been so far from uniform and so often dependent upon the language of particular treaties as not to afford any very useful guide. Commercial rates are so uncertain that, while their consideration may be useful, the umpire would not be justified in being controlled by them. The umpire believes it fair to take into special consideration the rate of interest paid in Venezuela by law in the absence of contract and also the rate accepted by foreign governments upon bonds given by Venezuela to pay obligations created by former arbitral tribunals.[177]

However the Germany and Italy–Venezuelan Commission did not accept this rate as generally applicable.[178] Certain individual arbitral tribunals also adopted the rate of the defendant state; the *Delagoa Bay Railway Company*, the *Orinico Steamship Company*, and the *Religious Properties* cases are all based on this rule. Other rates employed are that of the claimant state,[179] the commercial rate,[180] or the rate in the domicile of the creditor.[181] Often the relevant time for fixing the rate of interest is not mentioned, but in the *Lord Nelson*[182] the appropriate time was said to be that when the principal should have been paid, and in the *Del Rio*[183] it was the time of the conclusion of the contract. According to Whiteman, 'There are few rules within the scope of the subject of damages in international law that are better settled than the one that compound interest is not allowable.'[184] Perhaps this goes too far, for compound interest was awarded in *Fabiani's* case, and although it has been rejected in many other cases this was not invariably on grounds of principle but sometimes because it was not appropriate in those particular cases.[185] In *Dreyfus Brothers*[186] it was said, 'In fact the capitalization of interest can result only from a stipulation or from circumstances of fact making clear the consent of the debtor to assume such an onerous obligation.' Accordingly the law on this question is unsettled in the jurisprudence of arbitral tribunals.

As was mentioned above,[187] certain treaties provide that if payment of the award is not made by a certain date, then interest should be paid from this date. Some tribunals have followed this practice even where there is no such provision in the *compromis*.[188] Other tribunals have stipulated that if payment is not made by the due date then an increased rate of interest should be paid.[189] This is apparently intended partly as a sanction to encourage prompt payment rather than as compensation. However, a demand for such a decision was refused by the Permanent Court of Arbitration in the *Carthage* and the *Manouba*.

Some writers are not satisfied with this collection of contradictory decisions on the appropriate rate of interest in international claims. According to Subilia, the apparently random nature of the choice of the rate of interest is unsatisfactory, even 'choquante', as it is not designed to achieve the goal of full compensation. He argues that the rate of interest should depend on the profit the creditor would have made if he had had the sum of money, representing his loss, of which he was deprived.[190] Of course there are great difficulties involved in any such hypothetical calculations. Sohn and Baxter adopt a similar, perhaps slightly more realistic, approach in their draft codification.[191] Article 38(3) lays down that, 'The rate of interest shall be that prevailing with respect to obligations of analogous amount and duration at the time of the award in the place in which the injured alien was habitually resident at the time of injury'. This is based on the assumption that the alien will have been obliged to obtain financial replacement for his loss on the local money market. However unrealistic this assumption, it at least gives a fairly objective standard of assessment. But the arbitral tribunals themselves never came near to evolving a consistent set of rules on the award of interest. Nor can the differences between them be explained away as simply the result of differing facts; there are clear disagreements on the applicable rules.

(vi) TYPES OF INJURY

Damages have been awarded by international arbitral tribunals for many types of injury, almost all involving damage to interests comparable to those protected by municipal law, but the tribunals have not developed a consistent set of rules to govern the assessment of each type of loss. Reitzer, arguing that criteria such as the exclusion of indirect damage and the test of causation were too vague to ensure a consistent arbitral practice in the assessment of damages, said,

> Un progrès sensible serait réalisé si une certaine méthode d'évaluation venait à être adoptée au sujet de l'indemnité due en raison d'une catégorie déterminée d'actes dommageables. Un exemple de ce genre serait, par exemple, de trouver des règles communes à suivre en cas de saisie illégale d'un navire.[192]

But international arbitral tribunals never came anywhere near to achieving this goal.

(*a*) *Personal injury*

First, personal injury cases. Whiteman in her collection of the decisions on damages in such cases classifies the awards according to the type of injury involved.[193] This highlights the lack of uniformity in the awards.

Whiteman says, 'The most that can be said is that an effort is usually made to base the allowance of damages primarily upon the actual monetary loss shown to have been sustained'.[194] But it is doubtful whether this is so. In the majority of decisions no explanation at all is given for the amount awarded. The decisions of the 1916 United States–Panama Tribunal[195] are fairly typical in this respect. The award consists only of a list of the injuries inflicted and the amount of damages given for each. Apparently the amount depends on the gravity of the injury involved, and this suggests that the award is intended as pecuniary satisfaction for the injury rather than as compensation for the pecuniary losses resulting from it. Certain other tribunals quite clearly fix arbitrary sums as damages for personal injuries. For example, in the 1916 United States–Panama Commission the awards given were for $50, $75, and $100. However, there are also cases where damages are expressly based *inter alia* on the actual financial loss of the victim.[196]

Sohn and Baxter's codification allows for both these approaches. Article 28 lays down that:

> Damages for bodily or mental harm, for mistreatment during detention, or for deprivation of liberty shall include compensation for past and prospective:
> (*a*) harm to the body or mind;
> (*b*) pain, suffering and emotional distress;
> (*c*) loss of earnings and of earning capacity;
> (*d*) reasonable medical and other expenses;
> (*e*) harm to the property or business of the alien resulting directly from such bodily or mental injury or deprivation of liberty; and
> (*f*) harm to the reputation of the alien, resulting directly from such deprivation of liberty.

Express provision is thus made for compensation for 'pain, suffering and emotional distress', even where there is no physical injury to the claimant.[197] There are a few instances of this in international arbitral practice—this head of damages is used in *Janes's* case to enable the tribunal to give damages based on the state's own act—but they remain exceptional. The codification reflects the Western view that such harm is a proper subject of compensation. This is rejected in many communist legal systems. Also Article 28 (*f*) allows damages for injury to reputation, a commonplace in municipal legal systems but exceptional in international arbitral practice. Damages were allowed for such injury in *Maal's* case[198] and also in *Fabiani*.

Article 37 of Sohn and Baxter's draft codification provides for the deduction from the award of compensation received from other sources. This is to include compensation awarded to the alien by any other international tribunal, by any social security system, and through insurance payments. In general arbitral tribunals were not concerned with this problem of preventing over-compensation of the victim and thus they did not often examine the possibility of other sources of compensation. Of course these arbitrations preceded the creation of the welfare state and so the problem of payments from the state was not important. However, tribunals also usually ignored the possible existence of compensation through an insurance policy. There has been very little discussion by arbitral tribunals of the position of the insurer as regards claims under international law, potentially a very important question.[199] In fact this question appears to have been considered only by claims commissions and not at all by tribunals deciding individual cases. As regards life insurance, it was held by Umpire Parker in the United States–German Mixed Claims Commission[200] which decided the *Lusitania* cases that money received for this shall not be deducted from the damages awarded as life insurance is not an indemnity contract. Moreover, life insurers who had paid out could not recover their net loss on the ground that such payments constituted injury to United States property under the *compromis*. In the *Provident Mutual Life Insurance Company* case, Parker held that such claims could not be made. The maturing of life insurance contracts was too remote from the unlawful act of Germany. The same decision was reached by the Sweden and Norway–Venezuelan Claims Commission of 1903,[201] but this body gave no explanation for its refusal of such claims.

Nor is there much practice on property insurance. Most of the decisions on this are by national claims commissions rather than by international tribunals. Where the injured alien and the insurer of his property share the same nationality, relatively few problems of principle arise, but nevertheless tribunals have come to conflicting conclusions. For example, the 1824 United States Commission set up under the Treaty of Florida would only allow claims by insurers where those insured had suffered a complete loss. It was held that there could be no subrogation when there was only partial loss. The 1831 United States Commission[202] rejected this practice. The Commission set up in 1872 to decide on the *Alabama* claims[203] decided this question in accordance with American law. They allowed the claims of American insurers of American property only where it was established that the amount of their loss in the war exceeded the amount of premiums and benefits resulting from the same risks, and only to the extent of this excess. The differences between these cases may be partly explained by the fact that there is no accepted theory among tribunals and writers on the question of subrogation. It is not settled whether this should be decided by reference to municipal or international law and, if the latter, then what is the international law on the subrogation of insurers to the rights of the assured. Finally, the nature of the insurer's right is in doubt. These problems become even more important in cases where the insurer and the assured are of different nationalities. It seems to be generally accepted that the national state of the assured may not bring a claim on behalf of an alien insurer. This is usually settled by the terms of the *compromis*, but may also be deduced from the rule of the nationality of claims. The 1922 United States–Germany Mixed Claims Commission followed this rule, as did the Mixed Arbitration Tribunal that decided *La Foncière's* case.[204]

The question whether the national state of an insurer may bring a claim for an injury to the national of another state is more controversial. There have been decisions where this has been allowed, such as the *Circassian*,[205] where no explanation was given for allowing compensation to the British insurers of French property, and the *Mechanic*.[206] In the latter it was asserted that the insurer possessed a 'droit propre et originaire'. For it is only if the insurer has such a right, original and not derived from subrogation, in the property at the time of the injury, that his state will be able to satisfy the rule of nationality of claims. However, there are other cases which state that the insurer has no such right. In *Quillin's* case[207] it was held that at the time of the loss the insurer had only a contingent and conditional interest in the destroyed property, and that this interest became absolute and fixed by payment of the indemnity. The 1824 and 1831 United States domestic Commissions[208] refused to recognize the *locus standi* of United States insurers of foreign property, and the *Alabama* Claims Commission[209] and the 1931 Great Britain–Mexico Commission[210] also accepted this approach. Thus arbitral tribunals and claims commissions are divided on this question.

(*b*) *Imprisonment, arrest, and expulsion*

As in personal injury cases, so in cases of imprisonment, arrest and expulsion there is little consistency between the various awards of damages. Of course, the factors involved in each case, the status and character of the person imprisoned or expelled, the degree of justification for the state's behaviour, the type of treatment given, differ and so the apparent anomalies may have their explanations. However, often these justifications are not clear. It is difficult to see, for example, why George MacManus, who was arrested without grounds and detained for two hours without cruel treatment by Mexico in 1868, should receive $245.75, while Melvin B. Lander, arrested in Mexico at the same time, detained for ten hours without grounds, and subject to ill-treatment, should receive only $98.30. This is only one of many such strange contrasts; there is no need to make an exhaustive list as a glance at Whiteman's collection of awards[211] is enough to make the point. Therefore, Eagleton appears to be mistaken when he says, 'Precedents have fixed with fair accuracy the amount to be allowed for false imprisonment'.[212] It is possible that he was misled by *Faulkner's* case,[213] to which he refers. The United States–Mexico Commission there discussed *Topaze's* case[214] which itself contained a consideration of false imprisonment cases and where the tribunal came to the conclusion that in such cases the average award was $100 a day, and made this the basis of its own award. In *Faulkner's* case this was increased to $150 a day to allow for inflation. These two cases are unusual in their consistency. For even the United States–Mexico Commission did not continue to adhere to the standard it had adopted. As far as other tribunals are concerned, perhaps the only common factor is that many of their awards appear very generous.

Sometimes, especially where the imprisonment was only for a short period, the award was calculated on the basis of a fixed amount per hour or day.[215] This method was criticized in *Chevreau's* case,[216] where it was said,

> Le calcul de l'indemnité d'après un certain taux par jour n'est qu'un moyen pratique pour éviter de tomber dans l'arbitraire. En principe, il s'agit de fixer, en tenant compte des circonstances individuelles de chaque affaire, la somme globale qui compenserait d'une manière équitable le dommage moral ou matériel subi. Ce serait méconnaître ce principe que de vouloir déterminer l'indemnité à allouer en calculant simplement le nombre des jours et en y appliquant un taux qui a pu être consideré comme équitable dans les conditions qui ont régné en Amérique.

Here and in other cases of long periods of detention a lump sum was awarded. The decision as to a suitable award is necessarily somewhat arbitrary, but it seems reasonable to infer that in awards for short periods of imprisonment the primary intention of the tribunal is to indicate its disapproval of the unlawful act, whereas in those for longer periods the tribunal is more concerned with reparation.[217]

(c) *Death*

Eagleton also says that 'accumulated precedents will be of much help to the judge in assessing the amount of damages in death cases'.[218] This again is doubtful. As in personal injury cases, tribunals often gave no explanation of the basis of their awards—it is not made clear whether damages are being assessed for the loss of the dependants or of the deceased. But when the arbitrator considers this question expressly he bases his award on the injury to the dependants.[219] The United States–German Mixed Claims Commissions drew up detailed rules for the assessment of damages in case of death on this basis.[220] This method involves a calculation not only of what the deceased would probably have earned if he had survived, but also of what part of these earnings would have been paid to the claimants. Obviously such calculations are extremely hypothetical. The set of rules of the United States–German Commission referred to above lay down fairly exhaustively the factors to be taken into account in making these calculations. In certain cases damages were given even when there was no evidence that the deceased had in fact supported, or would support, the claimant. Thus, in the cases of the *Heirs of Jean Maninat* and the *Heirs of Jules Brun*[221] Umpire Plumley assumed in the absence of evidence that a son would have supported his mother had he lived. In some cases there is no attempt at a precise evaluation of the claimant's loss. For example, the Portugal–Germany Tribunal[222] said that in claims for loss of life, although strictly a tribunal should in each case work out the material and moral harm for the heirs, it would not do that here. Rather it divided the claims into four categories according to the type of victim and allowed a fixed amount for each category.

There are also many cases where damages have been given to relatives of the deceased although they have not suffered any pecuniary loss. It seems clear that this is intended partly as a solatium for moral injury (*Davis's* case,[223] which declared that such an award is not possible under international law, was not generally accepted), and partly as a sanction. Thus damages have been given for the death of wives and children who had not made any pecuniary contributions to the claimant and were not likely to have done so in the future.[224]

(*d*) *Property damage and loss*

Again arbitral tribunals have used many different methods to assess the loss resulting from damage to real and personal property. For example, the many cases on the award of damages for the destruction of ships adopt various different standards such as the original cost of the ship less depreciation as in the *Masonic*,[225] or fair value as in the *Commodore Stockton*.[226] The ship may be valued as at the start of its voyage, as in *United States* v. *The Two Sicilies*,[227] or as at the date of loss, as in the *Canada*.[228] Similarly, different methods of evaluating the lost cargo are employed; reference may be made to invoice value, replacement value, market value, or fair value. Damages may also be given for lost profits but as has been shown there is no uniformity in the methods of assessing these. If the ship is detained rather than destroyed the loss here again may be assessed in different ways; calculations have involved reference to factors such as demurrage, interest on the purchase money, freight, a percentage of the freight, payments to the crew, the trouble to the owner, lost profits. Even a single commission may vary its methods of assessment in different decisions. The quantification of damage resulting from injuries to other chattels is no more uniform. Whiteman lists the different types of rights in real property, the different types of property, and the different means of interference with such property.[229] But her collection of decisions on such interference again reflects no uniformity in the methods of assessment of damages. Sometimes the cost of repair is relevant, sometimes the decrease in the value of the property. Lost profits are generally allowed where these are probable, but tribunals' standards of probability vary as do their methods of calculation.

The expropriation of real property, or the interference with a business, including farming, conducted on that property, raises complicated questions of evaluation. There have been few arbitral decisions on expropriation alone not involving any breach of contract, and these cases provide very little clear guidance on standards of compensation or methods of assessment. In the *Religious Properties*, *Walter Fletcher Smith*, and *De*

Sabla[230] cases the tribunal attempted to work out the 'value' of the land, but value is a word whose meaning depends on the context and its meaning in these cases is not made clear. Indeed in the last two cases the tribunal reported simply that it reached its final figure by 'taking into account' a list of factors and gave no more detailed explanation than this. Certain cases on breach of contract have also been treated by tribunals as essentially cases of expropriation of property rights.

(*e*) *Contract*

Here, as in delictual claims, the general rule is that of full compensation: that the victim should be put in the position he would have been in if the breach had not occurred. As in municipal law, tribunals generally awarded damages to put the victim in the position he would have been in if the contract had been performed. For example, in *Cheek's* case the arbitrator said, 'I think Dr Cheek's estate is entitled to be put as nearly as possible in the same position as it would have been in had the Siamese government done nothing but had allowed the Agreement of April 1889 to run its course.'[231] But occasionally the aim is to re-establish the claimant in the position he would have been in if the contract had never been made. This approach was adopted in the *Oliva* case[232] as most favourable to the alien because there was little probability of future profits.

It is this question whether to allow lost profits and how to measure these that caused the most difficulty to tribunals. Where the breach of contract could be seen as a taking of property generally arbitral tribunals did not expressly concern themselves with the differences, if any, in compensation for lawful and for unlawful takings. In some cases it is not obvious whether the taking was lawful or unlawful under international law.[233] In all the cases on breach of contract it was apparently expressly accepted or implicitly assumed that lost profits should be compensated. When tribunals refused to award damages for this it was because lost profits were too remote or speculative. The awards for lost profits show a variety of methods of assessment but there is very little discussion of appropriate methods and generally it is not at all clear how the amount awarded was determined. In the *Martini* and *Deutz*[234] cases the extent of lost profits was certain as it was fixed under the contracts, but in most cases the assessment was more difficult. In some cases the net profits to be earned in the remaining period of the concession are calculated; this was the method adopted in *Shufeldt*[235] and *Cheek*. In contrast, sometimes compensation is based on the value of the concession at the time of the breach. Thus the unlawful action is treated as a taking of property. This was the basis of the award in several cases, including the *Compagnie Générale of the Orinoco* and the *Norwegian Shipowners* case. Probable future profits would be taken into account in this assessment of the value of the concession. The award in the

Delagoa Bay Railway Company case shows the complexities involved in this type of calculation; in fact experts were employed to assist in the calculations. In this case damages were based on the capitalized average income of the enterprise taking into account the prospects of a gradual increase in income over the period of the concession. And in general it seems that the role of lawyers and rules of law in the valuation of complex enterprises must be limited to laying down general principles and guidelines on methods of assessment. But early international arbitral practice shows that no one method is dominant; there is a choice of possible methods under international law.

And today the status of arbitral decisions on expropriation and breach of contract is controversial. These more than any of the vast mass of arbitral decisions are the subject of continuing debate. Developments inside and outside the United Nations—the recognition of permanent sovereignty over natural resources and the right to nationalize, the making of lump sum settlements providing less than the traditional prompt, adequate, and effective standard of compensation for nationalization—have led some states and writers to reject the authority of arbitral decisions on the appropriate standard of compensation and methods of assessment for nationalization of property. Most importantly, the aim of full compensation and the award of compensation for lost profits are being questioned. It is significant that in recent international commercial arbitration tribunals have not relied on the earlier arbitral decisions to guide their assessment of compensation for termination of concessions. In *Aminoil* v. *Kuwait*[236] the arbitrator did not even refer to international arbitral decisions on the assessment of compensation. In *Liamco* v. *Libya*[237] the arbitrator did survey the cases on the award of damages for lost profits but held that in the light of subsequent developments he could not hold that they were still decisive. He said that the question whether lost profits should be compensated in cases of nationalization was controversial in international law.

So divisions between writers and states on the right to nationalize and the standard of compensation affect the significance that they attribute to the early arbitral decisions on breach of contract and the taking of property as far as nationalization today is concerned. It is, however, conceivable that in principle the early arbitral decisions in this area could still provide guidelines in cases of simple breach of contract or limited expropriation of private property, but even here the brevity of the decisions and the variety of methods of assessment limit the guidance that they can give.

(f) *Currency of damages*

There seems to be no general rule as to the currency in which damages should be paid. According to Nussbaum,[238] out of the 114 cases between 1794 and 1938 that he examined, in 60 damages were payable in the currency of the creditor, in 33 in that of the debtor, in 18 in that of a third state, and in 3 in gold. The question has never been given much consideration by tribunals. It was briefly discussed in the *Pious Fund* arbitration,[239] where it was held that since the method of payment does not relate to the basis of the right in litigation but only to the execution of the award, the decision of an earlier umpire on the currency in which damages should be paid was not *res judicata*, and future payments could be made in silver rather than in Mexican gold dollars. Other tribunals do not provide any greater enlightenment on this question of currency.

Sometimes the question arises as to what is the appropriate rate of exchange to be adopted by a tribunal when the loss has been totally or partly assessed in one currency, and payment of damages is ordered in another currency. Sometimes treaties make express provision on the relevant rate of exchange,[240] but more often this is left to the tribunal. The question of the date at which the rate of exchange is worked out is important as this may affect the amount of the award because of changes in the relative values of the currencies involved. On these questions also there is no uniformity among the decisions of international arbitral tribunals. Certain writers have extracted rules, or suggested rules, on these questions on the basis of principle rather than of any consistent decisions by tribunals. They single out the decisions that seem reasonable to them and say that these are, or should be, the law.[241]

Finally, arbitral tribunals are not consistent in their awards of costs. An alien or his state may have incurred considerable expense in the pursuit of his claim. Some decisions have allowed damages for this as part of full compensation—certain awards involve calculations of actual expenses,[242] others allow an apparently arbitrary amount.[243] Costs have also been refused, and not just because of delay or other negligence on the part of the claimant.[244]

(g) *Satisfaction*

The vast bulk of international arbitral decisions on damages clearly concern claims by states for injury to their nationals. In the law of state responsibility a distinction is commonly drawn between injuries to individuals, which are called 'private' or 'economic' injuries, and injuries to states, which are called 'public' or 'political'.[245] The latter are usually conceived as consisting in harm to a state's honour and dignity, and the appropriate remedy for such injury is often said to be 'satisfaction'. But the exact juridical status of this remedy and its relation to pecuniary compensation for direct injury to a state and to punitive damages are not clear.[246]

According to Bissonnette, who has made a detailed study of satisfaction,[247] the function of satisfaction is to repair moral injury to a state, but on this question as to when such injury exists Bissonnette unfortunately closes his circular argument by saying that there is a moral injury when the appropriate remedy is satisfaction. Under the traditional theory of state responsibility every injury to a foreign national involves a moral injury to his state. In arbitral practice, however, states apparently claimed almost exclusively for injury to their nationals and rarely included separate claims on their own behalf. Bissonnette more helpfully goes on to list the types of injury for which satisfaction is typically allowed in diplomatic practice. These include attacks on a state's territory, on its agents, official residences, ships, and flag. The most common types of satisfaction for these injuries may be divided into four groups: apologies, punishment of the guilty, assurances as to the future, and pecuniary satisfaction.

State practice on the award of satisfaction shows the lack of objective standards in this area. Obviously exact correspondence between the injury and satisfaction is often not possible; the form of satisfaction given depends on political factors.[248] And in the extensive diplomatic practice on satisfaction the emphasis is on the affront to the state, however caused, rather than on any breach of international law. Many of the diplomatic claims for satisfaction listed by Bissonnette were brought for acts by individuals without any involvement by the state against whom the claim was made,[249] and this casts considerable doubt on its status as a legal remedy for breaches of international law. Satisfaction is much less common in arbitral practice but there are a few possible examples of its award.

In diplomatic practice the distinction between satisfaction and pecuniary compensation for injury to a foreign national is usually clear as the typical measures of satisfaction are non-pecuniary. In arbitral decisions, however, it is sometimes more difficult to make this distinction. Here again where the satisfaction is non-pecuniary there is no problem. Thus in the *Carthage* and the *Manouba* a declaratory judgment was held to constitute adequate satisfaction for violation of state sovereignty, and in the *I'm Alone*[250] the tribunal recommended that the United States should apologize to the Canadian Government for its unlawful action in sinking a Canadian ship. It is obviously more difficult to distinguish pecuniary satisfaction from damages. Unlike the latter, pecuniary satisfaction is not necessarily calculated on the basis of the extent of the injury involved. But where there has been a moral or personal injury to the individual it is difficult to decide whether an award apparently in excess of mere compensation for his financial loss includes an element for the satisfaction of the state or is just compensation for moral injury. Indeed the question arises whether it is possible to separate the two and, further, to distinguish them from punitive damages. The only means of achieving this is to examine the expressed intention, if any, of the arbitrators. However, arbitrators apparently sometimes confuse pecuniary satisfaction and punitive damages. Thus in *Stevenson's* case,[251] where Great Britain demanded damages for injury to herself through the injury to Stevenson, the tribunal refused because this would be wholly punitive. Again in the *Carthage* and the *Manouba* the Permanent Court of Arbitration refused France's claim for one franc for the violation of her sovereignty and for one thousand francs for her moral and political injury because it regarded this as a pecuniary sanction. Certainly satisfaction is closely related to punitive damages in that both are used to express disapproval of the unlawful act, satisfaction to appease the claimant state, and punitive damages to punish the wrongdoing state.

Pecuniary satisfaction has never been explicitly awarded by an international arbitral tribunal. When claims expressly based on indignity to the state have been made, as in *Miliani*[252] and *Stevenson*, these have been refused. There are cases where the amount awarded seems greater than necessary to compensate the injury to the alien, and in some of these it might be possible to infer an intention to provide pecuniary satisfaction for the state. However, it is doubtful whether cases such as the *Compagnie Générale des Asphaltes* and *Mallén*,[253] cited by Bissonnette as instances of the award of pecuniary satisfaciton by arbitral tribunals, in fact involved the award of money to the claimant state as opposed to its national. Rather it seems that in both these the money was intended for the individual and the terms of the decision were supposed to constitute satisfaction for the state. This may be seen also in the case of the *Heirs of Jean Maninat*. Here Umpire Plumley allowed 100,000 francs to a sister not dependent on her deceased brother. He said,

> The more important feature of this case is the unatoned indignity to a sister republic through this inexcusable outrage upon one of her nationals. It is for this tribunal to speak the voice of regret and to tender atonement for a sad result.[254]

Indeed, it is doubtful whether any decision apart from the *I'm Alone* has ever awarded pecuniary satisfaction to a state in the form of an award of money for itself rather than in the form of an increased award to its national from which the state is to derive more intangible satisfaction. In the *Arends* case[255] the umpire allowed only minimal damages for the detention by Venezuela of a Dutch ship,

> But the respondent government is willing to recognize its responsibility and express regrets for such an act in the only way that it can now be done, through the action of this Commission by an award on behalf of the claimant sufficient to make full amends for the unlawful delay.

He accordingly allowed $100 to take the place of the expression of regrets by Venezuela to the Dutch Government. Even here it is not beyond question that the money was intended for the state itself and the same is true of *Weile's* case.[256] Therefore it may be true that the *I'm Alone* is the only case where an arbitral tribunal awarded pecuniary satisfaction to a state. Here the tribunal said that the United States ought formally to acknowledge the illegality of its actions in sinking the Canadian ship and to apologize to the Canadian Government, and as a material amend in respect of the wrong the United States should pay $25,000 to the Canadian Government. The apparent intention of the tribunal was that the United States should provide pecuniary satisfaction for its unlawful act rather than damages based on any material injury to Canadian nationals.

All this discussion of international arbitral practice on judicial remedies may seem rather outdated for since the Second World War there has been a marked decrease in the number of arbitrations between states. Between 1945 and 1970 there were only 23 arbitrations. That is, fewer than one a year, in comparison with the average (admittedly misleading as it is taken for a much longer period) of three a year between 1794 and 1945.[257] Nor has the rate increased since 1970. Apart from the cases before the conciliation Commissions set up under the 1947 Peace Treaties[258] and the Austrian–German Arbitral Tribunal,[259] almost all post-Second World War arbitrations involved requests for declaratory judgments. Requests for damages were rare and their award even more so.[260] And the Conciliation Commissions set up to decide claims against Italy were controlled by the detailed provisions in the Peace Treaty.[261] It was not open to the Commissions to use methods of calculation other than those stipulated in the Treaty. Thus in *Suermondt and Dumont*[262] the Franco-Italian Commission said,

> Article 78 (4) *a* du Traité de Paix prévoit, dans l'hypothèse, où la restitution du bien est impossible, un mode particulier de calcul d'indemnisation, et l'interprète doit s'en tenir là, sans pouvoir recourir aux principes généralement admis pour la détermination du dommage.

Often the agents of the two states involved would agree on an appropriate amount of compensation so that there was no need to call on a third member of the Commission to decide between them.[263] But in cases where the two agents could not agree, the main problem facing the Commission was that of evidence, or lack of evidence. In accordance with the practice of international arbitral tribunals the inadequacy of available evidence did not necessarily lead the Commissions to reject a claim completely; rather they estimated the amount of compensation '*ex aequo et bono*'[264] or 'acting in a spirit of conciliation'.[265] Thus in *Theodorou's* case[266] the United Kingdom–Italian Commission said,

> The Conciliation Commission after a thorough examination of the various pieces of evidence has arrived at the conclusion that the loss has in principle been proved, but that the exact amount cannot be established or is difficult to determine, partly because of the same events which caused the damage and partly by reason of the fact that the evidence adduced is not sufficiently precise. The Conciliation Com-

mission has decided in these circumstances to determine equitably the amount of the compensation being guided by certain precedents in the decided cases of the Italo-French Conciliation Commission.

In many cases very little explanation of the amount of the award was given.[267] Often experts were called in to assess the amount due to the claimant, and almost invariably their calculations were accepted by the Commission.[268]

The 1951 Peace Treaty with Japan also provides for reparations. But unlike the 1947 Peace Treaties the detailed rules on the damage for which compensation is to be paid and on the principles of assessment are contained in a Japanese law to which reference is made in the Peace Treaty. Under a 1952 Agreement on the Settlement of Disputes, disputes over Article 15 were to be dealt with by Property Commissions. Four of these were established, of which three in fact made a small number of decisions. These decisions were based on the Japanese law and the Treaty, not made *ex aequo et bono*.[269]

But apart from these tribunals set up under Peace Treaties almost all modern interstate arbitrations involve requests by the parties for declaratory judgments stating their legal position. Personnaz, writing in 1938, had predicted the extension of the right to reparation to match the increase in scope of the rules of state responsibility.[270] In fact, as is now clear, interstate arbitration as he had known it had had its day, and awards of judicial remedies other than declaratory judgments had become exceptional.

What has been the impact of this substantial international arbitral practice? Do these decisions have any continuing significance? Developments in the law concerning expropriation have undermined or reduced the status of cases on this question as far as standards of compensation and methods of assessment are concerned. But the decisions on arrest, expulsion, personal injury, and so on have not been similarly affected. The question is whether it is possible to extract rules from this arbitral practice and what effect, if any, these decisions have had on later tribunals.

Awards of remedies other than damages were so exceptional that any deductions as to the law, apart from the availability of *restitutio in integrum*, must depend on later developments. As far as damages are concerned writers still cite early arbitral decisions as authoritative. But it is striking that those writers who have made detailed studies of this arbitral practice stress the uncertainty and lack of uniformity; they are very hesitant about the extraction of general rules. For even this brief survey of arbitral practice on the assessment of damages reveals a considerable variety of methods of assessment. Nor is there any consistency between decisions given at any particular time within the longer period. Even selecting only twentieth-century cases does not produce consistent sets of rules. Other writers dealing with this topic as part of a wider subject, or more briefly than the detailed studies mentioned above, have found greater certainty. It is not justifiable to assume that this is simply a case of the first group of writers being too close to their subject, unable to see the wood for the trees; it could equally be the case that the latter are making woods out of single trees. Probably we should abandon this metaphor and recognize that here, as often in international law, the difference between those who see rules and those who see chaos is essentially one of temperament.

However, what remains obscure is the process by which those who extract specific rules from the mass of arbitral practice choose between the cases. This does not, or not consistently, seem to be a simple matter of numbers—of taking the rule adopted in the majority of cases. The choice of particular cases as authoritative appears to rest, whether expressly or impliedly, on principle, that is, on the writer's view of what the law should be. Almost all writers, including both those who have made detailed studies and those who discuss this question in a wider context, agree on certain general rules. They agree that in principle lost profits should be compensated. They agree that in principle interest on, or as part of, awards should be allowed. And they agree that the test of proximate causation should be adopted to limit the award of damages. The first two rules seem justified on the basis of the preponderant arbitral practice, though their content is not certain. The last is a policy preference, supported by some cases but not others. By contrast, writers strongly disagree as to whether punitive damages are permissible in international law, arguing on the basis of opposing cases and of principle.

Of course there is nothing very strange about this process of extracting rules, whether general rules like those mentioned above or more specific rules about precise methods of assessment. This approach to a mass of cases can be seen in municipal law textbooks also. But there is a difference between international and municipal law here in that in the latter courts do not operate in isolation but develop consistent approaches over time. The relatively smaller number of international claims has not produced greater certainty.

On this question of the impact and continuing significance of international arbitral practice it is instructive to consider the pleadings in cases involving claims for damages before the World Court. Many make no mention of arbitral or judicial decisions on damages.[271] Others refer only to the *Chorzów Factory* case and/or the *Corfu Channel* case.[272] But in its pleadings in the *Aerial Incident* case, Israel invoked the *Lusitania* claims.[273] It did not offer any explanation or justification for its choice of this particular set of claims. It adopted the general approach of the United States–German Commission.

In five cases the pleadings show more extensive reliance on arbitral decisions. Thus in the *Anglo-Iranian Oil Company* case[274] the United Kingdom cited the cases where *restitutio in integrum* had been allowed or mentioned as possible. On the assessment of damages it chose the *Shufeldt* case as authority for the award of compensation for lost profits. In the *Aerial Incident* case[275] the United States sought not only damages on behalf of the next of kin of those killed but also 'additional amends'; by this they apparently meant punitive damages and they went on to invoke the *Lusitania* cases, the *I'm Alone*, the diplomatic claim in *Imbrie's* case, and Anglo-American case-law. In *Nottebohm* Liechtenstein said that

> An examination of the practice of international tribunals in awarding damages for [sc. unlawful arrest, detention and expulsion], though it reveals the existence of certain factors to be taken into consideration, does not provide rules which can be applied by the Court without the exercise of a substantial degree of discretion.[276]

It went on to discuss a number of relevant cases, saying that the standards applied in these cases should not be applied automatically but that they could give guidance. So in *Nottebohm* there is a fairly wide survey of cases and an attempt to explain the significance of those cases, but in the *Anglo-Iranian Oil Company* and *Aerial Incident* cases the choice of cases, relatively uncontroversial in the former but not in the latter, is made without discussion. The respondent state did not enter pleadings in the last two cases, and in *Nottebohm* Guatemala challenged the amount of the claim, not the relevance of the arbitral cases invoked by Liechtenstein. Disagreements in the pleadings on the rules to be derived from arbitral practice rather than merely on the amount of the claim can be found in only two cases. Not surprisingly these are the *Wimbledon*[277] and the *Chorzów Factory* case,[278] the two cases where the Permanent Court of International Justice actually considered the question of damages. In the former France claimed damages for lost profits in French currency. When Germany rejected this on the basis of general principle, France cited arbitral awards to back its claim. Subsequently in the *Chorzów Factory* case Poland used *ad hominem* arguments against Germany: in reply to Germany's claim for lost profits Poland cited Germany's arguments in the *Wimbledon*. But it is significant that Poland relied on a watered down version of the original argument. It apparently did not attempt to argue—though there is some ambiguity—that there was an absolute rule against the award of lost profits but only that there were many cases refusing lost profits where these were too remote and speculative and that these decisions were applicable on the facts of the case before the Court. Again, on the question of interest Poland cited those cases where this had been refused. Germany relied on the contrasting cases where damages for lost profits and interest had been awarded. Clearly arbitral practice offers a wide variety of cases, and states, like writers, may pick and choose between them. The crucial question of the attitude of the World Court and of other tribunals to this arbitral practice will be examined in the following chapters.

NOTES

1. For studies of earlier arbitrations see J. H. Ralston, *International Arbitration from Athens to Locarno* (1929); M. N. Tod, *International Arbitration amongst the Greeks* (1913); W. E. Darby, *International Tribunals* (4th edn. 1904).
2. J. Personnaz, *La Réparation du préjudice en droit international public* (1939); L. Reitzer, *La Réparation comme conséquence de l'acte illicite en droit international* (1938); F. V. García-Amador in F. V. García-Amador, L. B. Sohn, and R. R. Baxter, *Recent Codification of the Law of State Responsibility for Injuries to Aliens* (1974); M. Whiteman, *Damages in International Law* (1937); B. Bollecker-Stern, *Le Préjudice dans la théorie de la responsabilité internationale* (1973).
3. Moore *Int. Adj.*, iv. 194, 240.
4. Moore *Int. Adj.* iv. 372, at 400.
5. See the Opinions of Nicholls and Pinkney in the *Betsey*.
6. Most recently the Iran–United States Claims Tribunal displayed a very cavalier approach to the question of the law governing its awards of damages. See Ch. 5 Section 1.
7. García-Amador, op. cit. in n. 2, at 89. See also Reitzer, op. cit. ibid., at 111.
8. See, for example, E. M. Borchard, *The Diplomatic Protection of Citizens Abroad* (1928); F. S. Dunn, *The Protection of Nationals* (1932).
9. See below at n. 44.
10. According to F. K. Nielsen, *International Law Applied to Reclamations* (1941), at 61, 'In connection with the adjustment of international reclamations, rules and principles of municipal law are often invoked. This is frequently useful and indeed necessary in fixing the amounts of pecuniary losses. Principles of municipal law common to the systems of jurisprudence of nations may be said to have been applied so frequently as to have become accepted as international law. This is naturally so in cases in which losses consequent on acts or omissions of authorities attributable to a state are the same as losses resulting from acts which are tortious under domestic law.'
11. See I. Brownlie, *System of the Law of Nations: State Responsibility*, Part I (1983), at 223–4.
12. See, for example, García-Amador, 89, Reitzer, at 159.
13. 1912 Russia/Turkey 11 RIAA 421, at 442.
14. 1928 France/Mexico 5 RIAA 327, at 448.
15. La Fontaine, 398, Moore, 1865.
16. 1909 United States/Venezuela 9 RIAA 181.
17. 1920 France, Great Britain and Spain/Portugal 1 RIAA 7.
18. 1902 United States/Russia 9 RIAA 51, at 65.
19. 1903 France/Venezuela, La Fontaine, 343.
20. 1839 United States/Mexico, Moore, 2859.

21. 1900 Guatemala/United States 15 RIAA 47.
22. *Metzger* 1903 Germany/Venezuela 10 RIAA 417.
23. The *Canadienne* and the *Sidra* 1910 United States/Great Britain 6 RIAA 29 and 53. See also J. H. Ralston, *The Law and Procedure of International Tribunals* (1926), 98 ff.; *International Arbitration from Athens to Locarno* (1929), 84. And agreements such as those of 1923 between Mexico and various European states are exceptional. These provided that the amount of damages awarded for personal injuries should not exceed that obtainable in the claimant state. In fact this provision was never applied. See A. H. Feller, *The Mexican Claims Commissions* (1935), at 292.
24. See F. A. Mann (1957) *BYBIL* 20; R. B. Schlesinger (1957) *AJ* 734.
25. Bin Cheng, *General Principles of Law as Applied by International Courts and Tribunals* (1953).
26. Ibid., at 239.
27. See especially Vol. vii, *Contracts in General*, Ch. 16; Vol. xi, *Torts*, Chs. 4, 7, 8, 9, 10, 11; Vol. xvi, *Civil Procedure*, Ch. 4.
28. See (1985) *Texas ILJ*, 267.
29. See above at n. 20 ff. In their draft codification Sohn and Baxter (op. cit. in n. 2, at 333) suggest that in cases of breach of contract damages should be assessed in accordance either with the law of the respondent state or with an international standard. The obligation should be measured by the higher of these two standards. This is an innovatory suggestion but Sohn and Baxter unfortunately give no explanation as to why this approach should be adopted in contract cases but not for delicts. They do not discuss whether damages may be assessed in accordance with the local law even if this is not the proper law of the contract.
30. A. A. C. Trindade, *The Application of the Rule of Exhaustion of Local Remedies in International Law* (1983).
31. See, for example, A. I. Ogus, *The Law of Damages* (1973); H. McGregor, *Damages* (14th edn. 1980); H. Stoll, *IECL* Vol. xi, Ch. 8; H. Street, *Principles of the Law of Damages* (1962).
32. A. V. Dicey and J. H. C. Morris, *The Conflict of Laws* (10th edn. 1980), 1175 ff.; Halsbury's *Laws of England* (4th edn.), Vol. viii, §779.
33. E. Rabel, *The Conflict of Laws: A Comparative Study* (1958–64), Vol. ii (2nd edn.), 276–283, 544.
34. League of Nations Publication 1930, xvii. 234.
35. For example, the 1923 United States–Mexico General Claims Commission in *Faulkner's* case referred to *Topaze*, a decision of the 1903 Great Britain–Venezuela Commission on the appropriate measure of damages in cases of false imprisonment (4 RIAA 67). However, the Commission did not consistently adhere to this standard. See A. H. Feller, *The Mexican Claims Commission* (1935), Ch. 17. Other cases in which reference was made to the decisions of specific earlier tribunals include *Martini* 1930 *Italy* v. *Venezuela* (2 RIAA 975), *Shufeldt* 1930 *Guatemala* v. *United States* (2 RIAA 1081), and the Portuguese claims against Germany (2 RIAA 1013).

36. J. B. Moore, *Collected Papers* (1944), 200, quoted in K. S. Carlston, *The Process of International Arbitration* (1946), 259.
37. On express provision for the award of remedies other than damages see below at n. 44 ff.
38. Parry, lxxix. 397.
39. Collected in Feller, op. cit. in n. 23, at 412. The Treaty made on 18 April 1892 between the United States and Great Britain on the arbitration of the Behring Sea claims gave detailed guidance in Article 5 on the assessment of damages, but the parties did not follow its guidelines in practice. Moore, 755, at 804.
40. Those cases which do contain more detailed discussion of the assessment of damages have, understandably, attracted greater attention from writers, but they do not seem to have had any greater impact on other tribunals.
41. J. Subilia, 'L'Allocation d'intérêts dans la jurisprudence internationale' (1972), Lausanne, thesis.
42. A. M. Stuyt, *A Survey of International Arbitrations* (1972).
43. See Ch. 2 Section 1.
44. 3 RIAA 1905.
45. (1917) AJ 674.
46. By the arbitrator in *BP* v. *Libya* (53 ILR 297). See F. A. Mann (1976–7) *BYBIL* 1, at 13; Ch. 5 Section 2, at n. 35 ff.
47. PCIJ Ser. A no. 17. See Ch. 2 Section 4.
48. See, for example, García-Amador, 100; Personnaz, 77.
49. Reitzer, 171.
50. See Mann, op. cit. in n. 46.
51. M. B. Alvarez de Eulate, 'La restitutio in integrum en la prática y en la jurisprudencia internationales' (1971–2) 29–32 *Revista de ciencia y técnica jurídica* 11, in his apparently exhaustive list of instances of *restitutio in integrum* in diplomatic and arbitral practice unfortunately does not make this distinction. However the arbitrator in *BP* v. *Libya* drew the distinction and his survey of those arbitral agreements where express provision was made for *restitutio in integrum* led him to conclude, 'such treaties and compromis are not numerous and consistent enough to be regarded as evidence of a uniform state practice'. For a discussion of restitution of property seized in war see I. Vasarhelyi, *Restitution in International Law* (1964), and criticism by A. Drucker (1966) *ICLQ* 263.
52. 1930 Italy/Venezuela 2 RIAA 977.
53. Ibid., 1002.
54. Loc. cit. in n. 45, at 696.
55. 1940 Levant States/Egypt 3 RIAA 1871.
56. The instances of annulment of unlawful measures listed by Alvarez de Eulate (op. cit. in n. 51, at 27) were all, except three cases, the result of diplomatic settlement not arbitral award. These three cases are the *Martini* case quoted above, the *United Fruit Company* case, and the *Hotel Metropole* case. In these last two cases express provision for restitution had been made in the *compromis*.

57. 1923 Spain/United Kingdom 2 RIAA 615, at 722.
58. Op. cit in n. 51, at 20 ff.
59. The jurisprudence of national prize courts provides many examples of orders for the restitution of ships unlawfully seized in war. See, for example, C. J. Colombos, *A Treatise on the Law of Prize* (1949). However, prize courts may be regarded as a special case; their wide powers should not automatically be attributed to general international arbitration tribunals.
60. For example, the *Macedonian* 1858 United States/Chile, Moore, 1449; the *Orinoco Company* 1903 United States/Venezuela 9 RIAA 297.
61. M. O. Hudson, *International Legislation*, iv (1931), 2529.
62. 1931 Greece/Bulgaria 3 RIAA 1389.
63. 1929 United States/Cuba 2 RIAA 913.
64. 1911 France/Great Britain 11 RIAA 243.
65. 1909 France/Germany 11 RIAA 119.
66. This was argued by H. W. Baade (1960) *AJ* 801 and also by Feller, op. cit. in n. 23, at 290.
67. On international commercial arbitration see Ch. 5 Section 2.
68. 1903 Italy/Venezuela 10 RIAA 499; 1903 Belgium/Venezuela 9 RIAA 328.
69. 1926 United States/Mexico 4 RIAA 41, 218.
70. Ibid., 219.
71. Op. cit. in n. 46, at 13.
72. J. H. Ralston, *International Arbitration from Athens to Locarno* (1929), at 61.
73. See Mann, op. cit. in n. 46, and see the discussion by the arbitrator in *BP* v. *Libya*, Ch. 5 Section 2.
74. I. Brownlie, *Principles of Public International Law* (3rd edn. 1979), 462.
75. See below at n. 148 ff.
76. This slow development of the declaratory judgment in international arbitral practice is mirrored in municipal legal sytems. The civil law systems have only gradually extended the Roman law actions of *lex diffamari* and *ex lege si contendat*, and in England it was not until the Judicature Acts of 1873 and 1875 and the 1883 Rules of the Supreme Court that the courts abandoned their restrictive attitude to the declaratory judgment and gave such judgments in cases where no other form of relief was possible. See E. M. Borchard, *Declaratory Judgments* (1941); P. W. Young, *Declaratory Orders* (1975); and I. Zamir, *The Declaratory Judgment* (1962), for accounts of the historical development and current importance of this remedy. And see *IECL*, Vol. xvi, Ch. 4.
77. 10 RIAA 754.
78. Ibid., at 755.
79. 1910 Great Britain/United States 6 RIAA, 173.
80. See Ch. 2 Section 4.
81. 1913 France/Italy 11 RIAA 449, at 460.
82. 1913 France/Italy 11 RIAA 463, at 475.
83. See, for example, R. B. Lillich in R. B. Lillich (ed.), *International Law of State Responsibility for Injuries to Aliens* (1983), Ch. 1.
84. 1871 United States/Great Britain, Moore, 495, at 651. Although the tribunal

made it clear which heads of damage were covered by the award it gave no details as to the methods of assessment it used in arriving at the lump sum. The tribunal had been given an express power under the *compromis* to make a lump sum award as were two of the other tribunals that made lump sum awards, the 1923 United States–Turkey Commission (G. Fr. de Martens, *Nouveau Recueil général de traités* 3rd series, xxx. 753) and the 1862 Great Britain, France–Uruguay Commission (Lapradelle and Politis, ii. 119).

85. 1 RIAA 307, at 338. For similar statements by other tribunals see *Cheek* 1898 United States/Siam, Moore, 1899 and 5068; *Delagoa Bay Railway Company* 1900 Great Britain/United States, Moore, 1865, La Fontaine, 398; *Union Bridge* 1910 United States/Great Britain 6 RIAA 138.

86. García-Amador, Sohn, and Baxter, op. cit. in n. 2, at 99 and 314. See also the American Law Institute Restatement of the Law Foreign Relations Law of the United States (Revised) Tentative Draft no. 5.

87. D. V. Sandifer, *Evidence before International Tribunals* (2nd edn. 1975).

88. Ibid., at 4.

89. H. Lauterpacht, *The Development of International Law by the International Court* (1958), at 366.

90. Sandifer, at 22.

91. 1869 United States/Great Britain, Moore, 237, at 261.

92. 1870 United States/Spain, Moore, 1007, at 1014.

93. 1903 France/Venezuela 10 RIAA 184, at 284.

94. The *Norwegian Shipowners*, loc cit. in n. 81; *Campbell* 1931 Great Britain/ Portugal 2 RIAA 1147. See H. Scheuner in *International Arbitration: Liber Amicorum for Martin Domke*, ed. P. Sanders (1967), 275, L. B. Sohn, ibid., 330.

95. *Mavrommatis (Palestine) Concessions*, PCIJ Ser. A no. 2, 12. The anomalies presented by this theory are well known. See García-Amador, 78; R. R. Baxter (1964–5) *Syracuse LR* 745.

96. However, B. Bollecker-Stern (op. cit. in n. 2) suggests that because of the existence of socialist states and the involvement of even capitalist states in trade and financial affairs, the theory that injury to a national constitutes an injury to his state is becoming more realistic.

97. 1923 United States/Mexico 4 RIAA 82.

98. See, for example, F. S. Dunn, op. cit. in n. 8, at 175; J. L. Brierly (1928) *BYBIL* 42.

99. Loc. cit. in n. 97, at 90.

100. 1923 United States/Mexico 4 RIAA 440.

101. See Feller, op. cit. in n. 23.

102. Personnaz, Reitzer, Whiteman, op. cit. in n. 2; Subilia, op. cit in n. 41; A. Hauriou (1924) *RGDIP* 203.

103. Whiteman, 1767.

104. Personnaz, 132.

105. H. Lauterpacht, *Private Law Sources and Analogies of International Law* (1927), at 220.

106. Loc. cit. in n. 44.

107. See *Hammaken*, *Rice*, and *Brooks* 1868 United States/Mexico, Moore, 3470, 3248, 4309.
108. See Brownlie, op. cit. in n. 11, at 225, Hauriou, op. cit. in n. 102; Personnaz, 127; G. Salvioli (1929) 3 *HR* 235.
109. 7 RIAA 29.
110. H. L. A. Hart and T. Honoré. *Causation in the Law* (2nd edn. 1985).
111. 1930 Portugal/Germany 2 RIAA 1013, at 1032.
112. 1903 France/Venezuela 10 RIAA 55.
113. 1902 Germany/Great Britain, United States 9 RIAA 15. On the differences between the directness and foreseeability tests see, e.g., A. I. Ogus, *The Law of Damages* (1973).
114. 1897 Great Britain/Netherlands, Moore, 4948.
115. 1822 United States/Great Britain, Lapradelle and Politis, i. 348.
116. Loc. cit. in n. 114, at 4953.
117. See detailed study by Bollecker-Stern, op. cit. in n. 2.
118. This is not the place for a discussion of whether state responsibility is based on fault, for that is a question about the nature and basis of state responsibility rather than the measure of damages. On this doctrinal controversy see, e.g. I. Brownlie, op. cit. in n. 11, at 38–46.
119. PCIJ Ser. A no. 17, at 75.
120. 1903 Germany/Venezuela 10 RIAA 417.
121. 1861 Great Britain/Portugal, Lapradelle and Politis, ii. 78.
122. 1864 France/Argentina, Lapradelle and Politis, ii. 290.
123. 1930 Italy/Venezuela 2 RIAA 975.
124. Op. cit. in n. 102, at 219 ff.
125. 1863 United States/Peru, Moore, 3405.
126. 1870 United States/Brazil, Moore, 1733.
127. 5 RIAA 309.
128. Loc. cit. in n. 18, at 65.
129. Op. cit. in n. 105, at 149.
130. 1868 United States/Mexico, Moore, 3134.
131. 1871 United States/Spain, Moore, 3782.
132. 1903 Germany/Venezuela 9 RIAA 389.
133. 1898 United States/Siam, Moore, 1899 and 5068.
134. For example, G. Schwarzenberger (1950) *CLP* 263; Bin Cheng, op. cit. in n. 26, at 234–6; Borchard, op. cit. in n. 6.
135. See Ch. 6, and discussion by the International Law Commission (*ILC Yearbook* from 1976).
136. Loc. cit. in n. 109.
137. C. Eagleton (1929–30) *Yale L.J* 52.
138. Loc. cit. in n. 109, at 41.
139. 1868 United States/Mexico, Moore, 4309.
140. 1868 United States/Mexico, Moore, 3462.
141. 1868 United States/Mexico, Moore, 3411.
142. 1935 Canada/United States 3 RIAA 1609.
143. See below at n. 245 ff.

144. Whiteman, 716.
145. Loc. cit. in n. 133, at 5072.
146. 1903 United States/Venezuela 9 RIAA 225.
147. Whiteman, 628.
148. 1910 Great Britain/United States 6 RIAA 109.
149. 1903 Great Britain/Venezuela 9 RIAA 390.
150. Ibid., at 398.
151. Moore, 1287.
152. 1956 France/Greece 12 RIAA 155, at 216.
153. Parry, cxxii. 233.
154. Parry, cxxvii. 165.
155. Loc. cit. in n. 38.
156. Parry, clxvii. 63.
157. 9 RIAA 11.
158. For example, 1910 Great Britain/United States 6 RIAA 5; *Delagoa Bay Railway Company*, loc. cit. in n. 15; *Illinois Central Railway* 1923 United States/Mexico 4 RIAA 134.
159. 1910 United States/Great Britain 6 RIAA 29.
160. Feller, 312.
161. 1875 United States/Colombia, Moore, 1421, at 1445.
162. As in the *Macedonian* 1863 United States/Chile, Moore, 1449.
163. For example, *Dundonald* 1873 Great Britain/Brazil, Lapradelle and Politis, iii. 441.
164. As in the *Russian Indemnity* case, loc. cit. in n. 13.
165. Thus where the award is for personal injury often no interest is allowed as the amount of the award is designed to cover the whole loss including that likely to result in the future. Also where lost profits are calculated by concrete as opposed to abstract methods an award of interest is not necessary.
166. 7 RIAA 70.
167. See Feller, 309.
168. Op. cit. in n. 41.
169. Loc. cit. in n. 162.
170. Loc. cit. in n. 167.
171. 10 RIAA 357.
172. 1903 Italy/Venezuela 10 RIAA 492.
173. 1868 Commission, Moore, 1287; 1923 Commission 4 RIAA.
174. The 1922 Austria–Germany Commission 7 RIAA and the 1926 Tripartite Commission 6 RIAA 195 are exceptions to this.
175. 1843 Great Britain/France, Moore, 4937, Lapradelle and Politis, i. 512.
176. 10 RIAA.
177. Ibid., at 498.
178. Ibid.
179. For example, in the *Macedonian*, loc. cit. in n. 162.
180. For example, the *Christina* 1903 Sweden/Venezuela 10 RIAA 765.
181. For example, the *Behring Sea* claims 1868 Great Britain/United States, Moore 2123.

182. 1910 Great Britain/United States 6 RIAA 32.
183. 1903 Mexico/Venezuela 10 RIAA 698.
184. Whiteman, 1997.
185. See list in Whiteman, ibid.
186. 1914 France/Peru 1 RIAA 215, at 220.
187. At n. 153 and 154.
188. *Cocoa Grove Riot* claims 1916 United States/Panama 1916 US For. Rel. 918; *Religious Properties* case, loc. cit. in n. 17.
189. For example, 1881 Great Britain–Transvaal Commission, La Fontaine, 231; the *Rhodope Forests* case, loc. cit. in n. 62.
190. Subilia, op. cit. in n. 41, at Part II, Ch. 4.
191. Op. cit. in n. 2, at 344.
192. Reitzer, 190.
193. Whiteman, 517 ff.
194. Whiteman, 627.
195. Loc. cit. in n. 188.
196. For example, *Coleman* 1928 United States/Mexico 5 RIAA 364; *McNeill* 1930 Great Britain/Mexico 5 RIAA 164.
197. Op. cit. in n. 2, at 321.
198. 1903 Netherlands/Venezuela 10 RIAA 731.
199. See J.-P. Ritter (1961) *RGDIP* 765; T. Meron (1974) *AJ* 628.
200. 7 RIAA 32.
201. 10 RIAA.
202. Moore *Int. Adj.*, v. 377.
203. Moore, 495.
204. TAM, ix. 400.
205. 1871 Great Britain/United States, Lapradelle and Politis, iii. 355.
206. 1885 United States/Venezuela, Moore, 3210.
207. 1922 United States/Germany 7 RIAA 299.
208. Loc. cit. in n. 202.
209. Moore, 4639.
210. 5 RIAA 10.
211. Whiteman, 287.
212. Op. cit. in n. 137, at 75.
213. 1923 United States/Mexico 4 RIAA 67.
214. 1903 Great Britain/Venezuela 9 RIAA 387.
215. As in *Faulkner* and *Topaze*.
216. 1931 France/Great Britain 2 RIAA 1115, at 1139.
217. See Personnaz, 210.
218. Op. cit. in n. 137.
219. For example, *Di Caro* 1903 Italy/Venezuela 10 RIAA 597, *Standish* 1868 United States/Mexico, Moore, 3004; *Davis* 1915 United States/Panama 1916 US For. Rel. 918.
220. 7 RIAA, at 32.
221. 1903 France/Venezuela 10 RIAA 24.
222. 2 RIAA 1037.

223. Loc. cit. in n. 219.
224. There are many such instances among the *Lusitania* cases (loc. cit. in n. 109). For example, *Ferguson* and *Condon*.
225. Moore, 1055.
226. 1868 United States/Mexico, Whiteman, 1033.
227. Whiteman, 1023.
228. Loc. cit. in n. 126.
229. Whiteman, 1355. Damages are not generally based on unjust enrichment. *Lena Goldfields* (see below, Ch. 5 Section 2 at n. 51) and *William Parker* (4 RIAA 35) are exceptional in their employment of this method and it was expressly rejected in *Union Bridge* (6 RIAA 138) and *Dickson Car Wheel Company* (4 RIAA 669). See C. H. Schreuer (1974) *AJCL* 281.
230. 1926 United States/Panama 6 RIAA 358.
231. Loc. cit. in n 133, at 5069.
232. 1903 Italy/Venezuela 10 RIAA 600.
233. Compare the different divisions between the cases made in *Liamco* v. *Libya* ((1981) ILM 1), by J. Fischer-Williams (1928) *BYBIL* 1, and in UN Doc. A/AC 97/5. See discussion by R. Y. Jennings (1961) *BYBIL* 156. And see below Ch. 5 Section 1, at n. 35, Ch. 5 Section 2, at n. 55.
234. 1923 United States/Mexico 4 RIAA 472.
235. 1930 Guatemala/United States 2 RIAA 1081.
236. (1982) ILM 976.
237. (1981) ILM 1.
238. A. Nussbaum, *Money in the Law, National and International* (1950 rev. edn.). See also F. A. Mann (1959) 1 *HR* 7, at 104; *The Legal Aspect of Money* (1982), at 531 ff.
239. 1903 United States/Mexico 9 RIAA 1. See also the *Diverted Cargoes* arbitration 12 RIAA 65 and discussion by Mann, op. cit. in n 24.
240. See list in Whiteman, 1877 n. 1.
241. See Brownlie, op. cit. in n. 11, at 230; García-Amador, Sohn, and Baxter, op. cit. in n. 2, at 344.
242. As in *El Triunfo* 1902 United States/Salvador 15 RIAA 463.
243. As in *Moke*, loc. cit. in n. 141.
244. For example, *Delagoa Bay Railway Company*, loc. cit. in n. 15; *Cerruti* 1897 Italy/Colombia, Moore, 2120.
245. García-Amador, 91, Personnaz, 16.
246. See P. A. Bissonnette, *La Satisfaction comme mode de réparation en droit international* (1952), Part II Ch. 3, Brownlie, op. cit. in n. 11, at 208.
247. Op. cit. in n. 246. See also García-Amador, 89; Personnaz, Part III Ch. 2; and F. Przetacznik (1974) *RGDIP* 919.
248. Bissonnette, Part II Chs. 1 and 2.
249. Bissonnette, Part I Ch. 1. García-Amador, 94, also accepts this.
250. 3 RIAA 1609.
251. 1903 Great Britain/Venezuela 9 RIAA 494, at 506.
252. 1903 Italy/Venezuela 10 RIAA 584.
253. 1923 Mexico/United States 4 RIAA 173.

254. Loc. cit. in n. 221, at 81.
255. 1903 Netherlands/Venezuela 10 RIAA 729, at 730.
256. 1868 United States/Peru, Moore, 1653.
257. See A. M. Stuyt, op. cit. in n. 42; R. B. Lillich and B. H. Weston, *International Claims: Their Settlement by Lump Sum Agreements*, Vol. i (1975), 25 ff. And see L. Caflisch (1979) *AFDI* 1.
258. 13, 14, 16 RIAA.
259. See I. Seidl-Hohenveldern, *The Austrian–German Arbitral Tribunal* (1972).
260. Damages were claimed in *Ambatielos* 12 RIAA 91, *Gut Dam* (1965) AJ 892 (settled by a lump sum payment), and the *Lighthouses* arbitration 12 RIAA 161. They were awarded only in the last. In most of the *Lighthouses* claims the amount claimed was not contested, or the amount claimed was accepted by the tribunal. Even so the damages were not paid in full; a compromise settlement was reached: (1959) RGDIP 248.
261. Loc. cit. in n. 258. See W. S. Surrey (1951) *Law and Contemporary Problems* 435. In the case of the United States the requirements of the Peace Treaty were elaborated and clarified by subsequent agreements. See 14 RIAA 67.
262. Decision no. 158, 13 RIAA 566, at 569.
263. For example, Decisions nos. 48. 120, 76, 195, 214, and 224 of the Franco-Italian Commission. 13 RIAA 34, 75, 88, 706, ad 761.
264. As, for example, in *Soc. Anonyme de Filatures de Schappe*, Decision no. 174, Franco-Italian Commission 13 RIAA 598; *Feldman*, Decision no. 28, United States–Italian Commission 14 RIAA 212.
265. As in *Weiss*, Decision no. 20, United States–Italian Commission 14 RIAA 184; *Cestra*, Decision no. 165, United States–Italian Commission 14 RIAA 307; *Batchelder*, Decision no. 25, United States–Italian Commission 14 RIAA 201.
266. Decision no. 190, 14 RIAA 53, at 64.
267. For example, *Shafer*, Decision no. 27, United States–Italian Commission 14 RIAA 205; *Bourdeillette*, Decision no. 16, Franco-Italian Commission 13 RIAA 73.
268. For example, *Lachenal*, Decision no. 36, Franco-Italian Commission 13 RIAA 117.
269. The decisions of the Japanese Commissions are collected in (1961) Jap. AIL 45 and discussed by K. Nishimura (1962) *Jap. AIL* 39; and L. M. Summers and A. Fraleigh (1962) *AJ* 407.
270. Personnaz, 330.
271. *Mavrommatis (Palestine) Concessions*, PCIJ Ser. C. no. 5 Vol. i; *Prince von Pless*, PCIJ Ser. C. no. 70; *Polish Agrarian Reform*, PCIJ Ser. C. no. 71; *Socobelge*, PCIJ Ser. C no. 87, *Electricity Company of Sofia*, PCIJ Ser. C no. 88; *Corfu Channel* (1949–50) ICJ Pleadings; *Anglo-Norwegian Fisheries* (1951) ICJ Pleadings; *Germany* v. *Iceland* (1975) ICJ Pleadings.
272. *Oscar Chinn*, PCIJ Ser. C. no. 75; *Panevezys–Saldutiskis Railway*, PCIJ Ser. C no. 86; *Aerial Incident*, United Kingdom claim (1959) ICJ Pleadings; *Barcelona Traction* (1962) ICJ Pleadings; *United Kingdom* v. *Iceland* (1975) ICJ Pleadings.

273. (1959) ICJ Pleadings 45.
274. (1952) ICJ Pleadings *Anglo-Iranian Oil Co.*
275. (1959) ICJ Pleadings 167.
276. (1955) ICJ Pleadings 21.
277. PCIJ Ser. C no. 3.
278. PCIJ Ser. C no. 13 Vol. i, no. 15 Vol. ii.

2

Remedies in the World Court

HAVE the Permanent Court of International Justice and the International Court of Justice developed a more coherent set of rules on the assessment of damages and the award of other remedies than was achieved by international arbitral tribunals? Is it now possible to speak more confidently of the international law of judicial remedies?

The Statute and the Rules of the Court give little guidance on appropriate or permissible methods of reparation or on the assessment of damages: apart from Article 36 of the Court's Statute, which provides that where the parties accept the jurisdiction of the Court under the Optional Clause the Court shall have competence to decide on the 'nature and extent of reparation', no guidance is given.

SECTION I

(i) JURISDICTION

First, the extent of the jurisdiction of the World Court[1] to award remedies should be considered. Of course it is open to the parties to a case expressly to give the Court the power to grant a particular remedy but even so they will not easily be able to induce the Court to exceed its judicial function.[2] More commonly no express provision is made; the extent of the World Court's power to give remedies in those cases where its jurisdiction is derived from an agreement not containing any express provision on this question of remedies will now be considered.

In its first contentious case, the *Wimbledon*,[3] the Permanent Court of International Justice derived its jurisdiction from Article 387 of the Treaty of Versailles which said, 'In the event of violation of any of the conditions of Articles 380–386 or of disputes as to the interpretation of these Articles any interested power can appeal to the jurisdiction instituted for the purpose by the League of Nations.' One of the claimant states, France, requested damages for injuries resulting from an alleged violation of the relevant Articles and the Court ordered that these must be paid even though the Treaty made no express provision for such an award. The defendant state did not contest the Court's jurisdiction to award damages.

A similar problem was given express consideration by the Permanent Court in the *Chorzów Factory* (*Jurisdiction*) case.[4] Here Poland raised the question of the Court's jurisdiction to award damages. The Court's jurisdiction was based on Article 23(1) of the Geneva Convention which provided that the Court could decide on 'Differences of opinion resulting from the interpretation and the application of Articles 6 to 22'. Poland argued that this 'Does not contemplate differences in regard to reparations claimed for violation of these articles'. Without reference to its earlier decision in the *Wimbledon*, the Court rejected this argument saying

> It is a principle of international law that the breach of an engagement involves an obligation to make reparation in an adequate form. Reparation therefore is the indispensable complement of a failure to apply a convention and there is no necessity for this to be stated in the convention itself. Differences relating to reparations which may be due by reason of failure to apply a convention, are consequently differences relating to its interpretation.[5]

And the Court has consistently maintained this approach in all its later decisions. The suggestion of Poland that compromissory clauses should be narrowly interpreted so as to exclude claims for reparation unless express provision was made for these was dismissed by the Court as not supported by earlier arbitral practice nor by any recent developments. For although some international arbitral tribunals were expressly given the power to decide on 'claims for pecuniary compensation', many more were only authorized to settle 'all claims'; not surprisingly the latter saw nothing to prevent their fulfilling what were obviously the intentions of the parties and making awards of damages. Even stronger evidence against the Polish argument may be drawn from those individual arbitrations where the arbitrator was expressly required to decide only the question of responsibility and where no reference was made to remedies. In several such cases the arbitrator assumed that he had jurisdiction to allow damages.[6]

Therefore, Judge Ehrlich's view, expressed in his Dissenting Opinion[7] that

> It seems indeed to have been an established practice long before the adoption of the Covenant of the League and of the Statute in cases in which an arbitral tribunal was to deal with the question of the amount of reparation or mode of payment as distinct from, or in addition to, a divergence of opinion as to the interpretation of a treaty or violation of a treaty or rule of general international law, to specify such powers of the tribunal in the compromise,

is not tenable. But the Permanent Court's interpretation of Article 23(1) does seem rather generous and Ehrlich's further criticism of the judgment has some justification. He said the Court should have looked at the intention of the parties to the Geneva Convention to see if they intended to confer jurisdiction to assess damages. Moreover nothing had been brought to the attention of the Court to prove that the phrase 'interpretation and application' was considered in the practice of nations to comprise jurisdiction in the matter of determining the nature and extent of reparation. In fact, in the *Mavrommatis (Palestine) Concessions* case[8] such a clause was assumed by the Permanent Court to give this jurisdiction,[9] but the question was not discussed by the Court there as this point was not raised by the defendant state even though it contested the Court's jurisdiction on other grounds.

In the *Chorzów Factory* case the Permanent Court of International Justice supported its interpretation of the words 'interpretation and application' by the argument that

> The decision whether there has been a breach of an engagement involves no doubt a more important jurisdiction than a declaration as to the nature or extent of reparation due for a breach of an international engagement the existence of which is already established. If Article 23(1) covers the disputes mentioned in the first and third categories by the two provisions above mentioned [sc. Article 13 of the Covenant and Article 36 of the Court's Statute] it would be difficult to understand why—failing an express provision to that effect—it should not cover the less important disputes mentioned in the fourth category.[10]

As Lauterpacht says,[11] this is not a completely satisfactory justification for the Court's decision to take jurisdiction over the question of damages. He argues that the 'true' reason for the Court's decision is to be found at the end of the judgment where it says,

> An interpretation which would confine the Court simply to recording that the Convention had been incorrectly applied . . . without being able to lay down the conditions for the re-establishment of the treaty rights affected would be contrary to what would, prima facie, be the natural object of the clause; for a jurisdiction of this kind, instead of settling a dispute once and for all, would leave open the possibility of further disputes.

Thus the *Chorzów Factory* case establishes that a clause that gives jurisdiction over questions of the 'interpretation and application' of a treaty includes the power to assess damages for the breach of that treaty when these are requested by the claimant state.

However, in its decision on the merits of this case,[12] the Court recognized that there were limits to its jurisdiction over the assessment of damages. Germany had asked for a decision of principle to prevent the set off of a counterclaim against the indemnity fixed in the judgment or to allow such a set off in defined circumstances only. The Court held that although jurisdiction as to the reparation due for a violation of an international convention involves jurisdiction as to the forms and methods of reparation, this principle may not be unjustifiably extended to enable the Court to take cognizance of any question of international law for the sole reason that the manner in which such a question is decided will have an influence on the effectiveness of the reparation asked for. Here the possibility of a liquidated and undisputed claim against the indemnity awarded would not necessarily prejudice the effectiveness of reparation. Judges Rabel and Nyholm in their Observations[13] disagreed with the Court's view on this point. The former stated that as the Court had decided that Article 23 of the Geneva Convention gave it jurisdiction to determine the form and method of reparation due this definition of its jurisdiction also covered the question whether in this case a money indemnity should be actually paid in money or in other values. Moreover,

> if . . . in an international case, the Parties are at issue as to the action to be taken by the defendant in complying with the judgment, it appears to me that the nature of this action must be defined in the judgment in order to avoid any possible uncertainty.

In fact Poland had not claimed a set off so that the Court was not obliged to make a decision on the German submission.[14]

This problem of where to draw the line between those questions directly affecting the form and method of reparation and those only remotely affecting its effectiveness has not arisen again before the World Court. It was, however, discussed by the European Court of Human Rights in the *Ringeisen* case,[15] where the Court took a wide view of its jurisdiction, similar to that of Judges Rabel and Nyholm.

The *Corfu Channel* case [16] follows the line of the *Chorzów Factory* case in its consideration of the power to assess the amount of damages, although the International Court of Justice did not rely on the earlier case and indeed made no reference to it. In the *Corfu Channel* case the Court had been given jurisdiction under a special agreement between Albania and the United Kingdom to decide,

> 1. Is Albania responsible under international law for the explosions in Albanian waters and for the damage and the loss of human life which resulted from them, and is there any duty to pay compensation?
> 2. Has the United Kingdom under international law violated the sovereignty of Albania by reason of the acts of its navy in Albanian waters and is there any duty to give satisfaction?

The United Kingdom claimed compensation for the loss of one ship and injury to another and for the pensions and other expenses incurred by the government in respect of the deaths and injuries of naval personnel. Albania contested the Court's power to decide on the amount of damages rather than just to establish the principle of responsibility. The Court held that it would be 'Incompatible with the generally accepted rules of interpretation' to decide that a clause which gives the Court jurisdiction to decide whether there is a duty to pay compensation did not also confer the power to assess the amount of damages payable. Moreover,

> If the Court should limit itself to saying that there is a duty to pay compensation

without deciding what amount of compensation is due, the dispute would not be finally decided. An important part of it would remain unsettled. As both parties have repeatedly declared that they accept the Resolution of the Security Council [sc. that they should refer the dispute to the Court], such a result would not conform with their declarations. It would not give full effect to the Resolution but would leave open the possibility of a further dispute.[17]

As Lauterpacht shows, this argument and the reasoning in the *Chorzów Factory* case are based on the principle of effectiveness as a principle of treaty interpretation. The interpretation of the jurisdictional clause necessary to give the power to assess the amount of damages in the *Corfu Channel* case is less extensive than that required in the *Chorzów Factory* case. But even so five judges dissented from the Court's finding that it had jurisdiction to assess the amount of compensation due to the United Kingdom.[18]

The question of the jurisdiction of the International Court of Justice to award damages arose again in the *Fisheries Jurisdiction* (*Germany* v. *Iceland*) case.[19] Unlike the United Kingdom in its action against Iceland,[20] Germany did not abandon its initial request for damages for the injury to German fishing vessels or to fishing operations caused by the interference of Icelandic coastal patrol boats. The Court's jurisdiction was based on an agreement of 1961 which provided that, 'In case of a dispute relating to such an extension [sc. of Iceland's fishing limits] the matter shall, at the request of either Party, be referred to the International Court of Justice'. The Court held that this covered Germany's fourth submission in its Memorial; this asked the Court to declare

That the acts of interference by Icelandic coastal patrol boats with fishing vessels registered in the Federal Republic of Germany or with their fishing operations by the threat or use of force are unlawful under international law, and that Iceland is under an obligation to make compensation therefore to the Federal Republic of Germany.

The Court in deciding whether it had jurisdiction to decide this question said very briefly that 'The matter raised therein is part of the controversy between the Parties and constitutes a dispute relating to Iceland's extension of its fisheries jurisdiction'.[21] Individual judges examined this question at greater length in their respective opinions; they are divided into those who favour the extensive interpretation of the jurisdictional clause and those who reject it. The latter argued that the damage and injury relied on by Germany derived from something other than the extension of Iceland's fishing limits; the unlawfulness of the activities of the Icelandic coastal patrol boats might be deduced from the fact that they occurred either *pendente lite* or in disregard of the Court's Order as to interim measures.[22] In contrast, Judge Waldock said,

It seems to me too narrow an interpretation of those words [sc. the compromissory clause] to regard them as confining the competence conferred on the Court to the question of the extension of jurisdiction as such. In my view, incidents arising out of Iceland's extension of her fishery limit and claims in respect of such incidents clearly form part of 'a dispute in relation to such extension'—words of a quite general character.[23]

Most recently in the *Iranian Hostages* case[24] the International Court of Justice has accepted without comment that agreements providing it with jurisdiction over disputes as to the interpretation and application of treaties give it the power to award damages. Thus the Court has consistently followed a liberal policy in its interpretation of compromissory clauses so far as the power to award damages is concerned. But, typically of this area of international law, it has done so without much reference back to its own or arbitral practice.

Article 36 of the Statute of the World Court confers the power to decide on the 'nature and extent' of reparation. However, just as with compromissory clauses of the *Chorzów Factory* type, it is not immediately clear what forms of relief are covered by this. Although there are no examples of the award of damages in cases where the Court's jurisdiction was based on the Optional Clause, it seems undeniable that such awards were intended to be covered by the power to decide on the 'nature and extent of reparation'. In cases where application was made for an award of damages the Court never questioned its power to make such an award, never declined jurisdiction on the ground that this would be outside its powers under Article 36(2) of its Statute; it apparently assumed that it would have jurisdiction to award damages but refused jurisdiction on other grounds or accepted jurisdiction but in the end did not have to decide on the award of damages.[25]

But the scope of the Court's power to order other remedies such as restitution or specific performance under a compromissory clause like that in the *Chorzów Factory* case or under the Optional Clause is not clear. In a few cases the claimant state has requested the Court to order the defendant state to act in a certain way but until very recently in the *Iranian Hostages* case (and possibly not even then) the Court has never made such an order, nor has it ever discussed its power to do so.

In the *Chorzów Factory* case Germany asked the Court to prohibit the export by Poland of certain products or, alternatively, to order that the Polish Government be obliged to cease working the factory for the production of certain chemicals. Because neither of these measures could be counted as a necessary part of the compensation due to Germany the Court held that it was not necessary for it to decide

Whether such a provision, although customary in contracts between individuals, might form the subject of an injunction issued by the Court to a government, even if that government were working as a state enterprise the factory of which export was to be limited, nor if the prohibition asked for would be fair and appropriate in the circumstances.[26]

In the *Free Zones of Upper Savoy and the District of Gex* case[27] the Court made an order to France to withdraw its customs boundary in order to comply with its treaty obligations:

That the French Government must withdraw its customs line in accordance with the provisions of the said treaties and instruments; and that this regime must continue in force so long as it has not been modified by agreement between the parties.

However, express provision had been made for the Court to do at least this much in the Special Agreement from which it derived its jurisdiction. In the *Nuclear Tests* cases[28] (where, in fact, the basis of the Court's jurisdiction was never decided as the question of the existence of a dispute was treated as prior to this) Australia and New Zealand both requested the International Court of Justice to order in its final judgment that France 'shall not carry out any further such tests'. Again in the *Rights of Passage* case,[29] where the International Court of Justice had jurisdiction under the Optional Clause, Pakistan asked that the Court should adjudge that India should put an end to its interference with Pakistan's right of passage. Finally, in the *Diversion of Waters from the Meuse* case,[30] the Netherlands asked the Permanent Court of International Justice to order Belgium to discontinue all the works whose legality the Netherlands denied and to restore to a condition consistent with the Treaty all the works constructed in breach of the Treaty. However, in none of these cases did the Court discuss or decide on its power to give such an order. There do not seem to be any logical reasons why Article 36(2) should not cover this type of order; the practical difficulties are obvious. The *Iranian Hostages* case finally raised this question of the Court's jurisdiction to issue an order to the parties rather than merely a declaratory judgment on the interpretation and application of a treaty, in a case where the agreements between the parties made no reference to remedies. But it raised the question only by implication: the Court gave no express consideration to the question. In its application the United States had asked the Court 'to adjudge and declare' that Iran had violated its legal obligations to the United States; that Iran 'is under a particular obligation immediately to secure the release of all United States nationals currently being detained within the premises of the United States Embassy in Tehran and to assure that all such persons and all other United States nationals in Tehran are allowed to leave Iran safely'; that Iran shall pay reparation to the United States; and 'that the Government of Iran submit to its competent authorities for the purpose of prosecution those persons responsible for the crimes committed against the premises and staff of the United States Embassy and against the premises of its Consulates'. This leaves it unclear whether a declaration or an order or both is being requested.

The Court found that Iran had violated its obligations to the United States and went on to say that it

Decides that the Government of the Islamic Republic of Iran must immediately take all steps to redress the situation resulting from the events of 4 November 1979 and what followed from these events, and to that end:

(*a*) must immediately terminate the unlawful detention of the United States Chargé d'affaires and other diplomatic and consular staff and other United States nationals now held hostage in Iran, and must immediately release each and every one and entrust them to the protecting Power (Article 45 of the 1961 Vienna Convention on Diplomatic Relations);

(*b*) must ensure that all the said persons have the necessary means of leaving Iranian territory, including means of transport;

(*c*) must immediately place in the hands of the protecting Power the premises, property, archives and documents of the United States Embassy in Tehran and of its Consulates in Iran;

Decides that no member of the United States diplomatic or consular staff may be kept in Iran to be subjected to any form of judicial proceedings or to participate in them as a witness.

But if this is the first case in which the Court has issued an order to a state party rather than merely declaring that there is an obligation on it to act in a certain way then the Court made this breakthrough with a remarkable lack of discussion. In the absence of express discussion some uncertainty remains; does the Court regard an order as simply equivalent to a declaratory judgment that there is an obligation to act in a certain way, does it simply assume that both are equally within its jurisdiction whether under a *Chorzów Factory* type compromissory clause or under the Optional Clause?

For although there is no specific provision for this in the Statute the Court has accepted that it has jurisdiction to give declaratory judgments. In the *Certain German Interests in Polish Upper Silesia* case,[31] the Permanent Court of International Justice rejected the argument of the Polish Government that the Court could not give a general interpretation of a Polish law rather than discuss its application in a particular case. In this it relied on Article 14 of the Covenant of the League which gave it power 'To hear and determine any dispute of an international character which parties thereto submit to it'. In support of its argument the Court also used Articles 36(2)*a* and 63 of its Statute; the former allows the Court to give interpretations of treaties in cases brought under the Optional Clause, and the latter enables states parties to treaties which form the subject matter of a dispute before the Court between two other states to intervene in such proceedings. The Court said that all these provisions constitute recognition of the possibility of a judgment having a purely declaratory effect. The World Court has not refused to give such judgments on the ground that this would be outside its jurisdiction, but has relied on grounds of propriety to justify its refusals. The Permanent Court of International Justice was generally not asked to do more than give an interpretation of a treaty or contract or to decide on disputed sovereignty over particular areas. It did not therefore award declaratory judgments stating that a State Party was under an obligation to act in a certain way. Obviously such a consequence might be implicit in the Court's declaration as to the applicable law, but it was not made explicit in the judgments of the Permanent Court of International Justice.

It was under the International Court of Justice that such a development took place. In several cases the International Court of Justice was asked to declare that the defendant state was under an obligation to act in a certain way. Such a declaration would obviously be based on a finding, perhaps implicit rather than explicit, on the law, such as that a treaty or contract or arbitral award is binding. Requests for this type of declaration were made in seven cases and allowed in two of these.[32] The *Temple of Preah Vihear* case[33] is also within this category; the Court's discussion of its jurisdiction in this case makes it quite clear that this judgment is again declaratory rather than a mandatory order as asserted by Mann.[34] In this case the Cambodian Government had added a fifth submission at the end of the oral proceedings and asked the International Court of Justice 'To adjudge and declare that the sculptures etc. which have been removed from the Temple by the Thai authorities since 1954 are to be returned to the Cambodians by the Thai government'. The Court held that, as regards this fifth submission,

> The request made in it does not represent any extension of Cambodia's original claim (in which case it would have been irreceivable at the stage at which it was first advanced)—rather is it, like the fourth submission, implicit and consequential on the claim of sovereignty itself.

Therefore, after it had found that the temple was situated in territory under the sovereignty of Cambodia, the Court held in consequence (but only by seven votes to five) that Thailand was

> Under an obligation to restore to Cambodia any objects of the kind specified in Cambodia's fifth submission which may since the date of the occupation of the Temple of Thailand in 1954 have been removed from the Temple or the Temple area by the Thai authorities.

The Court here was willing to do what it had refused in the *Haya de la Torre* case,[35] that is, to make clear what action was demanded by its declaratory judgment.

Therefore it remains unclear, even after the *Iranian Hostages* case, whether the generosity of the Court in asserting its jurisdiction to award damages does or should extend to making an order requiring or forbidding certain behaviour by states in cases where, as in the *Chorzów Factory* case, the Court has jurisdiction only to decide on the interpretation or application of a treaty, or where it has jurisdiction under Article 36(2) of the Statute of the Court. If it were not for the peculiar suitability of declaratory judgments in actions between sovereign states and the lack of precedents for mandatory orders by the Court, it would be easier to dismiss the difference between the two remedies as a narrow technical one, an unimportant matter of form.

NOTES

1. In this chapter where reference to both the Permanent Court of International Justice and the International Court of Justice is intended the term 'World Court' will be used.
2. See the *Free Zones of Upper Savoy and the District of Gex* case, PCIJ Ser. A no. 24, where the Court said, 'Even assuming that it were not incompatible with the Court's Statute for the Parties to give the court power to prescribe a settlement disregarding rights recognised by it and taking into account considerations of pure expedience only, such power, which would be of an absolutely exceptional character, could only be derived from a clear and explicit provision to that effect which is not to be found in the Special Agreement.' See also *Haya de la Torre* (1951) ICJ Reports 71, at 79.
3. PCIJ Ser. A no. 1.
4. PCIJ Ser. A no. 9. For the converse case see *Claim of the United States and the Paraguay Navigation Co.* 1860 US/Paraguay 2, Moore, 1485, at 1504.
5. PCIJ Ser. A no. 9, 21.
6. For example, *La Masica* 1910 Great Britain/Honduras 11 RIAA 551; *Tillett* 1898 Belgium/Great Britain, La Fontaine, 581; *Van Bokkelen* 1888 Haiti/United States, Moore, 1807. This may be seen also in the later *Rhodope Forests* case 3 RIAA 1389. Here the tribunal derived its jurisdiction from Article 181 of the Treaty of Neuilly. This said, 'In cases of disagreement as to the application of this Article, the difference shall be submitted to an arbitrator appointed by the Council of the League of Nations'. The Greek Government sought reparation for the confiscation of the property of their nationals and the arbitrator allowed this without any discussion as to the extent of his jurisdiction.
7. PCIJ Ser. A no. 9, 35, at 38.
8. PCIJ Ser. A no. 2.
9. Article 26 of the Mandate for Palestine provides: 'The Mandatory agrees that if any dispute whatever should arise between the Mandatory and another member of the League of Nations relating to the interpretation or the application of the provisions of the Mandate, such dispute if it cannot be settled by

negotiation shall be submitted to the PCIJ provided for by Article 14 of the Covenant of the League.'

10. Loc. cit. in n. 4, at 23.
11. H. Lauterpacht, *The Development of International Law by the International Court* (1958), 246.
12. PCIJ Ser. A no. 13, at 59.
13. Ibid., at 66 and 92 respectively.
14. On counterclaims and set offs see C. W. Jenks, *The Prospects of International Adjudication* (1964), 135–6; J. L. Simpson and H. Fox, *International Arbitration* (1959), 172–8.
15. Eur. Court H. R., Ser. A no. 16. In response to a request for the interpretation of its judgment of 22 June 1972 awarding Ringeisen 20,000 DM as just satisfaction, the Court made it clear that its award was to be paid to Ringeisen personally and free from attachment.
16. (1949) ICJ Reports 4.
17. Ibid, at 26.
18. Ibid, at 57, 67, 73, 96, 128.
19. (1974) ICJ Reports 175, at 203.
20. (1974) ICJ Reports 3.
21. (1974) ICJ Reports 175, at 203.
22. Judges De Castro, Gros, and Petrén, (1974) ICJ Reports, at 225, 234, and 240 respectively.
23. Ibid, 227. See also the Dissenting Opinion of Judge Onyeama, ibid, 244.
24. (1980) ICJ Reports 3.
25. As in the *Anglo-Norwegian Fisheries* case (1951) ICJ Reports 116.
26. PCIJ Ser. A no. 13, 57.
27. Loc. cit. in n. 2.
28. (1974) ICJ Reports 253 and 457.
29. (1969) ICJ Reports 4.
30. PCIJ Ser. A/B no. 70.
31. PCIJ Ser. A no. 6.
32. *Guardianship of Infants* case (1958) ICJ Reports 55; *Interhandel* (1959) ICJ Reports 6; *South West Africa* cases (1962) ICJ Reports 319 and (1966) ICJ Reports 6; *Aegean Sea* case (1978) ICJ Reports 3. Declaratory judgments were given in the *Arbitral Award of the King of Spain* case (1960) ICJ Reports 192 and the *Ambatielos* case (1952) ICJ Reports 28 and (1953) ICJ Reports 10.
33. (1962) ICJ Reports 6.
34. F. A. Mann (1976–7) *BYBIL* 1.
35. (1951) ICJ Reports 71.

SECTION 2

(i) INTERIM MEASURES OF PROTECTION

In contrast the World Court undoubtedly has very extensive powers so far as remedies are concerned at the stage of interim measures. Under Article

41 of the Statute of the International Court of Justice[1] the Court is empowered 'To indicate, if it considers that circumstances so require, any provisional measures which ought to be taken to preserve the respective rights of either party'.[2] The Permanent Court of International Justice and the International Court of Justice have, without express consideration, interpreted this to cover both what may be called positive and negative orders. That is, they have not only ordered governments to refrain, and ensure that others refrain, from certain behaviour likely to aggravate or extend the dispute or to prejudice the rights that might result from the final judgment, as in the *Electricity Company of Sofia and Bulgaria*,[3] the *Nuclear Tests* cases,[4] and the *Nicaragua* v. *USA* case,[5] but also have demanded certain positive actions by Governments. Thus, for example, in the *Anglo-Iranian Oil Company* case[6] the International Court of Justice ordered that, 'There should be established by agreement between the Iranian Government and the United Kingdom Government a Board to be known as the Board of Supervision' and set out in detail the composition and duties of the Board. Again in the *Fisheries Jurisdiction* cases[7] the International Court of Justice said that 'The United Kingdom should ensure that vessels registered in the United Kingdom do not take an annual catch of more than 170,000 metric tons of fish', and that 'The United Kingdom Government should furnish the Government of Iceland and the Registry of the Court with all relevant information, orders issued, and arrangements made concerning the control and regulation of fish catches in the area'. As was pointed out in Section 1 of this chapter, it remains doubtful whether the Court without express permission from the states parties could make such orders in its final judgment on the merits.

Such interim measures of protection, both positive and negative, in part fulfil the role of an interlocutory injunction in international law and thus help to mitigate the effects of the delays involved in the settlement of international claims. Much discussion has been devoted to interim measures of protection[8]—considerably more discussion in fact than has been given to final remedies—so there is no need here to provide more than a brief outline. Also this is an area of great uncertainty: many basic issues remain unresolved. There is controversy over the basis of the Court's jurisdiction to award interim measures, over whether the Court's indication of interim measures is binding on the parties, and especially over the difficult question of the Court's power to order interim measures when its jurisdiction to give a decision on the merits is not established.[9] The jurisprudence of the Court does not provide much enlightenment on these questions. The oracular brevity of the Court in the recent *Case concerning Military and Paramilitary activities in and against Nicaragua* is perhaps an extreme example of the general tendency of the Court to avoid involvement in theoretical discussion of the problems mentioned above.[10]

In fact neither the Permanent Court of International Justice nor its successor ever refused to allow interim measures on the ground of lack of jurisdiction on the merits. Rather they based their refusals on the ground that interim measures were not necessary 'to preserve the respective rights of either party'. How did the World Court interpret this requirement, and did it follow a uniform practice? The World Court's refusal to indicate interim measures where the effect of this would be to prejudice the merits of the main case, as in the *Chorzow Factory* case,[11] or where the protection requested in the application for interim measures would extend beyond the rights at stake in the main action, as in the *Polish Agrarian Reform* case,[12] or where the interim measures were no longer urgently required, as in the *Pakistani Prisoners of War* case,[13] or no longer necessary because of a declaration by the defendant state as to its future behaviour, as in the *Interhandel*[14] and *Prince von Pless*[15] cases, has been discussed by other writers and does not pose any particular problems.

The main remaining topic of importance is the relationship of interim measures and the remedy of damages. In some cases the Court has insisted that the provision that interim measures are designed to 'preserve the respective rights of either party' presupposes that the party seeking interim measures must show that its rights would be irreparably harmed in the absence of interim measures. The Court has not, however, been wholly consistent in its view of what constitutes such irreparable harm.

The case of the *Denunciation of the Treaty betwen China and Belgium*[16] is the earliest in which interim measures were granted by the Permanent Court of International Justice. Belgium claimed that the treaty was still in force and China denied this. Belgium asked the Court to indicate, pending judgment, any provisional measures to be taken for the preservation of rights which might subsequently be recognized to belong to Belgium or her nationals. It has been said that in this, its first award of interim measures, the Court introduced a limit on its power to indicate these, that it held that the award of such measures was improper where the eventual remedy for injury to the right concerned was damages.[17] For the Court said that an infraction of the rights of Belgium or her nationals under the Treaty of November 1865 could not be made good simply by the payment of an indemnity or by compensation or restitution in some other material form, and, accordingly, 'the object of the measures of interim protection to be indicated in the present case must be to prevent any rights of this nature from being prejudiced'. However, the rights in question are arguably those for injury to which damages had typically been awarded by international arbitral tribunals.[18] The Court seems in fact to have been concerned with the general inadequacy of pecuniary compensation and other judicial remedies as a method of repairing non-pecuniary interests. Thus the restriction of interim measures in this case to the protection of rights which could not be repaired by an indemnity, compensation, or restitution does not amount to a limitation different from any observed by the Court and its successor in later cases; here, as in later cases, interim measures were indicated to protect rights for whose prejudice the common remedy is damages because such a remedy cannot in any real sense make good the injured right. Certainly, in the *Electricity Company of Sofia and Bulgaria case*,[19] the only other award of interim measures by the Permanent Court of International Justice, when Belgium asked the Court not to allow the continuation of proceedings against a Belgian company in the Bulgarian courts, although the normal remedy for the injury involved would have been damages, the Court made no mention of this and granted the request for interim measures with very little discussion. There is no consideration here of the type of injury that must be shown for the Court to allow interim measures.

And in the *Anglo-Iranian Oil Company* case[20] and the *Fisheries Jurisdiction* cases,[21] the International Court of Justice indicated interim measures to protect rights whose violation would be clearly remediable by the award of damages.[22] However, the liberal attitude of the International Court of Justice to the award of provisional measures apparent in these cases and also in the *Nuclear Tests* cases[23] was not displayed in the *Aegean Sea* case.[24] In the *Anglo-Iranian Oil Company* case and the *Nuclear Tests* cases the Court apparently regarded any threatened breach of international law as justifying the award of interim measures to protect the respective rights of the parties; in the former the Court did not discuss the type of harm threatened, in the latter it accepted that this might be 'irreparable' but did not make explicit what it understood by this term. In the *Fisheries Jurisdiction* cases it said only that

> The immediate implementation by Iceland of its Regulations would, by anticipating the Court's judgment, prejudice the rights claimed by the United Kingdom and affect the possibility of their full restoration in the event of a judgment in its favour.[25]

The *Aegean Sea* case marks a retreat from this liberal attitude. Here the Court rejected the claim of Greece that that state's exclusive sovereign rights to research, explore, and exploit the continental shelf should be given interim protection. It held that the infringement of the exclusive right of a littoral state to explore its continental shelf did not by itself justify recourse to the Court's powers under Article 41 of its Statute; interim measures would be indicated only if these were necessary to preserve the respective rights of the parties. The Court decided that this was not so here, not on grounds similar to those governing the decision of the Permanent Court of International Justice in the *Eastern Greenland* case,[26] but because in the present instance, the alleged breach by Turkey of the exclusivity of the right claimed by Greece to acquire information concerning the natural resources of areas of continental shelf, if it were established, is one that might be capable of reparation by appropriate means.[27]

Accordingly the Court held that there was no risk of irreparable prejudice to the rights asserted by Greece. Thus the Court here adopts a much stricter view than it had in earlier cases. Because appropriate reparation for the threatened injury *might* be possible no interim measures were allowed. In fact it is difficult to imagine what form of reparation would be appropriate for the type of injury involved in this case.[28]

The *Aegean Sea* case also leaves unclear whether under Article 41 the Court has an independent power to indicate interim measures for the sole purpose of preventing the aggravation or extension of a dispute. In several cases interim measures had been indicated for this purpose in combination with the purpose of avoiding prejudice to the rights of either party in respect of carrying out the decision on the merits.[29] Earlier in the *Eastern Greenland* case the Permanent Court of International Justice had avoided giving a decision on the similar question whether it was competent to indicate interim measures for the sole purpose of preventing regrettable events and unfortunate incidents. It held that there was no need for it to take a final stand on this controversy as to interpretation as there was no reason to fear that the incidents contemplated by the Norwegian request would actually occur. In the *Aegean Sea* case also the Court held that it was not necessary to decide the question mentioned above because it was not to be presumed that the governments involved would take action leading to the aggravation or extension of the dispute in violation of their obligations under the Charter of the United Nations and of the recommendations of the Security Council. But in the *Case concerning the Frontier Dispute (Burkina Faso/Mali)*[30] the Court finally made it clear that it could indicate interim measures, independently of the requests submitted by the parties, with a view to preventing the aggravation or extension of a dispute whenever it considered that circumstances so required.

Perhaps the strict view of the International Court of Justice in the *Aegean Sea* case as to the requirements of Article 41 may be interpreted as the result of the Court's unwillingness to indicate interim measures that would then be disregarded by the state to whom they were addressed, as had been the Court's previous order in the *Nuclear Tests* cases. Nevertheless the Court's view that as reparation in some unspecified form might later be possible the threatened injury would not be irreparable and that therefore interim measures of protection were not required is not acceptable. Even on the municipal level this type of approach is not adequate in non-commercial or civil liberties cases.[31]

The most recent decisions of the Court on interim measures show a return to the earlier, more generous approach to the question of irreparable harm. In the *Iranian Hostages* case[32] this is implicit in the judgment. In *Nicaragua* v *USA* and the *Burkina Faso* v *Mali* cases the Court accepts that its power to indicate provisional measures presupposes that irreparable prejudice should not be caused to rights which are the subject of dispute in judicial proceedings. It returns to the more generous and realistic view of before the *Aegean Sea* case as to what constitutes irreparable harm: as in the *Denunciation of the Treaty between China and Belgium* it accepts that.

> Continuance of the situation the subject of the present requests exposes the human beings concerned to privation, hardship, anguish and even danger to life and health and thus to a serious possibility of irreparable harm.[33]

The many theoretical issues discussed by writers do not, then, receive much clarification in the jurisprudence of the Court. Its decisions on interim measures seem unpredictable. There is no strong correlation between eventual success on the merits and the award of interim measures. Factors other than those expressly avowed apparently, and not surprisingly, influence the Court. The question of the likelihood of jurisdiction on the merits, despite the adoption by the Court of the prima facie test, is still obscure and perhaps in fact unimportant. The Court's refusals of interim measures are explained at greater length, though not necessarily more satisfactorily or consistently than its awards. All this may perhaps be attributable to the peculiar nature of the remedy of interim measures; municipal courts also struggle to evolve adequate rules and rationalizations to govern their decisions in this area.

NOTES

1. Essentially the same as Article 41 of the Statute of the Permanent Court of International Justice.
2. For a discussion of international arbitral practice on interim measures of protection see M. H. Mendelson (1972–3) *BYBIL* 259; E. Dumbauld, *Interim Measures of Protection in International Controversies* (1932); P. Guggenheim, *Les Mesures provisoires de procédure internationale et leur influence sur le développement du droit des gens* (1931); J. B. Elkind, *Interim Protection* (1981). Many treaties providing for the peaceful settlement of disputes contain express provision on interim measures; examples of their award are rare.
3. PCIJ Ser. A/B no. 79, 194, Order of 5 Dec. 1939.
4. (1973) ICJ Reports 99 and 135.
5. (1984) ICJ Reports 168.
6. (1951) ICJ Reports 89.
7. (1972) ICJ Reports 12 and 30. See also the *Iranian Hostages* case (1979) ICJ Reports 7.

8. See works cited in n. 2 and P. J. Goldsworthy (1974) *AJ* 258; J. G. Merrills (1977) *CLJ* 86.
9. The International Court of Justice (the problem did not arise before the Permanent Court of International Justice) appears after earlier uncertainty to have settled on the test that the Court must have prima facie jurisdiction on the merits to be able to indicate interim measures. However, the content of this test, the exact degree of probability required, remains obscure. What is perhaps of greater practical significance is the fact that the Court has never refused interim measures on the ground of lack of jurisdiction on the merits. It is also still unclear whether the question of jurisdiction on the merits is just one of the circumstances to be taken into account, together with urgency and the threat of harm (as argued by Mendelson, op. cit. in n. 2) or is a decisive preliminary question (as argued by Merrills, op. cit. in n. 8).
10. See above, n. 5. The Court merely sets out the various arguments of the parties, it gives no indication as to which it accepts and which it rejects, but says simply, 'Whereas in the light of the several considerations set out above, the Court finds that the circumstances require it to indicate provisional measures, as provided by Article 41 of the Statute of the Court, in order to preserve the rights claimed'.
11. PCIJ Ser. A no. 12. Compare this case with the Court's decision in the *Iranian Hostages* case (1979) ICJ Reports 7. Here the United States requested that Iran release the hostages, clear the embassy, and guarantee not to allow a trial of the hostages, both as interim measures and as a final remedy. The Court allowed interim measures. Its explanation that this did not prejudge the merits of the case, that the *Chorzów Factory* decision was not to be followed because the circumstances there were entirely different, does not seem completely convincing.
12. PCIJ Ser. A/B no. 58, Order of 29 July 1933. But see the Dissenting Opinion of Judge Anzilotti on this point.
13. (1973) ICJ Reports 328.
14. (1957) ICJ Reports 105.
15. PCIJ Ser. A/B no. 54, Order of 11 May 1933.
16. PCIJ Ser. A no. 8, Order of 8 Jan. 1927.
17. M. H. Mendelson, op. cit. in n. 2. P. J. Goldsworthy, op. cit. in n. 8.
18. The Court ordered that the following rights should be protected:

    'I. As regards nationals:

    1. a right on the part of any Belgian who may have lost his passport or have committed some offence against the law, to be conducted in safety to the nearest Belgian consulate.

    2. effective protection of Belgian missionaries who have peacefully proceeded to the interior of the country; and, in general, protection of Belgians against any insult or violence.

    3. a right on the part of any Belgian who may commit a crime against a Chinese or any other offence against the law, not to be arrested except through a consul, nor to be subjected, as regards the execution of any penalty

involving personal violence or duress, to any except the regular action of Belgian law;

II. As regards property and shipping:

protection against any sequestration or seizure not in accordance with the generally accepted principles of international law and against any destruction other than accidental;

III. As regards judicial safeguards:

a right on the part of physical and moral persons of Belgian nationality to have any legal proceedings to which they may be parties before Chinese authorities heard by the modern courts, in conformity with the modern codes of law . . . with right of appeal, in accordance with the regular legal procedure and with the assistance of advocates and interpreters chosen by them and duly approved by the said courts.'

19. Loc. cit. in n. 3.
20. Loc. cit. in n. 6.
21. Loc. cit. in n. 7.
22. In fact the United Kingdom and German Governments had argued in the *Fisheries Jurisdiction* cases that the damage to their fishing and associated industries could not be made good by the payment of monetary compensation. Belgium produced a similar argument in the *Electricity Company of Sofia and Bulgaria* case. However, the Court did not discuss these arguments. Moreover the acceptability of such an argument as a reason for the award of interim measures does not necessarily make the reverse argument, that if damages are the normal remedy for injury to a particular interest then no interim measures will be allowed, also acceptable.
23. Loc. cit. in n. 4.
24. (1976) ICJ Reports 3.
25. Loc. cit. in n. 7, at 16.
26. PCIJ Ser. A/B no. 48, Order of 3 Aug. 1932. This was also a case of disputed sovereignty over territory. Here the Court held that it was not necessary to order Denmark to abstain from asserting jurisdiction over Norwegian nationals in the disputed area partly because such actions could not affect the rights at issue in the main case, that is, they could not be effective to alter the status of the disputed area. This reflects a narrow view of the rights at issue in the main action. See also *Case concerning the Frontier Dispute* (*Burkina Faso/Mali*) (1986) ICJ Reports 3.
27. Loc. cit. in n. 24, at 11.
28. In his Separate Opinion, Judge Elias criticizes the Court's judgment: 'The apparent acceptance by the majority of the Court that, once any damage resulting from the exploration and/or exploitation by Turkey is capable of being compensated for in cash or kind, Greece cannot be said to have suffered irreparable prejudice, does not seem to me to be a valid one. It means that the State which has the ability to pay can under this principle commit wrongs against another State with impunity, since it discounts the fact that the injury to itself might be sufficient to cause irreparable harm to the

national susceptibilities of the offended State. The rightness or wrongness of the action itself does not seem to matter. This is a principle upon which contemporary international law should frown: might should no longer be right in today's inter-State relations' (1976) ICJ Reports 27. This argument seems correct on precedent and principle.

29. *Electricity Company of Sofia and Bulgaria*, *Anglo-Iranian Oil Company*, *Fisheries Jurisdiction*, *Nuclear Tests* cases.
30. (1986) ICJ Reports 3.
31. See P. Wallington (1976) *CLJ* 82.
32. (1979) ICJ Reports 7.
33. Loc. cit. in n. 5, 20.

SECTION 3

(i) DAMAGES

Out of the thirty-eight contentious cases brought before the Permanent Court of International Justice, nearly one third involved a claim for damages, a proportion rather smaller than that in international arbitral practice.[1] All these cases concerned injuries to the interests of individuals whose claims were taken up by their national states, but in only one were damages actually awarded—in the *Wimbledon case*.[2] Germany had refused passage through the Kiel Canal to a French ship, in breach of the Treaty of Versailles. She was held to be responsible for the loss occasioned by this refusal and liable to compensate the French Government which was acting on behalf of the company which had sustained the loss. The other claimant states, Great Britain, Italy, and Japan, did not make any claim for damages, and the intervening state, Poland, expressly disclaimed the right to bring such a claim. The Permanent Court of International Justice in this case did not discuss the question of damages in general, it did not refer to past arbitral practice,[3] and gave no detailed explanation of its award.

The Court allowed damages for certain different headings of injury. First, the French government made claims for compensation for demurrage, deviation, and expenditure of fuel, all well-established heads of loss. With very little discussion the Court approved the claimant's estimates as to the amount to be awarded under each of these headings. These amounts had not been contested by Germany. The question of lost profits did not arise as it was clear that there was no possibility of the vessel making a profit. A claim for the repayment of the share of the vessel in the general expenses of the company was refused on the ground that such expenses were not connected with the refusal of passage. A claim for government stamp duty and other costs of recovery was also rejected. However, there was no general theoretical discussion of the problem of indirect or remote damage; the Court did not set out its policy on these questions. Finally,

As regards the rate of interest, the Court considers that in the present financial situation of the world and having regard to the conditions prevailing for public loans, the 6% claimed is fair; this interest, however, should run not from the date of the arrival of the Wimbledon at the entrance to the Kiel canal, as claimed by the applicants, but from the date of the present judgment, that is to say from the moment when the amount of the sum due has been fixed and the obligation to pay has been established.[4]

This ruling on the payment of interest apparently accepts the distinction made in certain arbitral decisions between liquidated and unliquidated claims; only on the former is interest allowed from the date of injury.[5] A claim was made here for interest from this date, but was rejected because at that time damages were not liquidated. It is of course possible that an element to cover this loss could be included in the principal award but no indication that this had been done was given in this case. Thus it seems that the claimant did not receive full compensation; he was not allowed damages for the loss of use of a sum of money representing his injury. No reference was made to the arbitral decisions where such an award was made.

Also the Court refused to award interest at a higher rate in the event of non-compliance with the judgment by Germany: 'The Court neither can nor should contemplate such a contingency'.[6] Here again there is no discussion of those arbitral decisions where such a ruling was allowed. Germany was given three months to pay and payment was to be in French francs: 'This is the currency of the applicant in which his financial operations and accounts are conducted, and it may therefore be said that this currency gives the exact measure of the loss to be made good.'[7] This express consideration of the question of the appropriate currency for payment is exceptional among arbitral decisions. The decision seems reasonable in this case but should not be assumed to represent a general rule universally applicable.

The *Wimbledon* case does not then give much reasoned explanation of the assessment of damages in international law. It does not provide any discussion of the general theoretical issues, nor does the Court seem concerned to lay down any general rules. The Court's approach in this, its first decision on damages, is typical of its later practice also in its brevity, its unwillingness to consider basic issues, and its lack of reference to earlier arbitral practice.

The next case in which a claim for damages was discussed by the Court was the *Mavrommatis (Jerusalem) Concessions* case.[8] Here Greece made a claim against Great Britain for the breach of a concession in violation of its international obligations under the Mandate for Palestine. The Court accepted that Great Britain had violated its obligations, but said that the Greek Government's claim for an indemnity must be dismissed because no loss to Mavrommatis resulting from this breach had been proved. Thus it seems that at least as far as responsibility for injury to nationals of other states is concerned, under international law no claim for damages will succeed unless there is loss to such nationals. Mavrommatis was not allowed nominal damages to indicate that he had been the victim of a breach of international law.

Although eventually the parties in the *Chorzów Factory* case[9] came to a settlement on the question of damages, the Court in this case discussed the problem at some length and raised several interesting points in its judgments. This case contains perhaps the most famous statement of the function of damages in international law and is certainly the most quoted case in this area. In fact, in many ways it is an unusual decision. As with the *Wimbledon* case it is not easy to extract any general rules. The case concerns a claim made by Germany for compensation for the expropriation of a factory by Poland. The Court was asked:

1. To declare that the Polish Government by reason of its attitude in respect of the Oberschlesische and Bayerische Companies, which attitude the Court had declared not to be in conformity with the Geneva Convention, is under an obligation to make good the consequent damage sustained by those Companies;
2. to award compensation, the amount of which is indicated in the application, for the damage caused to each of the Respective Companies;
3. to fix the method of payment, and amongst other things to order the payments to be made by the Polish Government to be effected to the account of the two Companies with the Deutsche Bank at Berlin.

The Court said that there were three fundamental questions for it to decide; whether there existed an obligation to make reparation, whether there was any damage to be repaired, and what was the extent of the damage. The first was easily established. For 'it is a principle of international law and even a general conception of law that any breach of an engagement involves an obligation to make reparation'. The second question reflects the view followed also in the *Mavrommatis (Jerusalem) Concessions* case that in cases of injury to foreign nationals actual loss is a necessary condition for the award of damages. The third question involves the most difficulties. The Court now for the first time discusses at some length 'The principles according to which the amount of compensation due may be determined'. Its starting-point is that the taking of the factory by Poland was not a lawful expropriation but an illegal seizure:

The action of Poland which the Court has judged to be contrary to the Geneva Convention is not an expropriation—to render which lawful only the payment of fair compensation would have been wanting; it is a seizure of property, rights and interests which could not be expropriated even against compensation, save under the exceptional conditions fixed by Article 7 of the said Convention.[10]

Accordingly, 'it follows that the compensation due to the German Government is not necessarily limited to the value of the undertaking at the moment of dispossession, plus interest to the day of payment'. Then follows what is probably the best-known statement on the role of damages in international law:

The essential principle contained in the actual notion of an illegal act—a principle which seems to be established by international practice and in particular by the decisions of arbitral tribunals—is that reparation must, as far as possible, wipe out all the consequences of the illegal act and re-establish the situation which could in all probability have existed if that act had not been committed. Restitution in kind, or if this is not possible payment of a sum corresponding to the value which restitution in kind would bear; the award if need be of damages for loss sustained which would not be covered by restitution in kind or payment in place of it—such are the principles which should serve to determine the amount of compensation due for an act contrary to international law.

As was shown in Chapter 1, any assertion of the primacy of *restitutio in integrum* as a remedy in international law is not supported by international arbitral practice. In the final section of this chapter it will be considered whether the decision in the *Chorzów Factory* case provides evidence to the contrary. In this case the parties were in agreement on the impossibility of restoring the factory to its original owners. Accordingly, the Court ordered that the claimant should receive the value of the property at the time of indemnification, 'Which value is designed to take the place of restitution which has become impossible'. This is an unusual decision. The Court in its concern that a wrongful seizure should be visited with a heavier penalty than a lawful expropriation—which might almost be depicted as a concern that the damages should be punitive—adopts an exceptional rule. For it decided that the relevant time for the assessment of the value of the property should be that of the judgment. Apparently it assumed that the factory would have increased in value between the date of dispossession and that of the judgment, otherwise its choice of date would not have benefited the claimant.

In international arbitral practice the date most commonly chosen by the tribunal in cases of seizures of vessels for the assessment of the value of the ship is that of the seizure, that is, the date of the unlawful act. Admittedly there are exceptions to this. However, in cases of the expropriation of land there is no international arbitral decision where the date of the assessment of value is explicitly stated to be that of adjudication. In a few cases the date of assessment is not made clear, as in the *De Sabla* claim,[11] but the majority of decisions adopt the date of injury. Thus in the *Rhodope Forests* case[12] the value of the forests was calculated as at the date of dispossession, and this is the rule that was adopted by the United States–German Mixed Claims Commission of 1922.[13] Therefore the Dissenting Opinions of Judges Finlay and Ehrlich seem justified on this point. Finlay says, 'Damages must be assessed according to the general rule as at the time of the wrong'.[14] So the authority of the decision on this point must be open to doubt.

The basic principle that damages should not lead to over-compensation of the victim may be seen at work in the Court's decision to assess the damages for the two injured companies in a lump sum rather than in two separate awards, because the two companies formed an economic unit and to attempt separate assessment would involve the risk of compensating the same loss twice.[15] The Court was faced with the task of 'Determining what sum must be awarded in order to enable it to place the dispossessed company as far as possible in the economic situation in which they would probably have been if the seizure had not taken place'.[16]

It was not satisfied with the data for assessment supplied by the parties and accordingly ordered an expert inquiry under Article 50 of its Statute.

In this case the Court submitted two questions to the experts:

> 1.(*a*) What was the value on 3 July 1922 of the undertaking in the state in which that undertaking was on the date indicated in the hands of the Bayerische and Oberschlesische Stickstoffwerke.
>
> (*b*) What would have been the financial results which would probably have been given by the undertaking thus constituted from 3 July 1922 to the date of the present judgment if it had been in the hands of the said companies.
>
> 2. What would be the value at the date of the present judgment of the same undertaking if that undertaking had remained in the hands of the Bayerische and Oberschlesische Stickstoffwerke and had either remained substantially as it was in 1922, or been developed proportionately on lines similar to those applied in the case of other undertakings of the same kind, controlled by the Bayerisch.

Thus the basis for the calculation of damages was decided on by the Court. It did not abandon its judicial function to the experts. Nevertheless the hypothetical nature of these two questions leaves a large amount of freedom to the experts. This led Judge Finlay in his Dissenting Opinion[17] and Judge Nyholm in his Observations[18] to question the value of recourse to expert opinion. The latter argued that if an expert report were made on a purely mathematical basis, then it would be of decisive assistance in arriving at a just settlement. But in this case the hypothetical nature of the question made an equally hypothetical answer inevitable, and therefore it would not be worthwhile to delay the settlement and incur the difficulties connected with an expert report. An immediate decision was possible. In fact the parties reached a settlement on the question of damages and so the expert report was unnecessary.

Experts had also been employed in a few earlier international arbitral cases to help assess the amount of damages, sometimes even where there was no express provision for this in the compromis.[19] In most cases their role was a limited one; the tribunal decided on the method of assessment appropriate in the circumstances and the expert's function was to make the detailed calculations. Thus in the *Delagoa Bay Railway Company* case,[20] the tribunal instructed the experts to determine the real value of the railway enterprise on the basis of its average income, taking into account the prospects of an increase in that income. However, in fact it is almost impossible to draw a clear line between the judicial function exercised by the tribunal and the subordinate fact-finding role of the experts. This can be seen clearly in the *Electricity Company of Warsaw* case.[21] Here the experts were asked to decide

1. The length of prolongation of the concession which should be granted en bonne justice, taking account of the conclusions of the parties, the reasoning in the award and the company documents; and
2. In what way should the rates and indemnity claimed by the company in respect of loss suffered since 1927 as the result of the imposition by Warsaw of reduced rates be determined and fixed, taking account of the conclusions of the parties, the reasoning in the awards, and company documents and accounts.

The arbitrator accepted the experts' recommendations.

In the *Corfu Channel* case,[22] the only one where experts were employed to consider the question of damages by the International Court of Justice, a similar freedom was allowed to the experts appointed by the Court. The Court had decided that the United Kingdom figures and estimates raised technical questions which called for the employment of experts. They were to 'Examine the figures and estimates stated in the last submission filed by the United Kingdom Government regarding the amount of its claim for the loss of the Saumarez and damage to the Volage'. No more precise instructions than this were given to them. The experts reached a higher figure than the United Kingdom for the loss of the *Saumarez* and a slightly lower figure for the injury to the other ship. Their conclusion was,

> During their enquiry and calculations and as a result of their experience and of the information placed before them, the experts have become convinced that the claim submitted by the United Kingdom Government may be taken as a fair and accurate estimate of the damage sustained.[23]

The Court accepted the United Kingdom estimates, and was criticized for this by Judge Ečer in his Dissenting Opinion; he argued that the Court had not given sufficient reasons for its choice.[24]

In the *Chorzów Factory* case, however, the Court itself discussed the question of the assessment of damages at some length; it did not leave the problem completely to the experts. The Court considered the award of damages for lost profits; it followed the predominant trend of previous arbitral practice, although without any express reference to this, in its decision that these were compensatable in principle, but said that in this case such profits would mostly have been absorbed by upkeep. Potential profits would be reflected in the present value of the undertaking. However, the Court accepted that if the experts could show that profits would have been made then this should be included in the compensation, minus deductions for any capital investment which would have been required for development under the second question submitted to the experts. It is obvious that such calculations are necessarily founded on conjecture; the difficulty of assessing the probable future development of a complex enterprise is clear.

The Court next considered whether the Bayerische Company had, owing to the dispossession, suffered any damage other than that sustained by the Chorzów Factory. It held that any possible damage to the company from competition was insufficiently proved, and 'Moreover it would come under the heading of possible but contingent and indeterminate damage which in accordance with the jurisprudence of arbitral tribunals cannot be taken into account'.[25] Germany also asked for a ban on the export by Poland of certain chemicals from the Chorzów Factory or, alternatively, that Poland should cease working the factory. The Court held that if the former request was designed to protect the Bayerische Company against competition then it was open to the same objection that this loss was too uncertain. If it was intended to prevent harm to licences issued by the company then insufficient details had been given. To prohibit export at the same time as allowing damages based on the present value of the factory as a going concern would amount to double compensation. A prohibition of the exploitation of the factory was open to the same objection. The Polish Government had acquired the right to continue working the undertaking as valued by the Court.

In fact the parties reached a settlement on the amount of damages, not surprisingly perhaps in view of the fact that the eventual outcome of the Court's deliberations on this question was left so uncertain. Detailed calculations were left to the experts. Nor did the Court contribute much to the theoretical issues involved; its assertions as to the governing principles remain unsupported, their content remains unclear.

The practice of the International Court of Justice is similar in these respects. A claim for damages was involved at some stage in several cases, almost all concerning injuries to foreign nationals.[26] In two cases, *Interhandel*[27] and the *Temple of Preah Vihear* case,[28] restoration of property was sought rather than damages. However, damages have been awarded only in the *Corfu Channel* case[29] and not much discussed in the other cases.

Like the *Chorzów* case, this decision contained unusual elements not found in earlier arbitral practice. The United Kingdom claimed damages for injury to two of its ships caused by explosions for which Albania was held responsible, and also for the pensions and other expenses incurred by the United Kingdom Government in respect of the deaths and injuries of naval personnel. As described above, the Court accepted the United Kingdom's estimates as to the amount of the loss resulting from the injury to its ships. For the loss of the *Saumarez* the United Kingdom based its calculations on the replacement value of the ship at the time of its loss after deducting the value of usable parts recovered and stores already consumed. The Court accepted the replacement cost at this time as the 'true measure of compensation'. The figure reached by the experts was slightly higher than that put forward by the United Kingdom, but the Court held that it could not award more than the sum claimed by the United Kingdom. This decision is apparently based on the *non ultra petita* principle familiar in English law but surely by no means a necessary rule in international law. The Court's reliance on this principle seems out of keeping with its readiness to characterize the parties' evidence as insufficient and to call on experts to 'supplement this in the *Chorzów Factory* case and with its decision in the *Corfu Channel* case also to call on experts. The Court also accepted the United Kingdom estimate for damage to the *Volage*.

In his Dissenting Opinion[30] Judge Ečer strongly criticizes the Court's judgments on these points. He says it did not give sufficient grounds for the amount awarded; it made hardly any reference to the United Kingdom documents accepted as evidence of damage. He considers that something should have been said on their value as evidence, and also that the Court should have examined the experts' report in more detail. 'For the amount of compensation claimed is essentially a point of substantive law and should have been dealt with less briefly.' More controversially, Judge Ečer asserts that the Court should have been more precise on the question of *culpa*; 'A few words might thus have been said on the relation between the degree of culpability and the amount of compensation.' He adds that 'The juridical value of the judgment would have been increased by a few short observations on causality as a judicial element for determining the amount of compensation'. Finally, he says that the Court should have given express consideration to the question of the time of the evaluation of loss—here assumed to be that of the illegal act with no explanation given, and no reference to the *Chorzów Factory* case—and to the question of the deduction of depreciation from the replacement value of the ship.

However, Judge Ečer makes no objections to the final part of the Court's judgment on damages for the United Kingdom. The Court allowed the United Kingdom's claims in respect of the deaths and injuries of naval personnel; the United Kingdom was awarded the cost of pensions and grants to victims and their dependants, and the costs of administration and of medical treatment. The United Kingdom here is claiming for loss to itself in its capacity as provider of social security benefits. Such claims by state social security systems against the wrongdoer for reimbursement of the benefits they have conferred on the victim of the wrongdoer's act are allowed in certain municipal legal systems, but this type of claim is by no means universally recognized and other states leave the loss to be borne by the state and thus give the wrongdoer the benefit of the claimant's social security entitlement.[31] The International Court of Justice in the *Corfu Channel* case gave no consideration to the diverse municipal practice; it simply assumed that in international law a state could recover damages for the welfare benefits it had given to the victims of a breach of international law. Such an award is unprecedented in international practice.

(*a*) *Damages as a remedy for direct injury to States*

There is basic disagreement between writers as to whether the *Corfu Channel* case is *sui generis*, as to whether damages are a proper remedy for tribunals to award in cases of direct injury to a state. Extreme positions have been taken on each side. For some writers not only may states claim damages for direct injury but also they may claim for any breach of international law whether or not the breach causes actual material damage or loss. According to Fitzmaurice,

> It would seem that, whereas under municipal law there may be an infringement of a right without any damages being recoverable, if none have in fact been suffered, under international law a government is always entitled to some damages in respect of breach of international law or treaty, irrespective of whether the breach has caused any actual material damage or pecuniary loss. In cases of breach of treaty, the writer's view is that the government against whom the breach is directed is always entitled to some damages even though the private persons affected by the breach do not happen to be its nationals. Cases may well arise in which a state is entitled to damages as the result of a breach of treaty even though it has not sustained any actual material damage. In the same way breaches of the general rules of international law will give rise to a right to recover damages even though no pecuniary damage is involved. For instance, if the frontiers of a country are intentionally violated by the armed forces of another, the first named country will, it is suggested, be entitled to substantial damages even though the troops have, in fact, retired without committing any material damage.[32]

Brownlie[33] and Sohn and Baxter[34] also accept this theory.

On the other side, Parry[35] asked the question, 'May a state recover substantial reparation where it has been damaged in its own sovereignty or property, as distinct from the persons or property of its nationals, by the agents of another state?', and his examination of judicial and arbitral practice before the *Corfu Channel* case led him to conclude

1. that in the *Alabama*, *Carthage* and *Manouba, Wimbledon* and *Trail Smelter* cases claims with respect to injury directly to the claimant state itself were either withdrawn or rejected; 2. that *Janes's* case is irrelevant because no claim of this type was either made or admitted; 3. that in consequence the *I'm Alone* and *Portuguese-German* awards stand by themselves as the only available precedents; and 4. that even these last two cases are but doubtful authority; the true basis of the award to Canada directly in the *I'm Alone* being rendered somewhat suspect by the simultaneous rejection of the indirect claim and the award in peculiar form and only questionably intra vires; and the *Portuguese-German* award being similarly obscure as to its juridical basis because of the impreciseness of the compromis, the reliance by the Tribunal upon principles of equity as distinct from law, and the apparent determination of the existence of a prior acceptance of responsibility by the respondent state.

Parry's suggested conclusion, drawn from arbitral practice before 1956 and from a study of the historical development of the law of state responsibility, is that there is 'No firm rule of international law to the effect that for one state to cause damage to another directly is to create a right to reparation in that other'. This conclusion applies both to breaches of customary international law and to breaches of treaties. Parry also puts forward a subsidiary hypothesis in contrast to the arguments of Fitzmaurice and Sohn and Baxter, that a bare violation of sovereignty does not give rise to a right to material compensation. The *I'm Alone* is the only case in which a substantial sum was awarded otherwise than in respect of material damage and the case is ambiguous in this regard as material damage had in fact occurred. Nor are there any examples of damages being awarded for breaches of treaties where there is no injury to rights of aliens protected by the treaty, that is, for a mere breach of treaty not leading to damage.

There are a very few pre-1956 arbitral decisions not discussed by Parry where damages were awarded for direct injuries to states. Some of the Mixed Arbitral Tribunals set up after the First World War recognized the right of governments to appear as claimants, often without any discussion, as in the first such claim to be made before a Mixed Arbitration Tribunal, *Greece* v. *Vulcan Werke*,[36] and in several later claims.[37] However, in two cases express consideration was given to the question of the government's standing to bring a claim. Thus in *Great Britain and France* v. *Bulgaria*[38] the tribunal held that because the government was acting as a trader it could be considered as a claimant even though the claims of individuals only were referred to in the relevant Peace Treaty, and in *Rumanian Minister of War* v. *Turkey*[39] the government's claim was admissible similarly because it was appearing not as an act of sovereignty but as a proprietor and, further, because 'Governments being able to appear as defendants there was no reason why they should not appear as claimants'. This latter explanation, although reasonable in the context, for the decisions of the Mixed Arbitration Tribunals settled private law claims, is hardly acceptable as a general proposition. However, in these cases the state was making the claim in its private capacity, as a person under municipal law and as the owner of property or as a trader. The initial basis of its claim was in an injury to a municipal law right. García-Amador included such cases in the category of private injuries, as distinct from cases of injury to the state's territory which constitutes a 'public' injury.[40] Therefore it is possible to accept Parry's contention that *Corfu Channel* was a case *sui generis* at the time it was decided.

There are various different conclusions that could be drawn from this arbitral practice.[41] First that claims concerning injuries to states other than through their nationals are not suitable for international arbitral decision. Second, 'the position may be that claims in respect of injuries of this sort are otherwise settled'. Parry asserts that up to 1956 only a few instances of settlement by payment for direct injuries are to be found and those of a somewhat trivial nature. There are now more examples of compensation being paid for this type of injury but such instances remain exceptional; the recently published Digests of State Practice of the United States, Switzerland, France, and the United Kingdom do not produce many examples. Even when compensation was paid on various occasions for harm caused by accidental bombings this was apparently intended to repair not the injury to the state's territory, but the damage to the property of individuals.[42] In one case compensation was paid to a government for its own loss, but this was for injury to its property, not to its territory.[43] Compensation for damage to embassies may similarly be put under this head.

Nor have writers managed to find many clear instances of the payment of compensation for injury to a state in the absence of injury to its nationals.[44] Verzijl lists a number of possible wrongs that could directly injure a state, but is unable to produce an example of compensation being paid for harm caused by such an unlawful act.[45] Brownlie, in search of evidence to support his theory that even in the absence of a peace treaty unlawful aggression involves a duty to pay damages apparently for direct injury to a state as well as for injury to its nationals, can find only one unequivocal example, and that one of intentional harm caused by a Greek attack on Bulgaria.[46] To settle the question of responsibility for this incident the Council of the League of Nations established a Commission of Inquiry which decided that 'The Greek Government is responsible for the expenses, losses and sufferings caused to the Bulgarian people and the Government by the invasion of Greek troops and on this account should make reparation to Bulgaria'.[47] If this is to be regarded as a judicial decision based on international law, and as such as evidence of a rule that a state may claim damages for injury to itself other than via its nationals—and the lack of any reasoned assessment of the damages involved decreases its importance as an example of such a claim—this raises various questions. Is it possible to argue that such a duty to pay compensation for a direct injury to a state other than through its nationals exists only in cases of intentional injury? The *Corfu Channel* case could be regarded as another example of intentional injury. However, it may not always be possible or desirable to make a distinction between intentional and unintentional acts of states. Alternatively this decision of the Commission of Inquiry could be regarded as somehow the equivalent of a peace treaty and so a special case.[48] Or perhaps the scope of the compensation awarded to the Bulgarian Government for injury to itself may be limited to repairing damage to government-owned property and possibly also repaying the expenses of the social security benefits, if any, provided by the government.

Brownlie has returned to this question in his work on state responsibility.[49] But his list of examples of claims for reparation in cases of direct injury does not provide decisive support for a general right of states to claim susbstantial damages for direct injury in the absence of any injury to a national. Some of his examples are mere claims;[50] of course these should not be completely discounted but their legal significance is less than that of actual awards or payments.[51] Others appear to involve damage to property of the state or of its nationals or injury to nationals.[52] The clearest example he cites of compensation for direct injury to a state is that paid by the USSR to Canada for the damage done by the disintegration of a Rusian satellite.[53] But even here there is some doubt as to exactly which injuries were covered by the payment. The Canadian claim for $12 million was made under both the Convention on Liability for Damage caused by Objects Launched into Outer Space (entered into force 1 September 1972)[54] and customary law. Article II of the Convention says, 'A launching state shall be absolutely liable to pay compensation for damage caused by its space object on the surface of the earth or to aircraft in flight.' But according to the definition section in Article 1, 'The term "damage" means . . . loss of or damage to property of states or of persons, natural or juridical'. This apparently covers only property damage and does not extend to claims for harm to territory. Nor does this provision appear to cover clean-up expenses. But the Canadian claim included an element for the cost of clearing up debris caused by the disintegration of the satellite and of ensuring the freedom from pollution of the areas of Canada affected.[55] As the USSR simply paid half of the amount claimed without explanation some uncertainty must remain.[56]

More recently, France agreed to pay compensation of $US7 million to New Zealand for the sinking by French agents of the *Rainbow Warrior* in New Zealand waters.[57] Here again it is not entirely clear which injuries are being compensated. Moreover, the general problem mentioned in the Introduction remains: the problem of the significance of such state practice for the law on remedies applicable by international tribunals, of the relationship between agreements made by states on compensation and the powers of tribunals to award damages.

Certain United Nations resolutions demand the payment of compensation by an aggressor state to its victim;[58] a few of these do not make clear the type of injury which is to be compensated,[59] but others require compensation only for damage to life and property.[60] In no case was the compensation demanded by the United Nations actually paid.

Lump sum settlements and the decisions as to their distribution by national claims commissions do not show any alteration from earlier arbitral practice so far as state claims are concerned.[61] Many of the lump sum settlements allow for claims by governments; about one third of those collected by Lillich contain express reference to state claims as a separate category from claims by individuals.[62] Lillich says, 'With varying degrees of specificity, quite a few agreements permit, or at least seem to permit, the allowance of claims by states qua states'. However, he apparently includes in claims 'by states qua states' all claims by states including those for injury to their nationals. Thus he says that 'among the clearest agreements on this score' (that is, providing for state claims) are four specified agreements.[63] In fact two of these appear to provide for compensation to be paid to a state for injury to its nationals; there is no indication that this payment is intended to compensate the states concerned for injury to themselves. Indeed it is clear that where provision is made for state claims it is private law claims that are envisaged—for damage to state-owned property, the payment of debts, and payment for government services. Even the agreement betwen the United States and Japan on the Marshall Islands[64] which allowed for *ex gratia* compensation, among other things, 'for the claims advanced by the government of Japan for their medical and hospitalization expenses', is exceptional. There is no express provision for this type of claim, similar to that in the *Corfu Channel* case, in any of the other lump sum agreements collected by Lillich, nor in any of the more recent agreements.

Have states gone further towards providing for the compensation of injuries to states other than via their nationals in other areas of treaty practice? Various treaties have been made to govern ultra-hazardous and polluting activities likely to cause harm to state territory.[65] Very few of these allow for responsibility under international law; the Convention on Liability for Damage caused by Objects Launched into Outer Space is the only one of these agreements with detailed provisions on international liability.

However, many treaties on ultra-hazardous and polluting activities provide for municipal law liability for damage caused by the activities concerned.[66] Those which allow for civil rather than criminal liability expressly include the state in the category of those entitled to sue. Thus, in the 1969 Convention on Civil Liability for Oil Pollution Damage[67] (entered into force 19 June 1975), 'person' is defined to include state. Under the same convention, pollution damage includes the cost of preventing harm—'the costs of preventive measures and further loss or damage caused by preventive measures', but the scope of this is not entirely clear; does it cover clean-up costs incurred after damage has occurred, or is no distinction possible between such costs and those incurred in taking measures to prevent harm? Certainly, after the *Torrey Canyon* Disaster—and the 1969 Civil Liability Convention was drawn up in response to this disaster—compensation was paid by the shipowners and charterers to the United Kingdom and French Governments for their clean-up expenses. Similarly, after the *Amoco Cadiz* disaster in March 1977 the French Government and local authorities brought claims against the tanker owners for the costs of preventive and clean-up measures.[68] The Tanker Owners' Voluntary Agreement concerning liability for oil pollution[69] and the Offshore Pollution Liability Agreement (OPOL)[70] also provide for state claims to cover the costs of the remedial measures taken in the event of an oil spillage from a tanker or offshore facility covered by the agreements. Remedial Measures are defined in clause 1.14 of OPOL as

> reasonable measures taken by any Party from whose designated offshore facility a discharge of oil occurs and by any state to prevent, mitigate or eliminate pollution damage following such discharge of oil or to remove or neutralize the oil involved in such discharge of oil, excluding, however, well control measures and measures taken to protect, repair or replace such designated offshore facility.

The conventions designed to deal with pollution caused by nuclear installations[71] are less precise on this question of the type of loss for which claims might be brought, for although they include states in the definition of nationals allowed to bring claims, compensatable loss is described only by reference to its origin.

Therefore, under these conventions dealing with ultra-hazardous and polluting activities states are allowed to bring claims in the appropriate municipal court for damage to their property, and often also for the costs of preventive and clean-up measures. The possibility of payment for this latter type of claim decreases the importance of the fact that none of these conventions allow claims for injury to territory. If claims for the costs of preventive and clean-up measures could be, or are already, recognized in international law as well as claims for injury to state-owned property, then the state would be able to claim damages for injury to itself in a wide range of cases.

If these settlements and agreements between states may be taken as evidence as to which state interests are given economic value and so as guidance for international tribunals as to when damages are an appropriate remedy for injury to states, then the *Corfu Channel* case, although unusual at the time it was decided, now seems an acceptable decision. And it is now difficult to reject completely the possibility of state claims for damages for direct injury. On the other hand the limited practice does not justify the assumption that all direct injuries should be compensated by the award of damages. One reasonable interpretation of the practice could be that a state is able to claim damages in international law for those injuries for which the same remedy would be available in municipal law, or rather under a 'generalized municipal law standard'. Specifically it is clear that there is no compelling authority to support the claim that a mere breach of international law without injury to nationals or material damage to the state should be met by an award of damages by a tribunal.

Since the *Corfu Channel* case the International Court of Justice has been asked to award damages for direct injuries, but it has not made such an award or discussed this question. In the *Aerial Incident* case as mentioned above[72] the United States made a claim for 'additional amends' but did not make it clear whether by this they meant punitive damages for the injured individuals or damages for the state itself. Next, in the *Fisheries Jurisdiction (Germany* v. *Iceland)* case[73] Germany asked the Court to declare 'That Iceland is, in principle, responsible for damage inflicted upon German fishing vessels and under an obligation to pay full compensation for all the damage which Germany and its nationals have suffered thereby'. In the absence of any more detailed explanation of this claim it is not clear whether Germany was indeed assuming that it was possible for it to bring a claim for injury to itself other than via its nationals. In fact the Court refused to make such a declaration on grounds to be described in the next section.

The question of damages for direct injury to a state arose less ambiguously in the *Iranian Hostages* case where the United States asked the Court to declare,

> That the Government of Iran shall pay to the United States in its own right and in the exercise of its right of diplomatic protection of its nationals, reparation for the foregoing violations of Iran's international legal obligations to the United States, in a sum to be determined by the Court.[74]

That is, the claim assumes that damages may be awarded for direct injury to the United States but does not specify in any detail the nature of the claim. In fact the claim for reparation was not pursued at this stage and the Court did not pronounce on it.[75] There is only a rather tantalizing, throw-away suggestion that alleged United States activities in Iran, their long-term interference in the domestic affairs of Iran 'may later be found to have some relevance in determining the consequences of the responsibility incurred by the Iranian state with respect to that conduct, although they could not be considered to alter its unlawful conduct'.[76] This interesting indication by the Court that the amount of damages for unlawful activity may be affected by the behaviour of the claimant state is not further elaborated on. It might be explained as a novel extension of previous decisions on contributory negligence; damages payable to the United States might be reduced because its own behaviour contributed to causing the harm it ultimately suffered.

Finally, in the *Case concerning military and paramilitary activities in and against Nicaragua*[77] Nicaragua asked for a declaration that the United States had an obligation to pay Nicaragua 'in its own right and as parens patriae' reparations for damages to person, property, and the Nicaraguan economy. The Nicaraguan Agent in his final submissions in the Oral Hearings on the Merits requested the Court to deal with the question of compensation in a separate phase of the proceedings. Again, since Nicaragua reserved the right to introduce to the Court a precise evaluation of the damages, the scope of the last head of claim is uncertain. If it goes beyond a claim for damage to state-owned property then it goes further than any previous case. There is an opportunity here for the Court to pronounce on the controversial question of the scope of the right to claim damages for direct injury. But in the light of the Court's general approach to the question of damages and in particular of its lack of discussion of this question in the *Corfu Channel* case, probably we should not expect too much.

The Court in its decision on the merits declared that compensation was due 'for all injury caused to Nicaragua by the breaches of obligations under customary international law and by the breaches of the Treaty of Friendship, Commerce and Navigation', but reserved the question of the form and amount of such reparation for subsequent proceedings. To Nicaragua's request for an interim award of $370.2 million the Court replied that there was no provision in its statute specifically empowering or debarring it from making an interim award of the kind requested; it refused to accede to Nicaragua's request at that stage on the ground that in a case where one of the parties was not appearing before the Court it should refrain from any unnecessary act which might prove an obstacle to a negotiated settlement.

NOTES

1. *The Wimbledon*, *Mavrommatis (Palestine) Concessions*, *Chorzów Factory*, *The Lotus*, *Mavrommatis (Jerusalem) Concessions*, *Polish Agrarian Reform*, *Oscar Chinn*, *Phosphates in Morocco*, *Panevezys Railway*, *Electricity Company of Sofia and Bulgaria*, *Socobelge*, *Prince von Pless*.

2. PCIJ Ser. A no. 1. In fact no payment of these damages was ever made—PCIJ Ser. E no. 1, 167.
3. As H. Lauterpacht points out in *The Development of International Law by the International Court* (1958), 15, the International Court did not make a practice of referring to the decisions of international arbitrations. He lists only three references to specific cases and a few more references to general arbitral practice. Nor does later practice show any increase in such references.
4. Loc. cit. in n. 2, at 32.
5. See Ch. 1, at n. 166.
6. In fact France never received the damages awarded in this case. The Reparation Committee refused permission for Germany to pay the damages. PCIJ Ser. E, 167.
7. Loc. cit. in n. 2, at 32.
8. PCIJ Ser. A no. 5.
9. PCIJ Ser. A no. 13.
10. Ibid., at 46.
11. 6 RIAA 358.
12. *Greece* v. *Bulgaria* (1931) 3 RIAA 1389.
13. 7 RIAA 13.
14. Sohn and Baxter also accept the date of dispossession as that relevant for the assessment of the value of property, whether its expropriation was lawful or unlawful. See Articles 10 and 32 of their draft codification and explanatory notes.
15. Thus the Court here was willing to do what it later refused in the *Barcelona Traction* case (1970) ICJ Reports 4; to lift the corporate veil and look beyond the corporate entity to the underlying economic reality.
16. Loc. cit. in n. 7, at 49.
17. PCIJ Ser. A no. 13, 70.
18. Ibid., 92.
19. For example, the *Lighthouses* case 1956 *Greece* v. *France* 12 RIAA 155. See G. M. White, *The Use of Experts by International Tribunals* (1965).
20. 1900 Great Britain and United States/Portugal, La Fontaine, 38.
21. 1929 France/Poland 3 RIAA 1669.
22. (1949) ICJ Reports 4.
23. Ibid., at 249.
24. Ibid., at 252.
25. PCIJ Ser. A no. 13, 57.
26. *Corfu Channel*, *Anglo-Norwegian Fisheries* (claim for damages later dropped), *Anglo-Iranian Oil Company*, *Nottebohm*, the various *Aerial Incident* cases, *Barcelona Traction*, *United Kingdom* v. *Iceland* (claim for damages later dropped), *Germany* v. *Iceland*, *Iranian Hostages*, *Nicaragua* v. *USA*. In the *Arbitral Award of the King of Spain* the right to claim reparation was reserved.
27. (1959) ICJ Reports 6.
28. (1962) ICJ Reports 6.
29. Loc. cit. in n. 22.

30. (1949) ICJ Reports 115.
31. See J. Fleming, 'Collateral Benefits', *IECL*, Vol. xi Ch. 11, 21.
32. G. G. Fitzmaurice (1936) *BYBIL* 82, at 109.
33. I. Brownlie, *International Law and the Use of Force by States* (1963), 379 ff.; *System of the Law of Nations: State Responsibility*, Part I (1983), 236 ff.
34. p. 143. A. P. Lester (1963) *AJ* 828 criticizes this view in the context of state responsibility for pollution. He argues that substantial injury should be necessary for an international claim as the need for a reasonable compromise is greater than that for a purely formal definition of legal rights.
35. (1956) 2 *HR* 653.
36. 5 TAM 887.
37. *Turkey* v. *Grazie and Co* 8 TAM 235; *Greece* v. *Vulcan Werke*, ibid., 837; *Turkey* v. *Armstrong Whitworth*, ibid., 996; *Turkey* v. *Vickers*, ibid., 1002.
38. 6 TAM 943.
39. 7 TAM 993.
40. In Garcia-Amador, Sohn, and Baxter, 92.
41. See Parry, op. cit. in n. 35.
42. Whiteman *Digest*, viii. 974.
43. Ibid., at 979.
44. See also the discussion of satisfaction in Ch. 1.
45. J. H. W. Verzijl, *International Law in Historical Perspective* (1968), vi. 645.
46. Brownlie, *International Law and the Use of Force by States* (1963), at Ch. 7.
47. Whiteman, *Damages*, ii. 1372.
48. See Ch. 5 Section 1, at n. 5.
49. Brownlie, *System of the Law of Nations: State Responsibility*, Part I (1983), 236.
50. At 238, examples (*c*) the *Baron de Borchgrave* case and (*d*) the *Aerial Incident* cases.
51. Compare the arguments on the legal significance of claims for *restitutio in integrum*. See Ch. 2 Section 4.
52. Examples (*a*) German Violations of Swiss neutrality, 1914–16; (*e*) United Kingdom claim against Indonesia for destruction of its embassy, 1963. On examples (*g*) Provisions in Lump Sum Settlements and (*h*) Waiver Clauses see text at n. 62 below.
53. See (1979) ILM 899; (1981) ILM 689.
54. (1971) ILM 965.
55. See (1979) ILM 899.
56. See (1981) ILM 689, and discussion by C. Q. Christol (1980) *AJ* 346.
57. See 1986 Keesing's Contemporary Archives 34565–8.
58. For a more detailed discussion of these resolutions see Ch. 6, at n. 21 ff.
59. For example, SC Res. 262 (1969) *UN Monthly Chronicle* no. 1, 19 said that the Lebanon was entitled to redress for the damage it had suffered as a result of the Israeli attack on Beirut airport, without indicating the extent of the compensable loss. Again, the 1964 SC Res. (1964) *UN Yearbook* 145 required only that Vietnam should pay Cambodia 'just and fair compensation' for its invasion.

60. For example, SC Res. 290 (1971) *UN Monthly Chronicle* no. 1, 18 asked Portugal to pay Guinea compensation for damage to life and property. Under SC Res. 387 (1976) *UN Monthly Chronicle* no. 4, 5 South Africa was to meet Angola's just claims for full compensation for damage and destruction on its territory and restoration of equipment seized.
61. For a very brief discussion of lump sum settlements see Ch. 5.
62. R. B. Lillich and B. H. Weston, *International Claims: Their Settlement by Lump Sum Agreements* (1975). Lillich, perhaps rather ingeniously as he himself was responsible for a considerable part of the previous literature, observed at 106 that, 'Completely overlooked in the literature on lump sum settlements, however, have been the provisions in many such agreements rendering claimant states eligible to claim, so to speak, on their own behalf'.
63. Ibid.
64. Ibid., Vol. ii, no. 29.
65. See Ch. 6.
66. See Ch. 6, at n. 42 ff.
67. (1970) ILM 45.
68. *The Times*, 13 Nov. 1978.
69. (1969) ILM 497.
70. (1974) ILM 1409.
71. Brussels Convention relating to Civil Liability in the Field of Maritime Carriage of Nuclear Material (1972) ILM 277; Vienna Convention Supplementary to the Paris Convention on Third Party Liability in the Field of Nuclear Energy (1962–3) ILM 685; Paris Convention on Third Party Liability in the Field of Nuclear Energy (1961) AJ 1082.
72. Ch. 1, at n. 275.
73. (1974) ICJ Reports 175.
74. (1980) ICJ Reports 4.
75. Ibid., §90. See Section 4 below, at n. 67.
76. Ibid., 41.
77. (1986) ICJ Reports.

SECTION 4

(i) OTHER REMEDIES

(*a*) *Restitutio in integrum and injunctions*

As was described in Section 1 of this chapter, the jurisdiction of the International Court of Justice to give remedies such as specific performance or injunctions where there is no express provision for this in the agreement from which the Court derives its jurisdiction is not clear. The *Iranian Hostages* case[1] is possible authority for such a power but some doubt must remain because of the failure of the Court expressly to consider the question, and the ambiguity of its judgment. It may be that, given the doubt, the Court deliberately chose not to go into this problem, and the absence of Iran enabled it to do this.

Nor is the Court's power to order *restitutio in integrum* settled. Again the *Iranian Hostages* case is the only direct authority to support such a power. Otherwise this remedy has never been awarded by the International Court of Justice or its predecessor. It was requested by the claimant state in a few cases, the *Anglo-Iranian Oil Company*,[2] *Nottebohm*,[3] and *Interhandel*[4] cases, but none of these cases was decided on its merits. In the *Barcelona Traction* case,[5] Belgium said that she would not ask for this remedy as its award would be practically and legally impossible.

It is the *Chorzów Factory* case[6] that has been mainly relied on by writers to support their assertions that *restitutio in integrum* is not merely a possible remedy, but the primary remedy in international law. The passage quoted is as follows:

> The essential principle contained in the actual notion of an illegal act is that reparation must, as far as possible, wipe out all the consequences of the illegal act and re-establish the situation which would, in all probability, have existed if that act had not been committed. Restitution in kind, or if this is not possible, payment of a sum corresponding to the value which a restitution in kind would bear; the award if need be of damages for loss sustained which would not be covered by restitution in kind or payment in place of it—such are the principles which should serve to determine the amount of compensation due for an act contrary to international law.[7]

However, not only was restitution not requested by the claimant state in this case, but also the treaty which the Court had to apply gave the injured party the treaty right to demand restitution in kind.[8] In the light of these facts and of earlier arbitral practice, arguments that the dictum quoted above represents a generally applicable theory of the primacy of *restitutio in integrum* in international law do not appear very convincing. But writers and arbitrators remain divided on the authority of the Court's pronouncement, and the *Iranian Hostages* case is not clear enough to settle the issue either way.

(*b*) *Declaratory Judgments*

In the decisions of the Permanent Court of International Justice and of the International Court of Justice the declaratory judgment is the commonest type of award. As was shown in Chapter 1 the declaratory judgment was not used by international arbitral tribunals as a remedy for breaches of international law; that is, with a very few exceptions—comprising awards of nominal damages, which could possibly be represented as declaratory judgments, and the grant of satisfaction in the form of a declaratory judgment—arbitral tribunals were not requested simply to declare that there had been a breach of international law and did not in fact make such declarations. The same is largely true of the practice of the Permanent Court of International Justice; it gave declaratory judgments mostly for the purpose of interpreting a treaty or contract or settling a question of territorial sovereignty. Obviously there can be no absolutely clear-cut distinction between such a judgment and a declaration that there has been a violation of international law,[9] but the form of the judgment is different.

In every award of damages there are two stages, first the determination or admission of responsibility and second the assessment of appropriate reparation. This distinction is clear even when both questions are brought before the Court at the same time as in the *Lotus* case[10] and the *Mavrommatis (Jerusalem) Concessions* case.[11] It has been said that the latter is an example of the Permanent Court of International Justice giving a declaratory judgment that there has been a breach of international law.[12] Such an interpretation is probably not justified. The Court decided that as there had not been any loss to M. Mavrommatis the claim for damages must fail. There was no indication that it considered the first part of its judgment to be a declaratory judgment that there had been a breach of international law, in itself a remedy for the claimant state. Rather the Court completely rejected the claim on behalf of M. Mavrommatis. Thus the Permanent Court of International Justice apparently did not at this stage recognize or use the declaratory judgment as a remedy for an international wrong. Later it apparently came to accept this possibility, though there is no clear instance of this type of remedy. But the declaratory judgment did from early in the jurisprudence of the Permanent Court of International Justice emerge as a separate preliminary stage.

In certain cases the Court was asked to decide on the first stage only, on the existence of responsibility—at least initially. However, it seems clear that the claimant states in these cases were interested also in eventual pecuniary compensation. The problem of assessing this was left to the parties or to a later judgment of the Court. Thus in *Certain German Interests in Polish Upper Silesia*[13] the Court was at first asked to give a purely declaratory judgment as to the legality of the behaviour of the Polish Government.[14] Only at a later stage was the Court requested to award damages. Again, in the *Eastern Greenland* case[15] the Permanent Court of International Justice was asked to declare that the acts of the Norwegian Government were in violation of its obligations under international law. The claimant state, Denmark, expressly reserved its right to claim reparation.[16] In the *Diversion of Waters from the Meuse* case[17] the declaratory judgment does seem to have been requested as an end in itself, but even here the Netherlands asked the Court not only to make a declaratory judgment that Belgium's projects would violate its treaty obligations but also for a consequent order that Belgium should discontinue work on those projects. In fact the Court rejected both claims. And in the *Borchgrave* case[18] it is true that the application of the claimant state to the Court was apparently not concerned at all with reparation. Belgium asked in its

Memorial that the Court should 'Adjudge and declare that the responsibility of the Spanish Government is involved on account of the crime committed on the person of Baron Jacques de Borchgrave; to adjudge and declare that the Spanish Government is responsible for not having used sufficient diligence in the apprehension and prosecution of the guilty', but earlier Belgium had sought pecuniary reparation from the Spanish Government. The case was later withdrawn by Belgium.

Although the declarations as to responsibility sought in these cases were clearly closely related to the desire of the applicants for pecuniary compensation, this question of reparation was left open. The parties to the case are free to work out the detailed implementation of the award. This has led writers to consider the declaratory judgment as a particularly suitable remedy for international law as it strikes a balance between third-party settlement and the sovereignty of states. Obviously the degree of freedom left to the parties will depend on the terms of judgment. In those cases such as the *Serbian Loans*,[19] *Lighthouses*,[20] and *Socobelge*[21] cases where the Court declares that a contract has been duly entered into and is binding on the parties or that an arbitral award is binding, although this is not formally an order for specific performance it is clear what the parties ought to do. The declaratory judgment has the further advantage that it is undoubtedly available as a remedy for injury to a state whereas some controversy remains as to the availability of damages for direct injuries to a state.

This does raise the question whether there is a duty on the claimant state to exhaust local remedies in certain actions for direct injury,[22] and the more general question whether exhaustion of local remedies is necessary before an action for a declaratory judgment is admissible. The World Court has not provided an answer to these questions.[23] Writers disagree on whether it is necessary to exhaust local remedies in all actions for a declaratory judgment, or whether this is necessary only if there is a subsequent action for damages based on the declaratory judgment.[24] In those cases before the Court where a declaratory judgment was requested and harm to individuals was involved so that a later award or agreement on damages would be conceivable this question of local remedies was not raised by the parties or discussed by the Court.[25] On principle it would seem that if an international claim is based on injury to a national then it is necessary for the claimant state to show that legal remedies have been exhausted, whether the international claim is for damages or merely for a declaration.

It is in the practice of the International Court of Justice that the declaratory judgment takes on a new importance. As before it is used to settle disputes as to the interpretation of contracts and treaties and to settle boundary disputes. It is also used to give satisfaction. Thus in the *Aerial Incident* case[26] Israel asked the Court to declare that 'Bulgaria is responsible under international law for the destruction of Israeli aircraft and for the loss of life and property and all other damage that resulted therefrom'. Israel requested damages for the financial loss incurred 'By the persons whose cause is being adopted by it', but stated 'That a declaration by the Court regarding the international responsibility of Bulgaria . . . would be sufficient satisfaction and that it was waiving any further claim to reparation' as far as injury to Israel herself was concerned. Again, in the *Corfu Channel* case[27] the Court was asked, 'Has the United Kingdom under international law violated the sovereignty of Albania by reason of the acts of the navy in Albania's waters and is there any duty to give satisfaction?' Albania did not allege that she herself had suffered any material damage from the acts of the British navy. The Court declared that Albania's sovereignty had been violated, 'And that this declaration by the Court constitutes in itself appropriate satisfaction'.

Also, the International Court of Justice unlike its predecessor has given declaratory judgments that there is an obligation on the defendant state to act in a certain way. This gives more guidance to the states parties than does a simple interpretative judgment. The latter has its drawbacks, as may be seen in the *Haya de la Torre*[28] case. The Court was asked to determine the manner in which effect should be given to its declaratory judgment in the *Asylum* case.[29] There the Court had decided that a state granting diplomatic asylum did not have the right unilaterally and definitively to qualify an offence for the purpose of asylum, nor was Colombia entitled to claim guarantees for the safe departure of the man to whom she had given asylum. On the other hand this man was held to be a political refugee. Not surprisingly the parties asked for further guidance. In the *Haya de la Torre* case the court took a restrictive view of its competence and held that it would only decide on questions submitted to it in the earlier case and that therefore it was not in a position to state how Colombia should terminate the asylum it had granted. It said,

> Having thus defined in accordance with the Havana Convention the legal relations between the parties with regard to the matters referred to it, the Court had completed its task. It is unable to give any practical advice as to the various courses which might be followed with a view to terminating the asylum, since by doing so it would depart from its judicial function.[30]

Lauterpacht suggests that this unsatisfactory solution was the product of the parties' failure to request the Court to give judgment finally and unequivocally adjudicating upon the issue involved.[31] This seems unconvincing as an explanatioin for the Court's failure to take a liberal view of its jurisdiction.[32]

The recent agreement between Libya and Tunisia to submit their differences over the delimitation of the boundary between their continental shelves to the International Court of Justice[33] was apparently designed to avoid this sort of difficulty and to obtain from the Court a judgment of greater immediate practical application than that requested and given in the *North Sea Continental Shelf* case.[34] In Article 1 of their Agreement Libya and Tunisia asked the Court to decide on the principles and rules of international law to be applied in the delimitation of their continental shelves. They further requested the Court to specify precisely the practical way in which the aforesaid principles and rules apply in this particular situation so as to enable the experts of the two countries to delimit those areas without any difficulties.[35]

A declaratory judgment may give detailed guidance to states on their future conduct rather than merely state their relative legal positions. Thus in the *Temple of Preah Vihear* case,[36] where there was a dispute between Cambodia and Thailand as to which had sovereignty over the temple, Cambodia requested not only a declaration as to its sovereignty but also a declaration based on this finding, that Thailand was under an obligation to withdraw its troops and return sculptures and other objects taken by it from the temple. The Court gave a declaratory judgment to this effect. And similarly, if the judgment in the *Iranian Hostages* case is to be regarded as a declaratory judgment rather than as an order to the parties, it gives clear guidance as to what Iran was to do.

The International Court of Justice has also used declaratory judgments to state that there has been a breach of international law, either as a substitute for the award of damages or where damages would not be available. In several cases[37] there was some possibility of injury to the nationals of the claimant state, but the claimant states apparently felt it more appropriate not to seek pecuniary compensation; what was important to them was a declaration of their legal rights. In both the *United Kingdom* v. *Iceland*[38] and the *Anglo-Norwegian Fisheries* cases the initial request for damages was later withdrawn.

Lauterpacht argues that the Court should be careful to keep the rendering of declaratory judgments within limits, for otherwise the contentious jurisdiction of the Court might be used by states to obtain Advisory Opinions.[39] He says that the Statute of the Court wisely made no provision for this, for 'Whereas it may be assumed that an organ of the United Nations or a specialized agency would act upon an Advisory Opinion of the Court, there may be no such assurance in the case of individual states'. Apparently he fears that states might not comply with an Advisory Opinion because these are not binding. But as both Advisory Opinions and judgments in contentious cases state the law, surely the fact that the latter are expressly said to be binding while the former are not is of little significance. The binding quality even of the latter depends on the willingness of the states concerned to comply with the judgment; the provisions of Article 94 of the United Nations Charter have little practical importance. In fact, there is little distinction in substance and effects between Advisory Opinions and judgments; the major differences are merely procedural.[40]

However, it has been suggested that there is one fundamental difference between Advisory Opinions and declaratory judgments; that the former relate to the future whereas the latter bear on the past.[41] As far as Advisory Opinions are concerned there are certain clear exceptions to this suggested rule. The *Certain Expenses of the United Nations* case,[42] for example, obviously related to the past. Moreover, there does not seem to be any necessary reason why Advisory Opinions should not concern the past. Is a declaratory judgment necessarily limited to making a statement about the past? Where the dispute concerns the interpretation of a treaty this is obviously not so. A declaratory judgment may be delivered on the legality of a proposed course of action under the treaty. Thus in the *Diversion of Waters from the Meuse* case,[43] the Netherlands requested a declaration that certain water works proposed by Belgium were illegal under a treaty. It was implicit in the Court's decision that such a judgment was permissible. The *Interpretation of the Statute of the Memel Territory* case[44] also involved a declaration as to future conduct. Certainly in municipal legal systems declarations as to future conduct are possible. Borchard distinguishes two types of action where declaratory relief may be invoked:[45] first, those where the plaintiff seeks a declaration that he may act, or that he is immune from the liability asserted by the defendant, or where he requests a construction of a disputed contract before a breach has taken place; in such cases no award of damages would be possible. Second, there is the type of action where the plaintiff contents himself with a declaration although he could sue for an executory judgment. Of course there are limits on the award of the first type of declaratory judgment in municipal law;[46] such judgments must not be awarded to decide purely hypothetical questions. In international law, the existence of a dispute between the parties is a necessary condition of the award of a declaratory judgment. There seems to be no compelling reason, given this limitation, why the International Court should not give declaratory judgments as to the legality of a proposed course of conduct.[47] In municipal law it is not necessary to wait for the destruction of the status quo before allowing a declaratory judgment. Why should this be necessary in international law? Borchard criticizes the narrow view which limits the concept of wrongs and cause of action to committed delicts, and limits the concept of judicial process to their redress.[48] This limitation obscures the fact that harm is done and rights impaired by a mere dispute without the occurrence of a physical attack.

Ritter argues that to the extent that a declaratory judgment goes beyond consideration of the past, it is no longer a judgment but a method of proclaiming a norm; he says future conduct cannot be the object of litigation.

This is a very limited view. It is true that simple intention is not illegal but it does not follow from this, as Ritter claims, that a declaratory judgment necessarily bears only on the past. The declaration concerns the legality of the proposed course of conduct, not of the intention to carry it out. Also the Court may clarify the content of a rule of international law and, so far from being limited merely to proclaiming the norm, may rule on its application to the facts of a particular case. Therefore Ritter's proposed distinction between Advisory Opinions and declaratory judgments on the basis of the time to which they relate is not tenable. He and Lauterpacht (in his arguments against the declaration being used to obtain an Advisory Opinion) ignore the important policy considerations involved in this question; they seem to forget that it is desirable to prevent unlawful acts from taking place. If an international organization may obtain a ruling on the legality of proposed actions and adjust its behaviour accordingly, why should not a state also?

However, the effectiveness and importance of the declaratory judgment as a remedy for breaches of international law have been limited by the strict approach of the Court. It has refused to award declaratory judgments on the grounds that to do so in the circumstances would not be a proper exercise of its judicial function. The *Northern Cameroons* case[49] has been much discussed. Cameroon sought a declaration from the International Court of Justice that the United Kingdom in its application of the Trusteeship Agreement which governed its rights and duties towards the Northern Cameroons had failed to respect certain obligations. However, the claimant state did not seek any pecuniary compensation for this. The Court held that there was a dispute in existence so it had jurisdiction to decide the question put to it by the Northern Cameroons, but that it was entitled to examine the propriety of giving a judgment in this case. It said that there are inherent limits on the exercise of the judicial function. Because the Trusteeship Agreement had now ended, and the claimant state did not attack the validity of the General Assembly resolution which declared the legality of the United Kingdom's actions, and did not seek reparation for the allegedly unlawful acts, the Court held that it was impossible to render a judgment capable of effective application.

> That the Court may, in an appropriate case, make a declaratory judgment is indisputable. The Court has, however, already indicated that even if, when seized of an Application, the Court finds that it has jurisdiction, it is not obliged to exercise it in all cases. If the Court is satisfied, whatever the nature of the relief claimed, that to adjudicate on the merits of an Application would be inconsistent with its judicial function, it should refuse to do so.[50]

Moreover, the Court observed that if in a declaratory judgment it expounds a rule of customary law or interprets a treaty which remains in force, its judgment has a continuing applicability. But in this case there was a dispute about the interpretation and application of a treaty—the Trusteeship Agreement—which had been terminated, was no longer in force, and there would be no opportunity for a future act of interpretation or application of that treaty in accordance with any judgment the Court might render.

This decision has been much criticized. Judge Morelli, in his Separate Opinion,[51] argued that the Court was wrong once it had established the existence of a dispute to refuse to give a decision on the ground that this would not be a proper exercise of the judicial function.

Since a dispute is regarded as existing, the usefulness of the decision resides precisely in the very settlement of the dispute. Such a decision has undoubted legal effects; it produces precisely the specific legal effects of res judicata which consist of placing an obligation on the parties to regard the dispute as having been settled in a particular way. These effects are produced for the future. Although the conduct by one of the parties which is the subject of the decision is past conduct, the legal effect of this decision, that is to say the obligation deriving from it for the parties, concerns their future conduct.

Judge Badawi in his Dissenting Opinion[52] made the point that this case is very similar to that of the *Corfu Channel* where a declaratory judgment was allowed as satisfaction for Albania. So here if the Cameroons had claimed a declaration as a form of satisfaction, presumably the Court would not have been able to refuse to make a decision on the ground that this would have no practical application. Moreover,

To declare that the present case is inadmissible as a result of the termination of the trusteeship, because it could not lead to any practical application, is to assume that the essential feature of any legal action is that it must have a practical application. This assumption is undeniable where a judgment is sought for the purposes of execution, but it is more than questionable in the case of declaratory judgments.[53]

Gross discusses this case in detail and makes three main criticisms of it.[54] First, he points out that the Court relies on different dates for different purposes—that of the application, when the Trusteeship Agreement was still in force, to establish the existence of a dispute, but that of the decision of the Court, after the Agreement had come to an end, to back up its assertion that a judgment would be without effect. Secondly, a judgment on the interpretation of a treaty no longer in force may have continuing application just as much as a judgment on customary international law or an existing treaty. Thirdly, the Court's speculation as to the future conduct of the parties was not within its judicial function and was definitely out of place in a decision whether to allow a declaratory judgment. In the *Rights of Passage* case the Court was not concerned with the probability that its declaration would have no practical application.

The *Nuclear Tests* cases[55] also show the Court taking a restrictive view of its power to award declaratory judgments. Australia requested a declaration that 'the carrying out of further atmospheric nuclear tests in the South Pacific Ocean is not consistent with applicable rules of international law'. This obviously refers to the legality of future acts. The New Zealand application was different in that she requested a declaration 'That the conduct by the French government of nuclear tests in the South Pacific Region that give rise to radioactive fall-out constitutes a violation of New Zealand's rights under international law, and that these rights will be violated by any further such tests'. This could be interpreted as referring also to past acts. Neither claimant state sought damages for injury caused by the alleged breaches of international law. Not only would this have been very difficult to prove, involving difficult technical questions and problems of causation, but also it was more important for Australia and New Zealand to obtain an assurance as to future behaviour than compensation for the past. The Court held that it had the right to interpret the submission of the parties in order to identify the object of the claim. This power is uncontroversial. But the Court's use of it led them to a strange conclusion. It decided that both Australia and New Zealand in spite of the differences between their submissions were seeking the same thing:

> It is clear that the *fons et origo* of the dispute was the atmospheric nuclear tests conducted by France in the South Pacific region, and that the original and ultimate objective of the Applicant was and has remained to obtain a termination of those tests.[56]

The Court held in the Australian case that

> While the judgment of the Court which Australia seeks to obtain would in its view have been based on a finding by the Court on questions of law, such a finding would be only a means to an end, and not an end in itself. The Court is of course aware of the role of declaratory judgments, but the present case is not one in which such a judgment is requested.

France had given unilateral undertakings not to conduct further tests and the Court decided that these were binding: 'Thus the Court faces a situation in which the objective of the Applicant has in effect been accomplished, in as much as the Court finds that France has undertaken the obligation to hold no further nuclear tests in the atmosphere in the South Pacific.' This leads the Court to conclude that 'The dispute having disappeared, the claim advanced by Australia no longer has any object. It follows that any further finding would have no raison d'être.' The Court seems to have been anxious to avoid making a decision on the merits of these cases, perhaps understandably, but it seems a pity that they achieved this by reinterpreting the parties' submission in such a way as to deny their obvious intention of seeking a declaratory judgment. As the Joint Dissenting Opinion of Judges Onyeama, Dillard, Arechaga, and Waldock[57] said, 'While the court is entitled to interpret the submissions of the parties it is not authorised to introduce into them radical alterations'. These judges rejected the Court's view of the real aim of Australia and New Zealand. They also point out that

> The Judgment, while it reiterates that the Applicant's objective has been to bring about the termination of atmospheric nuclear tests, fails to examine a crucial question, namely from what date the Applicant sought to achieve this objective.[58]

The court considered only events after the French undertaking; it ignored those between this time and the date of the application.

> Such a view of the matter takes no account of the possibility of Australia seeking to claim compensation in respect of the 12 tests conducted in 1973 and 1974. It is true that the Applicant has not asked for compensation for damage in the proceedings which are now before the Court. However, the Australian government has not waived its right to claim them in the future.

The Court also ignored the possibility of a declaration constituting satisfaction for the violation of Australian rights under international law. So here, as in the *Northern Cameroons* case, if Australia and New Zealand had specifically asked for a declaration as a form of satisfaction, or else had requested damages, then it seems unlikely that the Court would have been able to reach the same decision that there was no longer any dispute in existence. It seems unfortunate, to say the least, that the only way in which a state can be certain that its claim for a declaration will be received is for it to make a claim for material compensation. One of the main advantages of the declaratory judgment is that its use avoids the decree for reparation which could injure the dignity of the respondent state. It is noticeable that in those cases where pecuniary reparation was involved the World Court had difficulty in securing compliance with its judgments.[59]

The Court also took a restrictive view of its power to give a declaration in the *Germany* v. *Iceland* case.[60] Germany's fourth submission was a request for a declaration that

> The acts of interference by the Icelandic coastal patrol boats with fishing vessels registered in Germany or with fishing operations by the threat or use of force were unlawful under international law and that Iceland is under an obligation to make compensation therefore to Germany.

Germany reserved all its rights to claim full compensation for all the unlawful acts that had been committed or might yet be committed. It did not submit a claim for payment of a certain amount of money as compensation for the damage already inflicted.

However, she requests the Court to adjudge and declare that Iceland is in principle responsible for damage inflicted upon German fishing vessels and is under an obligation to pay full compensation for all the damage which Germany and its nationals suffered thereby.

Here again the Court used its powers of interpreting this submission in such a way that it concluded it had no power to give the declaration requested. It held that this submission did not ask for the assessment of compensation for certain specified acts, but for a declaration of principle that Iceland was under an obligation to make compensation to Germany in respect of all unlawful acts of interference with German fishing vessels. The Court said that although it was possible to request a general declaration establishing the principle that compensation was due this was conditional on the claimant's asking the Court to receive evidence and to determine in a subsequent phase of the same proceedings the amount of damages to be assessed. The claimant had not done so here. Accordingly,

it would not be appropriate for the Court while acting under Article 53 of the Statute and after the applicant has stated that it is not submitting a claim for the payment of a certain amount of money as compensation, to take the initiative of requesting specific information and evidence concerning the indemnity which in the view of the applicant would correspond to each incident and each head of damage. In these circumstances the court is prevented from making an all embracing finding of liability which would cover matters as to which it has only limited information and slender evidence.[61]

But the Court's interpretation is not the only permissible one. As Judge Waldock points out in his Separate Opinion,[62]

In so far as the submission may be understood as merely claiming a declaration of principle that Iceland is under an obligation to make reparation for any acts of interference established as unlawful, I do not see the same difficulty in the Court's acceding to the claim.

Here again the Court refused to give a declaratory judgment where this was requested as a substitute for, or possibly preliminary to, a request for damages.

The Court's attitude in the *Temple of Preah Vihear*[63] had been more liberal. Here Cambodia[64] had put forward a fifth submission asking for a declaration that the sculptures and other objects which had been removed from the temple by the Thai authorities since 1954 were to be returned to the Cambodians by the Thai Government. Having decided that this claim was admissible, the Court said,

On the other hand no concrete evidence has been placed before the Court showing in any positive way that objects of the kind mentioned in this submission have in fact been removed by Thailand from the Temple or Temple Area since Thailand's occupation of it in 1954. It is true that Thailand has not so much denied the allegation as contended that it is irreceivable. In the circumstances, however, the question of restitution is one on which the Court can only give a finding of principle in favour of Cambodia without relating it to any particular objects.[65]

In contrast with the flexible approach in this case, the restrictive decisions in the *Northern Cameroons*, *Nuclear Tests*, and *Icelandic Fisheries* cases represent unacceptable limitations on the declaratory judgment. There is no reason why the Court should not pronounce on the question of responsibility alone, or state in principle that there is an obligation to reparation.[66] A state should not be forced to make a claim for damages for its claim to be admissible, but should have the option of leaving the question of possible reparation for later negotiations. The unnecessary restrictiveness and excessive formalism of the Court's position in *Germany* v. *Iceland* is highlighted by the later decision in the *Iranian Hostages* case. Here the United States' request that the Court declare that Iran was under an obligation to pay reparation of an amount to be determined escaped the fate of Germany's claim in the *Icelandic Fisheries* case, possibly because the United States took the precaution of expressly asking the Court to determine the amount of reparation in a subsequent phase of the proceedings.[67] Nicaragua made a similar request in its recent case against the United States.[68]

(*c*) *Conclusion*

So the jurisprudence of the World Court is some way from creating an international law of remedies. The Court treats each case in isolation, it does not refer back (or only briefly and partially) to previous arbitral practice or to its own decisions. There is little general discussion of basic rules, and what there is—in the *Chorzów Factory* case—is controversial. Of course the Court's function is to decide cases, not to write general essays on the law of remedies. Clearly it is difficult to lay down general rules that will produce predictable results in all cases; to some extent the case by case approach is unavoidable. Maybe pronouncements on the calculation of lost profits or remoteness of damage will not have much content when not applied to particular facts, but other issues such as interest, currency questions, the availability or primacy of *restitutio in integrum* could be settled by the Court. In theory it would be possible for the Court, and helpful to potential litigants, to clear up some of the uncertainty left by arbitral practice. But the decisions of the Court that did deal with these questions are unfortunately less than authoritative because they are brief, generally not fully reasoned, and made without reference to international arbitral practice. Of course it is always the tendency, sometimes the weakness, of academic writers to seek uniformity, to look for coherent sets of rules. The harm caused by the present confusion should not be exaggerated. But the differences between modern arbitral awards and between national claims commissions highlight the continuing uncertainty.[69] Like cases are not treated alike; results are unpredictable; litigants are not clear on their rights. And the World Court has not contributed much. Its treatment of remedies seems somewhat perfunctory in contrast with its approach to substantive issues. For it, as for most writers, remedies are an afterthought. The conception of an international law of remedies seems weak; remedies are something to be invented anew in each case.

NOTES

1. (1980) ICJ Reports 4.
2. (1952) ICJ Reports 93.
3. (1955) ICJ Reports 4.
4. (1959) ICJ Reports 6.
5. (1970) ICJ Reports 3.
6. PCIJ Ser. A no. 13.
7. Ibid., at 47.
8. See, for example, H. W. Baade (1960) *AJ* 801.
9. This can be seen in the application of Article 177 of the EEC Treaty. This gives the European Court of Justice the power to make preliminary rulings on the interpretation of Community law, but the distinction between such interpretation and the application of Community law to a particular set of facts cannot be absolute. See L. Collins, *European Community Law in the United Kingdom* (3rd edn. 1984), at 123 ff.; J. de Richemont, *Integration of Community Law within the Legal Systems of the Member States* (1978), 47.
10. PCIJ Ser. A no. 10.
11. PCIJ Ser. A no. 5, at 51.
12. García-Amador in García-Amador, Sohn, and Baxter, at 98.
13. PCIJ Ser. A no. 6.
14. It was also asked to state what attitude should have been adopted by the Polish Government, but held that it was not necessary for it to give an answer to this question.
15. PCIJ Ser. A/B no. 53.
16. In this case the Court decided that 'The declaration of occupation promulgated by the Norwegian Government on 10th July 1931, and any steps taken in this respect by that Government, constitute a violation of the existing legal situation and are accordingly unlawful and invalid'. This apparently represents a finding, one of the first in international arbitral and judicial practice, of the nullity of an unlawful action by a state. See n. 38.
17. PCIJ Ser. A/B no. 70.
18. PCIJ Ser. A/B no. 72.
19. PCIJ Ser. A nos. 20/21.
20. PCIJ Ser. A/B no. 71.

21. PCIJ Ser. A/B no. 78.
22. See Section 3 above, at n. 31 ff.
23. The only defendant state to object to the Court's jurisdiction to make a declaratory judgment on this ground of non-exhaustion of local remedies was Spain in the *Borchgrave* case (loc. cit. in n. 18). Belgium had asked the Permanent Court of International Justice to declare that Spain was responsible for its involvement in the crime committed against Baron Jacques de Borchgrave and also for its lack of diligence in the apprehension and prosecution of the guilty. Spain argued that 'The Belgian Government's claim cannot be entertained in regard either to the first or to the second of the submissions contained in its Memorial, owing to the fact that the remedies afforded by Spanish municipal law have not been exhausted'. However, Spain subsequently withdrew this objection to the jurisdiction of the Court and asked that it be joined to the merits of the case. Because Belgium abandoned its action this question was not settled by the Court.
24. See the discussion reported in (1956) *AIDI* 299. Also T. Haesler, *The Exhaustion of Local Remedies* (1968), at 119.
25. Thus, for example, in the *Fisheries Jurisdiction* (*Germany* v. *Iceland*) (1974) ICJ Reports (jurisdiction), (1975) ICJ Reports (merits), Germany reserved the right to claim full compensation. It did not present a definite claim for damages in its action but sought a declaration that Iceland was in principle responsible and under an obligation to pay full compensation for injury to Germany and its nationals. The question of local remedies was not raised by Iceland nor discussed by the Court.
26. (1959) ICJ Reports 127.
27. (1949) ICJ Reports 4.
28. (1951) ICJ Reports 71.
29. (1950) ICJ Reports 266.
30. Loc. cit. in n. 28, at 83.
31. H. Lauterpacht, *The Development of International Law by the International Court* (1958), 148.
32. Writers today adopt a more sceptical approach to the Court's motives for refusing jurisdiction or not allowing a requested award. See, for example, J. Dugard (1975–6) *Virg. JIL* 463.
33. (1979) ILM 49.
34. (1969) ICJ Reports 3.
35. Even so Tunisia and Libya disagreed about the meaning of the agreement and the role of the Court, but the Court dismissed this controversy as of minor importance. (1982) ICJ Reports 4. See also the agreement for submission to the Court between Malta and Libya (1982) ILM 971.
36. (1962) ICJ Reports 6. See also the Joint Declaration of Judges Tanaka and Morelli at 37.
37. *Anglo-Norwegian Fisheries* (1951) ICJ Reports 116; *Rights of Passage* (1960) ICJ Reports 6; *South West Africa* (1962) ICJ Reports 319 and (1966) ICJ Reports 4; *Northern Cameroons* (1963) ICJ Reports 15; *Fisheries Jurisdiction* (1974) ICJ Reports 3 and 175; *Nuclear Tests* (1974) ICJ Reports 253 and 457.

In the *Arbitral Award of the King of Spain* (1960) ICJ Reports 192, Honduras reserved the right to claim compensation.

38. The decision in this case and in the case that Germany brought against Iceland include a finding that Iceland's Regulations on Fisheries Jurisdiction 'Are not opposable to the United Kingdom (or Germany)'. For in international law as in municipal law an unlawful act may be void or voidable (it is clear that this distinction may legitimately be drawn in international law as in municipal law in spite of the lack of compulsory jurisdiction in the former (see R. Y. Jennings in *Cambridge Essays in International Law* (1965), 64 and P. Cahier (1972) *RGDIP* 645)) and a finding to this effect may be sought as a remedy for a state. See also the *Eastern Greenland* case, PCIJ Ser. A/B no. 53 and the *Namibia* Advisory Opinion (1971) ICJ Reports 56. The Vienna Convention on the Law of Treaties contains detailed rules as to what makes a treaty void or voidable and rather less detailed rules on the consequences of this. There appears to be little, or at any rate little accessible, state practice on the operation of these provisions. State and arbitral and judicial practice on the nullity of international arbitral decisions and of the acts of international organizations is more accessible and has been much discussed. See, for example, W. M. Reisman, *Nullity and Revision* (1971); P. Cahier, op. cit.; E. Lauterpacht in *Cambridge Essays in International Law* (1965), at 88; F. Morgenstern (1976–7) *BYBIL* 241; E. Osieke, ibid., 259.
39. H. Lauterpacht, op. cit. in n. 31, at 250.
40. See D. Pratap, *The Advisory Jurisdiction of the International Court of Justice* (1972), 232.
41. J.-P. Ritter (1975) *AFDI* 278.
42. (1962) ICJ Reports 151.
43. PCIJ Ser. A/B no. 70.
44. PCIJ Ser. A/B no. 49.
45. E. M. Borchard, *Declaratory Judgments* (1941), 26.
46. See E. M. Borchard, ibid., 29 ff.; P. W. Young, *Declaratory Orders* (1975); I. Zamir, *The Declaratory Judgment* (1962).
47. Nor should such a judgment be interpreted as merely a decision on the legality of the past refusal of a state party to allow the proposed activity. This is Ritter's suggestion (op. cit. in n. 41). Such an interpretation seems highly artificial. The legality of the refusal is dependent on the legality of the proposed course of action. Also it may happen that, although there is a dispute as to a proposed course of action, there has not been any actual refusal or obstruction by a state party.
48. E. M. Borchard, op. cit. in n. 45, 5 ff.
49. (1963) ICJ Reports 15.
50. Ibid., 37.
51. Ibid., 131.
52. Ibid., 150.
53. Ibid., 151.
54. L. Gross (1964) *AJ* 415.

55. (1974) ICJ Reports 253 and 457.
56. Ibid., at 263 and 467.
57. Ibid., at 312 and 494.
58. pp. 318, 500.
59. See C. W. Jenks, *The Prospects of International Adjudication* (1964), 663.
60. (1974) ICJ Reports 175.
61. Ibid., 205.
62. Ibid., 227. Judge Dillard also makes this distinction between the two possible interpretations of Germany's submission, and Judge Onyeama argues in favour of the interpretation which would have allowed the Court to give the declaration requested. Ibid., at 207, 244 respectively.
63. Loc. cit. in n. 36.
64. See Section 1 of this chapter, at n. 33.
65. Loc. cit. in n. 36, at 36.
66. Or rather, there is some force in the argument that abstract declarations that there is an obligation to make reparation in the absence of actual evidence of loss are undesirable. But even the Court does not seem to base itself on this argument, as it admits that declarations in principle are acceptable provided only that the claimant state has asked the Court to receive evidence and decide the amount of damages later in the same case. Nor is this argument consistent with the Court's approach in the *Temple of Preah Vihear* case.
67. Even here Judge Lachs in his Separate Opinion argued that the finding by the Court that Iran was under an obligation to make reparation was redundant given the finding of the responsibility.
68. (1986) ICJ Reports.
69. See Ch. 5.

SECTION 5

(i) ADVISORY OPINIONS

Like interim measures of protection Advisory Opinions have been discussed by writers more often and at greater length than have judicial remedies awarded on the merits of a contentious case.[1] So here there is no need to do more than consider whether the Advisory Opinion may be regarded as a remedy for a breach of international law, and, if so, how it operates.

It is possible to conceive of an Advisory Opinion being used to give a remedy for or against an international organization, a remedy equivalent to a declaratory judgment that there has been a breach of an obligation under international law by the organization or by its member states. However, the effectiveness of such a remedy would be limited by the fact that only international organizations may request Advisory Opinions from the Court and so any dissatisfied state must be able to secure the majority necessary for a decision of the competent organ of the organization to request an Advisory Opinion. Moreover the suggested distinction between the organization and its member states is misleading. The dual nature of most international organizations should be recognized; the organization may be a separate legal entity under international law but, to an extent that varies according to the degree of autonomy and power of the organization's officials, it operates through the decisions of its member states. In fact in the light of the jurisprudence of the Permanent Court of International Justice and its successor it is more realistic to speak of an Advisory Opinion being requested to settle a dispute or difference of opinion between different member states or groups of member states rather than to say that the Advisory Opinion is a remedy for or against the organization.

The Statutes of the International Court of Justice and the Permanent Court of International Justice contain very little information about the nature and function of Advisory Opinions. It is necessary to consider how the Court has operated in practice; the Court itself makes little express comment. In a well-known passage in the *Interpretation of the Peace Treaties* case,[2] however, the International Court of Justice listed those characteristics which distinguish the Advisory Opinion from a judgment in a contentious case:

> The consent of States parties to a dispute is the basis of the Court's jurisdiction in contentious cases. The situation is different in regard to advisory proceedings even where the Request for an Opinion relates to a legal question actually pending between states. The Court's reply is only of an advisory character and as such it has no binding force. It follows that no State, whether a member of the United Nations or not, can prevent the giving of an Advisory Opinion which the United Nations consider to be desirable in order to obtain enlightenment as to the course of action it should take. The Court's Opinion is given not to the States but to the organ which is entitled to request it; the reply of the Court, itself an 'organ of the United Nations' represents its participation in the activities of the Organization and, in principle, should not be refused.

Do these characteristics make it impossible to regard the Advisory Opinion as a remedy for a breach of international law? Is the Advisory Opinion really so different from a declaratory judgment? The distinction has been made between those Advisory Opinions which are given to guide the conduct of international organizations and those given to settle a dispute between states.[3] A further category could be added: those Advisory Opinions which state the legal position so that one state may be brought to act lawfully in a situation where no harm to the legal interests of another state is involved. The Advisory Opinions on the *Danzig Legislative Decrees*[4] and the *German Settlers in Poland*[5] come under this heading. In the former the Court was asked to state whether Poland was bound by the Treaty of Versailles in its treatment of Polish nationals of German race and if so whether its behaviour was in conformity with its international obligations. In the latter the Court was asked to give an opinion as to whether certain decrees issued by the city of Danzig were consistent with its constitution. This type of Advisory Opinion might be said to go a little way towards the provision of an *actio popularis* in international law.[6]

The distinction between cases where an international organization is seeking guidance on the running of its affairs and those where there is a dispute between states is recognized in the Rules of the Court. Article 68 of the Rules of the Permanent Court of International Justice, introduced under the 1929 Amendment, provides for the assimilation of the advisory to the contentious procedure in appropriate cases. This says, 'In the exercise of its advisory functions, the Court shall further be guided by the provisions of the Statute which apply in contentious cases to the extent to which it recognizes them to be applicable'. This provision was retained by the International Court of Justice in Article 68 of its Statute, Article 87 of the Rules.[7]

More specifically, provision for the appointment of an *ad hoc* judge in advisory proceedings was first made in 1927, when the Court adopted an amendment incorporating in Article 71 of its Rules a paragraph stating that

> On a question relating to an existing dispute between two or more states or members of the League of Nations, Article 31 of the Statute [which provides for the appointment of an ad hoc judge in contentious cases where there is no judge of the nationality of one or both of the states parties to the dispute before the court] shall apply. In cases of doubt the Court shall decide.

The corresponding provision of the Rules now in force is Article 89 which allows the appointment of an *ad hoc* judge where there is 'A legal question actually pending between two or more states'. Neither the Permanent Court of International Justice nor the International Court of Justice has created a set of guidelines to enable it to decide in this context, for the purposes of allowing or refusing the appointment of an *ad hoc* judge, when there is an 'existing dispute' or a 'legal question actually pending' between two or more states.[8]

The Permanent Court of International Justice allowed the appointment of *ad hoc* judges in six cases. In the first of these the *Jurisdiction of the Courts of Danzig* case,[9] this was done without any discussion at all by the Court in its Opinion. In three of the remaining cases the initiative towards the appointment of an *ad hoc* judge apparently came from the Court itself.[10] The Court's statement in the *Greco-Bulgarian Communities* case[11] is typical. It said that

> In view of the fact that neither of the governments concerned had upon the bench a judge of its nationality and that—the request to the effect that an advisory opinion be obtained having, according to the terms of the letter addressed to the Secretary

General . . . been submitted 'on behalf of the two Governments'—the question related to an existing dispute between two states within the meaning of Article 71(2) of the Rules, the attention of the Parties to this dispute, namely the Bulgarian and Greek Governments, was drawn to their right under Article 31 of the Statute each to choose a judge of their nationality to sit in the case. The two governments availed themselves of this right.

In the last two cases where the appointment of an *ad hoc* judge was allowed[12] it seems that the initiative came from the state concerned. No more prolonged consideration is given to the question of the existence and nature of 'an existing dispute between two or more states' in any of these cases. It is clear from the judgments of the Court in the six cases in which it allowed *ad hoc* judges that there was in each of these cases a difference of opinion between two states; in the three cases involving Poland and the Free City of Danzig the Court in its Advisory Opinion considers the history of the disagreements between the two parties and examined the communications, assertions, and counterassertions of the parties (in the *Polish War Vessels in the Port of Danzig* and the *Polish Nationals in Danzig* these disagreements apparently took place almost exclusively within the League of Nations). Similarly in the *Railway Traffic between Lithuania and Poland* and the *Interpretation of the Greco-Bulgarian Agreement*, Poland and Lithuania, Greece and Bulgaria had clearly made opposing claims as to the legal obligations on Poland and Greece under international agreements. In the *Greco-Bulgarian Communities* case the dispute lay in the failure of the Greek and Bulgarian commissioners on a mixed commission to come to an agreement on the interpretation of a convention. However, the Court does not discuss what factors are necessary and sufficient for there to be an existing dispute under Article 71 of its Rules. Nor is there any more detailed discussion in two of the cases where the Court refused to allow the appointment of an *ad hoc* judge—the *Danzig Legislative Decrees* case and the *Minority Schools in Albania* case.[13] In both of these the Court simply stated that Article 71 did not apply as there was no existing dispute. In the *Customs Union* case[14] Austria and Czechoslovakia were refused *ad hoc* judges as there were already on the Court judges of the nationalities of states with the same interests as Austria and Czechoslovakia.

The International Court of Justice has allowed the appointment of an *ad hoc* judge in only one case. It has never on its own initiative suggested the appointment of an *ad hoc* judge to the parties concerned. No application was made by the interested parties unrepresented on the Court in the *Interpretation of the Peace Treaties* case[15] which could be regarded as a case where there was 'a legal question actually pending between two or more states', nor did the Court suggest this. Certain of the Allied and Associated Powers signatories to the Treaties of Peace with Bulgaria, Hungary, and Romania had charged the governments of those countries with violation of the Treaties of Peace and had called upon those governments to take remedial measures. The Bulgarian, Hungarian, and Romanian Governments rejected the charges and also refused to appoint representatives to sit on Commissions provided for under the Peace Treaties which could settle the disputes.

The Court had to decide on the appointment of *ad hoc* judges in two cases, the *Namibia* case[16] and the *Western Sahara* case.[17] In neither of these did it give much attention to the question of what constitutes 'a legal question actually pending between two or more states' and to what extent this requirement differs from 'an existing dispute between two or more states'. Indeed the Court apparently assimilated the former to the latter.[18] In the *Namibia* case the Court did not discuss separately the appointment of an *ad hoc* judge as requested by South Africa, but mentioned it in passing in its Advisory Opinion. First it considered whether it would be proper for it to give an Advisory Opinion in the light of the assertion of the South African Government that there existed a dispute between itself and other states.[19] Having rejected the South African argument on this point and concluded that there was no dispute, it went on to discuss its refusal to appoint an *ad hoc* judge. The Court said simply,

> This decision was based on the conclusion that the terms of the request for an advisory opinion, the circumstances in which it had been submitted as well as the other considerations set forth . . . above [that is, the discussion as to the existence of a dispute] preclude the interpretation that an opinion had been requested upon a legal question actually pending between two or more states.[20]

The Advisory Opinion in the *Western Sahara* case is equally unenlightening on this point. The Court here speaks exclusively of the existence or non-existence of legal disputes, with no definition of this, nor any justification for reliance on this criterion rather than on the existence or non-existence of a 'legal question actually pending between two or more states'. It said only that 'There appeared to be a legal dispute between Morocco and Spain regarding the territory of Western Sahara' and without further elaboration allowed Morocco an *ad hoc* judge. Similarly, as 'There appeared to be no legal dispute between Mauritania and Spain', the Court by 8 votes to 7 rejected Mauritania's application for an *ad hoc* judge. This seems rather unsatisfactory; the Court did not discuss the differences between the position of Morocco and that of Mauritania which might justify this difference in their treatment by the Court. It remains uncertain when the Court will allow the appointment of an *ad hoc* judge and when it will refuse this; the factors it takes into account are not made clear.

Those Advisory Opinions given to decide what is in reality a dispute between two or more states—whatever the form of the question put to the Court, however apparently abstract the Court's reply, and whether the

Court allows the appointment of an *ad hoc* judge or not—do not seem very different in substance from judgments in contentious cases; the main differences are procedural. Both declaratory judgments and Advisory Opinions merely state the law, they are not coercive remedies. In theory Advisory Opinions are not binding. Certainly studies of their effectiveness show that the record of compliance by states is far from perfect,[21] but the same is true of decisions in contentious cases,[22] and as Advisory Opinions purport to state international law it is difficult to see why they should be regarded as somehow less binding than declaratory judgments.

Seventeen out of the twenty-seven Advisory Opinions given by the Permanent Court of International Justice involved disputes between states.[23] A much smaller percentage of the Advisory Opinions of the International Court of Justice come within this category: 3 out of 18.[24] These are the *Peace Treaties* cases, the *Namibia* case, and the *Western Sahara* case. It has been said that the International Court of Justice has moved away from being a participant in a process for the peaceful settlement of interstate disputes towards becoming a constitutional court advising requesting organs of international institutions on matters which directly affect them. Obviously this is partly a reflection of the type of disputes which states acting through international organizations are willing to submit to the International Court for an Advisory Opinion, but it is certainly true that the International Court has preferred to treat the questions submitted to it for Advisory Opinions as abstract questions and has often given its Opinions without any discussion of the history of events which led up to the request for an Advisory Opinion.

The declaratory judgment is designed to settle disputes between states. As was shown in Section 4 of this chapter, the International Court of Justice has taken a narrow view of when it is proper to allow such a judgment. Moreover, consent of the parties is necessary to found the jurisdiction of the Court. It is clear that this is not necessary for the Court to assume jurisdiction in an Advisory Opinion, but it may possibly affect the propriety of giving an Opinion.[25] This was discussed in the *Namibia* case; South Africa had argued that the Court should refuse to give an Advisory Opinion as a matter of judicial propriety as the question before it related to an existing dispute between states. The Court seems to have been eager to give an Advisory Opinion. It discussed the factors that distinguished this case from the opinion in the well-known *Eastern Carelia* case[26] where the Permanent Court of International Justice had refused an Advisory Opinion as it related to a dispute between states: South Africa was a member of the United Nations and hence bound by Article 96 of its Charter which gave authorized bodies the power to request Advisory Opinions, it had appeared before the Court and addressed itself to the merits. More controversially the Court decided that the Advisory Opinion in this case did not concern a dispute between South Africa and other states; it was not the purpose of the request to obtain the assistance of the Court in the exercise of the Security Council's functions relating to the pacific settlement of disputes between two or more states, rather the request was put forward by a United Nations Organ with reference to its own decisions; it was seeking legal advice from the Court on the consequences and implications of these decisions. A similar, rather formalistic, approach was adopted by the Court in the *Western Sahara* case. The Court chose here also to portray the dispute as merely a difference of opinion in the General Assembly in order that it could assert jurisdiction without laying itself open to the charge of using the advisory procedure, 'as an alternative after the failure of an attempt to make use of the contentious jurisdiction with regard to the same question', and thus as a means of bypassing the consent of a state. In fact the dispute between states here does not seem different in kind from those where the Court has given judgment in contentious proceedings. Also, as described above, the Court had decided in an Order given before its Advisory Opinion, that 'For the purposes of application of Article 89 of the Rules of Court [providing for the appointment of an *ad hoc* judge] the advisory opinion requested . . . appears to be one "upon a legal question actually pending between two or more states" '. Of course it is possible that the conditions for the existence of a 'legal question' under Article 89 are different from those that would make it improper for the Court to give an Advisory Opinion without the consent of the state concerned. This can be argued more convincingly now that the requirement for the appointment of an *ad hoc* judge is the existence of 'a legal question actually pending between two or more states' rather than an 'existing dispute' as it was under the Rules of the Permanent Court of International Justice. Nevertheless this does not seem very satisfactory; if there exists 'a legal question actually pending between two or more states' such that the appointment of an *ad hoc* judge is necessary to protect the interests of the state concerned, it is difficult to argue that, for example, the dispute exists only within the General Assembly as a difference of opinion between various states and that therefore the consent of the states concerned is not necessary, especially in the light of the interpretation of 'legal question' by the International Court and its assimilation to 'legal dispute'. In the *Western Sahara* case where this situation arose, Judge Gros at any rate thought that there was an inconsistency between the Court's making an Order for the appointment of an *ad hoc* judge and its also making a decision that there was 'No bilateral dispute detachable from United Nations debate on decolonisation'.[27] This problem has arisen because of the anomalous nature of the provision allowing for *ad hoc* judges in Advisory Opinions although these opinions are in theory not binding decisions between disputing states parties. These difficulties did not arise in the cases of the

Permanent Court of International Justice as in those opinions where an *ad hoc* judge was appointed there was no refusal of consent to the Court's jurisdiction by the states concerned.

The International Court of Justice is very aware of its role as principal judicial organ of the United Nations; it has repeated its statement in the *Peace Treaties* case that an Advisory Opinion 'In principle should not be refused', in several later cases.[28] The *Western Sahara* case shows clearly that the International Court is anxious to respond to a request for an Advisory Opinion not only in cases when it has been asked to give guidance on the conduct of an international entity. This seems to have led it to interpret the dispute in this case as one solely within the United Nations so that Spain's refusal of consent to the jurisdiction would not affect the propriety of giving an Advisory Opinion. The Court's attitude to Advisory Opinions provides a marked contrast to its approach to declaratory judgments. Because of the theoretical differences in nature between the declaratory judgment and the Advisory Opinion the latter may be, and has been, used to obtain a remedy comparable to the declaratory judgment in circumstances where the Court would not give judgment in a contentious case.

NOTES

1. See K. J. Keith, *The Extent of the Advisory Jurisdiction of the International Court of Justice* (1971); D. Pratap, *The Advisory Jurisdiction of the International Court of Justice* (1972); M. Pomerance, *The Advisory Function of the International Court in the League and UN Eras* (1973).
2. (1950) ICJ Reports 65.
3. See Keith, op. cit. in n. 1; M. Pomerance (1973) *AJ* 446; L. M. Goodrich (1938) *AJ* 738.
4. PCIJ Ser. A/B no. 65.
5. PCIJ Ser. B no. 6. Possibly the *Acquisition of Polish Nationality* case, PCIJ Ser. B no. 7, may also be included in this category.
6. See Ch. 6.
7. See Pratap, op. cit. in n. 1, at 15.
8. See Pomerance, op. cit. in n. 3; D. Mathy (1976) *Rev. belge DI* 528.
9. PCIJ Ser. B n. 15.
10. The *Greco-Bulgarian Communities*, PCIJ Ser. B no. 17; *Railway Traffic between Lithuania and Poland*, PCIJ Ser. A/B no. 42; *Polish War Vessels in the Port of Danzig*, PCIJ Ser. A/B no. 43.
11. PCIJ Ser. B no. 17.
12. *Polish Nationals in Danzig*, PCIJ Ser. A/B no. 44; *The Interpretation of the Greco-Bulgarian Agreement*, PCIJ Ser. A/B no. 45.
13. PCIJ Ser. A/B no. 64.
14. PCIJ Ser. A/B no. 41.
15. (1950) ICJ Reports 65.
16. (1971) ICJ Reports 12.

17. (1975) ICJ Reports 6.
18. See Mathy, op. cit. in n. 8.
19. See below at n. 24.
20. Loc. cit. in n. 16, at 25.
21. See Pratap, op. cit. in n. 1, at 234; Keith, op. cit. ibid., at 196; Goodrich, op. cit. in n. 3; Pomerance, op. cit. in n. 1, at 330.
22. See, for example, C. W. Jenks, *The Prospects of International Adjudication* (1964), at 664.
23. *The Nationality Decrees of Tunis and Morocco*, PCIJ Ser. B no. 4; *Eastern Carelia*, Ser. B no. 5; the *Jaworzina* case, Ser. B no. 8; *Question of the Monastery of Saint-Naoum*, Ser. B no. 9; *Exchange of Greek and Turkish Populations*, Ser. B no. 10; *Polish Postal Service in Danzig*, Ser. B no. 11; *Treaty of Lausanne*, Ser. B no. 12; *Jurisdiction of the European Commission of the Danube*, Ser. B no. 14; *Jurisdiction of the Courts of Danzig*, Ser. B no. 15; *Greco-Turkish Agreement*, Ser. B no. 16; The *Greco-Bulgarian Communities*, Ser. B no. 17; The *German Minority Schools*, Ser. A/B no. 40; *Austro-German Customs Regime*, Ser. A/B no. 41; *Railway Traffic between Lithuania and Poland*, Ser. A/B no. 42; *Polish War Vessels in the Port of Danzig*, Ser. A/B no. 43; *Polish Nationals in Danzig*, Ser. A/B no. 44; *Interpretation of the Greco-Bulgarian Agreement*, Ser A/B no. 45; *Minority Schools in Albania*, Ser. A/B no. 64.
24. S. Rosenne discusses possible explanations for the relative infrequency of requests to the International Court of Justice for Advisory Opinions in (1963) *BYBIL* 1.
25. See the *Peace Treaties* case, loc. cit. in n. 15, and discussion in Keith, op. cit. in n. 1, at 98.
26. PCIJ Ser. B no. 5.
27. (1975) ICJ Reports, at 12.
28. For example *Reservations to the Genocide Convention* (1951) ICJ Reports 15, *Namibia* case, *Western Sahara*, *Application for Review of Judgment No. 273 of the United Nations Administrative Tribunal* (1982) ICJ Reports 325.

3

A Comparison of Judicial Remedies in the European Communities with Judicial Remedies in International Law

How does the use of judicial remedies in the international legal system compare with their role in the more closely integrated European Communities? Has the European Court of Justice been influenced by, or contributed to, the more general international law of remedies as developed by other international judicial and arbitral tribunals?

This chapter is primarily concerned with the functioning of the European Court of Justice under Articles 169–71 of the EEC Treaty and their equivalents in the ECSC and Euratom Treaties.[1] The judicial remedies available against Member States in breach of their community obligations will be examined. Of course the European Court's jurisdiction is not limited to actions against Member States and this represents only a minor part of its work. The Court also provides judicial review of the legality of the actions or inaction of Community organs, and either annuls the unlawful act or makes a declaration as to the illegality of the failure to act.[2] This provides a contrast with the practice of other international organizations where judicial decisions play a very small part, if any, in controlling the activities of the organs of the organization.[3] Similarly the Court's power to award damages, not only to injured officials[4] but also to other individuals and enterprises harmed by violations of Community law by the organs of the Community distinguishes the European Communities from other international organizations. The European Court of Justice may also under Article 177 of the EEC Treaty[5] give interpretations of Community law on application by the courts of Member States; it hears appeals against the imposition of penalties and sanctions on enterprises,[6] and it may give Advisory Opinions in a limited number of cases.[7]

Thus the jurisdiction of the European Court of Justice is more extensive than that of the International Court of Justice and than that of the normal international arbitral tribunal as regards the forms of action, the eligible parties, and the types of decision available to it. This was desirable because the organs of the European Communities have great power to affect municipal activities, and possible because the Communities are closely integrated so far as certain areas of national activity are concerned and their rules are designed to cover questions previously handled under the municipal law of Member States.

(i) ACTIONS AGAINST MEMBER STATES

It has been said that the European Court acts as an international court under Articles 169–71 of the EEC Treaty.[8] Is this accurate, or are the differences between its role and that of the International Court of Justice more pronounced than the similarities? How do their attitudes to remedies compare? Certainly the Member States of the European Communities are held responsible by the European Court of Justice for breaches of obligations binding on them under the constituent treaties. Article 169 of the EEC Treaty provides:

> If the Commission considers that a Member State has failed to fulfil an obligation under this Treaty, it shall deliver a reasoned opinion on the matter after giving the State concerned the opportunity to submit its observations. If the State concerned does not comply with the opinion within the period laid down by the Commission the latter may bring the matter before the Court of Justice.

Article 170 of the EEC Treaty establishes the procedure for such an action to be brought by a Member State. Articles 140–2 of the Euratom Treaty are essentially similar, but the procedure established under the ECSC Treaty differs from that under the other two Treaties. Article 88(1) and (2) provides:

> If the High Authority considers that a State has failed to fulfil an obligation under this Treaty, it shall record this failure in a reasoned decision after giving the State concerned the opportunity to submit its comments. It shall set the State a time limit for the fulfilment of its obligation.
>
> The State may institute proceedings before the Court within two months of notification of the decision; the Court shall have unlimited jurisdiction in such cases.

Here the High Authority issues a 'reasoned decision' rather than a 'reasoned opinion'. Proceedings may be taken against it before the Court if it fails to issue this decision; no such review of the Commission's failure to give a reasoned opinion is possible in the Economic Community or Euratom and this represents a weakness of the procedure against wrongdoing Member States of these two Communities, only partly mitigated by the existence of a right of action for Member States against other Member States under Articles 170 EEC and 142 Euratom. Also under Article 88 ECSC in the action before the court the Member State alleged to have committed a breach of its obligations seeks the annulment of the decision to this effect, made by the High Authority, whereas under the provisions of the other two Treaties the Commission brings the action before the Court and requests a declaration as to the illegality of the behaviour of the Member State.[9]

In contrast to the International Court of Justice, the European Court exercises compulsory jurisdiction over disputes concerning Member States. The provisions in the treaties of the European Communities on the judicial settlement of disputes concerning the obligations of Member States, unlike those in the constituent documents of other international organizations, have proved workable.[10] Furthermore it is open to the organs of the European Communities and not only to Member States to bring before the Court actions against against offending Member States. It is clear from an examination of the European Court's decisions that it conceives its function to be to help achieve the purposes of the European Communities. The International Court of Justice, the 'principal judicial organ of the United Nations',[11] could be said to operate on a comparable basis in its giving Advisory Opinions, but perhaps not in its decisions in contentious cases, for the purposes of the United Nations are more abstract than those of the European Communities, and the International Court's lack of compulsory jurisdiction makes its contribution to this much smaller than that of the European Court in its more limited sphere.

It should be clear from the preceding chapters[12] that the role of judicial remedies in the international legal system is limited not only because there is no compulsory judicial settlement of disputes, but also because of the nature of the entities involved. This latter consideration influences the role of judicial remedies in the European Communities also.

(i) JURISDICTION

It is commonly said that a judgment of the Court under Articles 169 and 170 of the EEC Treaty and their equivalents is purely declaratory, that the Court is restricted to stating that a Member State has or has not failed to fulfil its obligations, and that it is left to the Member State to decide on the measures necessary for it to perform the obligations incumbent on it as a result of the judgment.

As far as enforcement of the judgment is concerned, Article 171 of the EEC Treaty (Article 143 Euratom is identical) imposes a duty to comply with the judgment of the Court. It says, 'If the Court of Justice finds that a Member State has failed to fulfil an obligation under this Treaty, the State shall be required to take the necessary measures to comply with the judgment of the Court of Justice.' The effectiveness of such a provision in the face of non-compliance by a recalcitrant Member State appears limited. In fact the record of compliance with judgments of the Court addressed to Member States in breach of their obligations is quite impressive,[13] and only in two cases has the Commission brought an action to secure observance of

Article 171.[14] In the first of these—and the only case to be decided by the Court under Article 171—the Commission argued that the Italian Government had not taken adequate measures to comply with the judgment of the Court in Case 7/68, *Re Export Tax on Art Treasures No.1.*[15] The Court accepted this and said,

> In the present instance the efficacy of Community law, as held with binding effect against Italy, implied an absolute prohibition on the relevant national authorities applying a national provision which has been held incompatible with the Treaty and, where necessary, an obligation to adopt all measures necessary to facilitate the full efficacy of the Community law.[16]

The Advocate-General considered,

> Whether it is really judicious to condemn Italy when its Government and its Senate have shown their will to abolish the taxation system in issue and it may be hoped that the Parliament resulting from the recent elections will quickly put an end to the situation under discussion. To that question also it is not easy to reply in the negative. It is enough to remember that the Article 169 procedure, which is a feeble enough instrument, is the only means available to the Community to obtain the setting up of a situation which conforms to the Treaty. In those circumstances there is no doubt of the need to emphasise strongly the necessity of the Member States promptly carrying out the judgments delivered under that procedure and using all the means available to them to preserve the authority of the Community legal order and of the Community itself.[17]

It is only under the ECSC Treaty that there is provision for sanctions to be employed against Member States in the event of their violation of treaty obligations. These are to be imposed by the High Authority, not the Court. The second part of Article 88 ECSC says:

> If the State has not fulfilled its obligation by the time limit set by the High Authority, or if it brings an action which is dismissed, the High Authority may, with the assent of the Council acting by a two-thirds majority:
>
> (*a*) Suspend the payment of any sums which it may be liable to pay to the State in question under this Treaty;
>
> (*b*) take measures, or authorise the other Member States to take measures, by way of derogation from the provisions of Article 4, in order to correct the effects of the infringement of the obligation.

In fact the High Authority has never used this power; in the ECSC as in other international organizations the role of those sanctions for which formal provision is made in the constituent documents is in practice very limited. The lack of any such provision in the EEC and Euratom Treaties is not a serious weakness as far as the operation of the Communities is concerned.

As was mentioned above, under the ECSC Treaty it is for the Member State held by the Commission to be in breach of its obligations to ask the

European Court for the annulment of the decision of the Commission. The other two Treaties, however, say nothing about the type of judgment to be given in actions by the Commission against Member States. Writers have apparently assumed from the wording of Article 171 quoted above, and from the fact that Article 187 and 192 of the EEC Treaty, which provide for the enforcement of the judgments of the European Court of Justice in Member States, do not extend to the decisions given in actions against Member States, that the only type of ruling open to the Court under Articles 169 and 170 of the EEC Treaty is a declaratory judgment.[18] On the whole this view is supported by the practice of the Court for it has never gone beyond making a declaratory judgment that a Member State has violated its obligations; it has never attempted to annul acts, issue orders, award damages, or even declare that there is an obligation on a Member State to take certain measures. Admittedly it has never in an action against a Member State directly pronounced on this question of the extent of its jurisdiction to give remedies. But there are indications that the restrictive view of its jurisdiction is correct.

Reference is often made in this context to Case 6/60 *Humblet* v. *Belgium*,[19] where the Court was asked to interpret part of the Protocol on the Privileges and Immunities of the ECSC, and also to annul certain measures of the Belgian authorities. The Court said,

> Community law does not grant to the institutions of the Community the right to annul legislative or administrative measures adopted by a Member State . . . Under the terms of Article 31 of the ECSC Treaty it has responsibility for ensuring that Community law is observed and by Article 16 of the Protocol has jurisdiction to rule on any dispute relating to the interpretation or application of the Protocol but it may not, on its own authority, annul or repeal the national laws of a Member State or administrative measures adopted by the authorisation of that State. This statement of the limits of the jurisdiction of the Court may further be supported by an argument stemming from the Treaties of Rome, in particular from Article 171 of the EEC Treaty and Article 143 of the EAEC Treaty which merely attach declaratory effect to the decisions of the Court in cases of failure to comply with the Treaties, albeit obliging the Member States to take the necessary measures to comply with the judgment.[20]

And in a request for a preliminary ruling under Article 177, the Court has been asked to give guidance on the effect of an Article 169 judgment against a Member State and on the interpretation of Article 171.[21] The Court made it clear that its judgment could not directly give rights to individuals under national law.[22] Nor has it claimed the power under Article 169 to give an extension of the period allowed by the Commission to the Member State for fulfilling its obligations under Community law.[23]

Of course these cases are only indirect authority but combined with the consistent practice of the Court in Article 169 actions they do provide convincing evidence that the Court has no jurisdiction in this type of case to annul domestic acts or to issue orders to Member States. They support the view of the Advocate-General in Case 141/78 *France* v. *United Kingdom*[24] that an Article 170 action can only be for a declaration that a Member State has failed to fulfil its obligations under the Treaty and that it is not possible for the Court to declare a national rule of law illegal in such proceedings.

Nor has the European Court of Justice ever awarded damages against a Member State. Apparently only one writer has argued that it has the jurisdiction to do so.[25] The Court has not gone beyond the suggestion in Case 39/72 *Premiums for Reducing Dairy Production*[26] that a judgment under Article 169 might establish a basis of responsibility on a Member State to another Member State or the Community or an individual. It is true that the International Court of Justice has asserted jurisdiction to award damages even where there is no express provision for this; as was described in the preceding chapter, instruments conferring jurisdiction over disputes concerning the 'the interpretation and application' of treaties have been taken as giving jurisdiction to award damages. So Wyatt claims that Articles 169 and 170 and their equivalents similarly confer on the European Court the power to order Member States to pay damages, that Member States may claim for direct injury to themselves and, exceptionally, for injury to their nationals. But this claim must be doubtful on grounds of policy and of law. Against it is the weight of practice of the Court, the fact that Member States and the Commission have not attempted to pursue this remedy, the wording of Article 171, and the pronouncements by the Court and the Advocates-General as to the purely declaratory nature of the Court's judgments. And, as Wyatt himself says,

> A possible difficulty about allowing a Member State to pursue a right of action at all with respect to its nationals is that the Treaty does not seek to establish a network of bilateral rights and obligations for Member States, enforced by traditional bilateral means, but a régime calculated to bring about particular social and economic conditions for all natural and legal persons within the territory of the Member States, and equipped with institutional arrangements for enforcement.[27]

The nature of the Article 170 action as a remedy for breaches of Community law, designed to secure compliance with Community law rather than to prevent injury to Member States[28] and the scarcity of judicial and arbitral decisions allowing damages as a remedy for direct injury to states also militate against an extensive interpretation of the jurisdiction of the European Court.

Even the power of the Court to go beyond a mere statement of breach and to declare that a Member State is under an obligation to act in a certain way in order to comply with the requirements of Community law is controversial. Again the International Court of Justice has assumed that it has the power to make declaratory judgments of this type,[29] and again it has often been doubted whether the European Court would be competent to do so. Smit and Herzog argue that it is not so competent.[30] They say,

> This construction [that the Court has authority to specify what measures are needed] would seem to put too much strain on the language of Article 171. Furthermore, specification of the precise corrective measures a State must take would involve the Court in the intra-State distribution of powers. The better view appears to be that the Court must specify in appropriate detail which obligations under the Treaty the Member State has breached and that the Member State must take whatever corrective measures are appropriate. By making no effort to describe what corrective measures the Member States found guilty of violations should take, the judgments the Court has rendered thus far have indicated its sympathy with this view.

The Court itself has not settled this question. It was asked to do so in Case 70/72 *Re Investment Grants for Mining*,[31] where Germany argued that

> it follows from Article 171 of the Treaty that in the course of an action directed against a Member State the Court of Justice must limit itself to finding a failure to fulfil an obligation, and has no power to order the Member State to take any specific steps, so that it is in fact the responsibility of the Member State alone to determine the necessary measures to comply with the judgment of the Court so as to eliminate the results of its failure to comply.

But the Court did not decide on its own competence, only on that of the Commission. It accepted that the Commission could apply for a declaration that in omitting to take specific measures a Member State has failed to fulfil an obligation under the Treaty.[32] Clearly this means that a finding by the Court of a breach by a Member State because it has failed to take specific measures does not differ in substance from finding that there is an obligation to take those specific measures. But the Court has not yet taken the step from the former to the latter type of declaratory judgment. And the Advocate-General in Case 61/81 *Equal Pay for Men and Women*[33] clearly subscribes to the orthodox view that it is not for the Court, having found a breach, to indicate how the United Kingdom should adapt its legislation in order to ensure equal pay.

All this leads to the seemingly paradoxical result that the European Court of Justice under Articles 169–71 and their equivalents has a less extensive jurisdiction over Member States than that of the International Court of Justice under the Optional Clause or treaties giving jurisdiction over the interpretation and application of agreements; less extensive in that the European Court has not awarded damages, nor has it given declaratory judgments that there is an obligation to act in a certain way. Of course in the absence of an express ruling by the European Court some doubt must remain; much turns on the interpretation of Article 171. But the apparent paradox that the Court of the more integrated community should have in this respect narrower jurisdiction may help towards a proper understanding of the role of judicial remedies on the international level; rather than advocate a more extensive jurisdiction for the European Court of Justice it might be wiser to recognize the peculiar suitability for international relations of the narrow type of declaratory judgment used by the European Court of Justice. It is not clear that it would serve the purposes of the Community or be conducive to good relations between Member States or between Member States and Community organs for the European Court to abandon its restrictive approach, to go beyond the declaratory judgment with its implicit recognition of state sovereignty, and to issue orders or awards of damages.

(i) THE DECLARATORY JUDGMENT

However, the role of the declaratory judgment in the European Communities is in many ways not as circumscribed as it is in the jurisprudence of the International Court of Justice and to some extent it resembles an Advisory Opinion in its scope and function. For it is designed not to remedy harm to individual Member States caused by the violation of Community law by other Member States, although this may be the incidental result of an action under Article 169 or 170 of the EEC Treaty or their equivalents, but to bring to an end such violations in order to ensure the achievement of the objectives of the Communities. Also many of the actions against Member States brought before the Court arise not out of deliberate breach by a Member State but out of disagreement as to the requirements of Community law. Thus it is not necessary for the award of a declaratory judgment by the European Court that there should be a dispute in existence at the time of the judgment or even at the time of the bringing of the case to court. In Case 7/61 *Re Quantitative restrictions on imports of pork products into Italy*,[34] Italy finally fulfilled its obligations under Community law although not within the time laid down by the Commission in its reasoned opinion. The Court had to decide whether the application had become purposeless so that the case should be dismissed. The Commission argued that the object of the action was,

> to obtain a ruling by the Court that a Member State has failed to fulfil an obligation under the Treaty [Article 171 of the EEC Treaty]. When a matter has been brought before the Court, it is for it to decide ex tunc whether the failure was committed, without being bound to examine whether, subsequent to the submission of the application, the State in question took the measures necessary to bring the infringement to an end. In cases where the infringement has come to an end, the Commission retains an interest in obtaining the Court's decision on the issue whether a failure was indeed committed. The argument to the contrary would enable a State

to denude the action of its purpose by means of terminating its illegal conduct just before judgment, and to re-apply the disputed measures thereafter, no judgment having been given to sanction its failure.[35]

The Court accepted the Commission's argument that the case was admissible and declared that the Italian Government had failed to fulfil its obligation under the Treaty. The Court has consistently followed this approach in its later judgments.[36]

Moreover the fact that retroactive compliance with a decision of the Court would not be possible, that it is too late to put right past breaches of Community law, does not make it possible for the Member State responsible to escape judicial proceedings. In Case 39/72 *Re Premiums for Reducing Dairy Production,*[37] Italy had completely failed to comply with Community regulations. The Italian Government argued that, as 'The situation has become in the meantime irremediable, because it would no longer be possible physically to comply retroactively with the obligations which should have been performed during the period provided by the Community provisions in question', therefore the Commission's claim had lost its purpose and the Court should hold that there was no need to give a decision. The Court to the contrary held that

The defendant cannot in any case be allowed to rely upon a fait accompli of which it is itself the author so as to escape judicial proceedings. Moreover, in the face of both a delay in the performance of an obligation and a definite refusal, a judgment by the Court under Article 169 and 171 of the Treaty may be of substantive interest as establishing the basis of a responsibility that a Member State can incur as a result of its default, as regards other Member States, the Community or private parties,[38]

and rejected Italy's argument.

This willingness of the European Court to give a judgment even where there is no longer any dispute between a Member State and the Community organs, or where its declaratory judgment will not have any immediate practical effect, contrasts strongly with the attitude of the International Court to requests for declaratory judgments as seen in the *Northern Cameroons*[39] and *Nuclear Tests*[40] cases. In both these cases the International Court interpreted the aim of the claimant state in bringing the action before it in such a way that developments after the bringing of the case meant that their claims no longer had any object.[41] The Court held in both cases that there was no longer a dispute in existence and so there was no need for it to give a judgment. It ignored the possibility that all or any of the claimant states might have desired merely a declaration that there had been a breach of international law. In this respect the attitude of the European Court in its decisions finding violations by Member States of their obligations might be said to resemble that of the International Court to the giving of Advisory Opinions rather than that shown in the two decisions referred to above, for the former may be given for the guidance of an international organization and its Member States without any immediate practical consequences in view.

In this context the question has been raised whether in certain circumstances, although the Commission is entitled to bring an action and the Court to give a judgment, it would be proper for them both to renounce the exercise of their discretionary rights. In two cases[42] the Advocate-General has accepted that this might be proper in cases where the Member State has ended its breach before the judgment of the Court, or would do so shortly thereafter. But the Court did not in either case actually refuse a judgment and to have done so would seem inconsistent with the general trend of cases, for the Court itself appears to have allowed the Commission an unlimited discretion in deciding when it should bring a case against a Member State.[43] And in Case 128/78 *Commission* v. *United Kingdom*,[44] when the United Kingdom argued that the Court should not issue a declaration of breach as this would not substantially promote the achievement of the aims of the Treaty and might even tend to defeat its objectives, the Commission replied replied that it was not aware of the existence of such a power of dispensation and the Court implicitly rejected the United Kingdom's argument.

It has been asserted as a restriction on the discretion of the Commission that for the Commission's action to be admissible it must have an interest in the case,[45] but the Court does not appear to adopt this approach, at any rate not unequivocally. In general the Commission's interest in bringing a case is assumed; it acts on behalf of the Community. In this also an action under Article 169 of the EEC Treaty resembles an Advisory Opinion of the International Court rather than its contentious jurisdiction. The question of the Commission's interest in bringing an action has apparently been raised before the European Court in various cases,[46] but in fact all these could be regarded as concerned with matters of substance, with the question whether there is a case to answer, rather than with the question of admissibility. As the Court said in Case 167/73 *Re French Merchant Seamen*,[47] when the French Government challenged the existence of a legal interest on the part of the Commission, 'This plea may be understood either as aimed at the admissibility of the action or as denying the existence of the alleged default'. The same is true of the defendant states' objections in all the other cases where this point was raised. Moreover, in case the French Government really was questioning the admissibility of the Commission's action because of the latter's lack of *locus standi*, the Court decisively rejected this argument. It said,

The Commission in the exercise of the powers which it has under Articles 155 and 169 of the Treaty does not have to show the existence of a legal interest, since in the general interest of the Community its function is to ensure that the provisions of the Treaty are applied by the Member States and to note the existence of any failure to fulfil the obligations deriving therefrom with a view to bring it to an end.[48]

The European Court has only given one decision on an action under Article 170 of the EEC Treaty by one Member State against another.[49] It seems from this that the interest of a Member State in bringing an action against another Member State for breach of Community law was similarly presumed.

The right to bring an action before the European Court to ensure observance of Community law by Member States is not, however, given to private parties, but there is the possibility of a reference by national courts to the European Court under Article 177 of the EEC Treaty.[50] Although this procedure is not designed to enable the Court to decide whether the behaviour of a Member State is in accordance with EEC law, but merely to enable it to interpret a point of Community law, its existence means that an individual or enterprise may be able to secure compliance by Member States indirectly by bringing an action or defending a case before a municipal court. For even if there is a possibility of an action under Articles 169 or 170 of the EEC Treaty against a Member State before the European Court this does not rule out a reference to the European Court under Article 177.[51] Similarly, even if an act of the European Communities is directly applicable in the Member States so that those affected by its violation might be able to obtain a remedy in their national courts there is no requirement of the prior exhaustion of local remedies before an action based on that violation can be brought under Articles 169 or 170 before the European Court.[52]

The right of action against a Member State which is conferred on the Commission by Article 169 of the EEC and Article 141 Euratom may be exercised whether or not the breach complained of has affected or harmed the interests of another Member State—another factor that distinguishes this action from the declaratory judgment as used by the International Court of Justice as a remedy for breaches of international law. In Case 7/71 *Re The Euratom Supply Agency*,[53] the French Government argued that there was no breach of treaty as it had not been proved that its behaviour had damaged the interests of third parties and in particular affected the supply of enterprises in other Member States. The Advocate-General rejected this, saying that the essential condition for the success of proceedings under Article 141 of the Euratom Treaty is the failure to observe Community law, and that the Treaty does not make any reference whatsoever to any additional element such as interests prejudiced, or any similar condition. He rather weakens this by going on to say that 'Prejudice to substantial interests of other Member States or of the Community cannot be ruled out in the present case'. The Court's judgment confirms that 'Article 141 does not imply the existence of a prejudice suffered by the other Member States as a condition for the exercise of the procedure to establish a breach'.

Nor does the right of action against a Member State depend on harm to the Community having been caused by the Member State's unlawful action or omission. Or rather it seems that any breach is presumed to cause harm to the Community; no proof is required. In Case 141/77 *Commission* v. *Italy*,[54] the Advocate-General said, 'As the Court said in Case 95/77 it is of no importance that the failure to apply a directive has had no adverse effect on the functioning of the Common Market'. This seems a slight misinterpretation of what the Court actually said in Case 95/77,[55] which was, 'The argument that the failure to apply that directive has had no adverse effect on the functioning of the Common Market cannot be accepted in view of the objective pursued by that directive'.

It is clear that in these cases brought against Member States the emphasis is not on securing a remedy for other Member States whose interests might have been injured by the violation of Community law but on ensuring compliance with the obligations imposed by the Treaties. The same is true of decisions under Article 170 of the EEC Treaty; the process involved is not designed to compensate the Member State bringing the action for any loss but is merely an alternative process to an action by the Commission with the same aim of safeguarding the purposes of the Treaty.

(iv) ADVISORY OPINIONS

The European Court has no general power to give Advisory Opinions, but has limited powers under the Community Treaties to give Advisory Opinions in particular cases. There is no uniformity between the Treaties on this; the approach seems rather haphazard. The ECSC Treaty under the heading General Provisions in Article 95 says,

> If, after the end of the transitional period provided in the Convention on the Transitional Provisions, unforeseen difficulties emerging in the light of experience in the application of this Treaty, or fundamental economic or technical changes directly affecting the common market in coal and steel, make it necessary to adapt the rules for the High Authority's exercise of its powers, appropriate amendments may be made; they must not, however, conflict with the provisions of Articles 2, 3 and 4 or interfere with the relationship between the powers of the High Authority and those of the other institutions of the Community.

These amendments 'Shall be submitted to the Court for its opinion. In considering them, the Court shall have full powers to assess all points of fact and of law'. The Court has to decide whether the proposed amendments are compatible with the paragraph quoted above. The EEC Treaty does not contain any provision corresponding to this. But under the heading 'General and Financial' it includes Article 228. The first paragraph deals with the treaty-making power of the Community and establishes the procedure to be followed. It goes on, 'The Council, the Commission or a Member State may obtain beforehand the opinion of the Court of Justice as to whether an agreement envisaged is compatible with the provisions of this Treaty'. Where the opinion is adverse the agreement may enter into force only in accordance with Article 236 (that is, the EEC Treaty must be amended). The Euratom Treaty also provides for Advisory Opinions on treaties, but there are some significant differences between it and the EEC Treaty. Under the heading 'External Relations' Article 103 deals with both treaties and contracts by Member States.

> Member States shall communicate to the Commission draft agreements or contracts with a third State, an international organisation, or a national of a third State to the extent that such agreements or contracts concern matters within the purview of this Treaty. If a draft agreement or contract contains clauses which impede the application of this Treaty, the Commission shall within one month of receipt of such communication, make its comments known to the State concerned.
>
> The State shall not conclude the proposed agreement or contract until it has satisfied the objections of the Commission or complied with a ruling by the Court of Justice, adjudicating urgently upon an application from the State, on the compatibility of the proposed clauses with the provisions of this Treaty. An application may be made to the Court of Justice at any time after the State has received the comments of the Commission.

Articles 104 and 105 contain comparable provisions on agreements made after the entry into force of the Treaty and on prior agreements. In both these it is for the Commission rather than the Member State (as in Article 103) to go to the Court for its ruling on compatibility.

Thus, only the EEC provision is optional, the ECSC and Euratom Treaties require resort to the Court. The Euratom Treaty covers both treaties and contracts, unlike the EEC Treaty, and it is concerned with agreements by Member States rather than those of the Community as in the EEC Treaty. The ECSC Treaty does not contain any provision comparable to those in Euratom and the EEC Treaty; it does not even include any provision giving treaty-making powers to the Community—apart from the general provision in Article 5, 'In international relations the Community shall enjoy the legal capacity it requires to perform its functions and attain its objectives.' In fact treaty-making by the Community alone is not common, there are only three agreements made by the High Authority alone and these appear to bind it rather than the Community as a whole. More commonly the ECSC makes agreements jointly with Member States.[56]

All these provisions are limited; the Advisory Opinion is a stage in particular types of executive action. Nor have they been much used in practice. Relatively little attention has been paid to the cases from a procedural point of view, attention has centred mainly on what they say about the external relations powers of the EEC and Euratom.[57] But the cases raise some interesting questions, in particular on the scope of the Treaty provisions: has the Court transformed these limited provisions into something more like general Advisory Opinions? Is there a need for a power to give general Advisory Opinions?

Three cases were decided under Article 95 ECSC in 1959, 1960, and 1961.[58] It seems that further changes in the powers of the High Authority have proved unnecessary. The Court is empowered to approve amendments that 'adapt the rules for the High Authority's exercise of its powers'. All the opinions discuss the meaning of this. In all of them the Court drew a distinction between amendments that give new powers to the High Authority and are thus impermissible, and those that merely change the conditions for the exercise of the High Authority's powers and are permissible. Clearly this is a difficult distinction to draw. In Case 1/60 it had been argued that any change in the substantive powers of the High Authority would not be permissible under Article 95. The Court rejected this as it would mean that Article 95 could only be used to amend the procedural rules and formalities to be observed by the High Authority:

> Such an interpretation of the phrase 'rules for the exercise of powers' confines the scope for the amendment of the Treaty within such narrow limits that it is no longer possible to understand how its authors could have considered the amendment provided for by the third paragraph of Article 95 as an adequate means of enabling the Community to deal with 'fundamental economic or technical changes'.[59]

Accordingly changes may be made to the definition of conditions for the exercise of powers. The difference between this and the creation of a new power is one of degree, the characterization of an amendment will necessary be somewhat subjective.

In its decisions under Article 95 the Court was clearly anxious to be helpful to the High Authority. In Cases 1/59 and 1/61 in which it refused to approve the proposed amendments the Court gave an elaborate and detailed discussion of their defects; in Case 1/59 the amendment fell at each of the hurdles set up by Article 95; it would have been possible for the Court merely to have mentioned one of the inadequacies and to have said that because of this the amendment could not be approved. The method it adopted enabled the High Authority to come back in Case 1/60 having altered its proposal to meet all the objections of the Court.

Thus the Court was generous in its interpretation of Article 95, took it to cover substantial as well as procedural amendments, and construed extensively 'A change in the conditions for the exercise of a power'; but clearly

Article 95 is a very limited procedure and cannot provide a general advisory opinion for the ECSC.

The three cases on Article 228 EEC are better known.[60] In the first the Court considered the purpose of the Article: it was designed to forestall complications which would result from legal disputes concerning the compatibility with the Treaty of international agreements binding on the Community. A possible decision by the Court that an agreement was incompatible would provoke serious difficulties in the Community context and in international relations. In order to avoid these the Treaty had recourse to the exceptional procedure of prior reference to the Court, to elucidate before the conclusion of an agreement whether it was compatible with the Treaty. (Because the procedure is optional the protection provided is, however, not complete.) This purpose led the Court to take an expansive view of its role; the Article 228 procedure must be open for all questions capable of submission for judicial consideration either by the European Court of Justice or possibly by national courts, in so far as such questions cast doubt on the substantive or formal validity of the agreement.

The references to the Court were all made by the Commission. As it turned out—perhaps contrary to the intention and expectations of the drafters of Article 228—the questions were mainly about procedural matters, about the appropriate method of concluding the agreement, rather than about the substance of the agreement envisaged and its compatibility with the Treaty. In Case 1/75 the main question put to the Court was whether the Community had exclusive powers to conclude the undertaking, in 1/76 and 1/78 the Court was asked to decide whether the participation of Member States in the agreement was permissible or necessary.

In the first case the Court accepted the admissibility of this type of question. It said that the fact that the Commission had raised the question of compatibility of an agreement with the Treaty in order to get an Opinion of the Court on the extent of Community powers was not sufficient of itself to make the request inadmissible. For the compatibility of an agreement with the Treaty must be assessed in the light of all the rules of the Treaty, both substantive rules and those on the extent of the powers of the institutions. The Court did not in this case or in the later cases refer to Article 107 of the Rules of the Court to justify its giving an Opinion, although it might have done so as this provides: 'The Opinion may deal not only with the question whether the envisaged agreement is compatible with the provisions of the EEC Treaty but also with the question whether the Community or any Community institution has the power to enter into that Agreement'.

In contrast the Court has taken a less extensive approach to the questions of substance that seem to be the main object of Article 228. In Case 1/76, in addition to the procedural question, the Commission consulted the

Court on the compatibility of the substance of the agreement envisaged with the Treaty. The Court did not give any unequivocal ruling on the question of substantive compatibility. It said only that the provisions in the agreement were perhaps incompatible with the Treaty, and that different interpretations were possible. 'It is not for the Court within the context of a request for an opinion under Article 228 to give a final judgment on the interpretation of texts which are the subject of a request for an opinion'. It is for the legal organs in question to make such an interpretation, and it is possible that they will come to different interpretations. The Court said only that it had reservations as to the compatibility with the Treaty. This caution provides a striking contrast with the attitude of the Court to questions of competence; it may have been inspired by an awareness of the problems involved in giving Advisory Opinions in this type of case.

The Court has taken a generous view of what is an 'agreement envisaged' under Article 228. Not surprisingly the formal designation of the agreement is not decisive;[61] what is required is an undertaking entered into by entities subject to international law which has binding force. Nor need there be an actual draft of the agreement in existence. In Case 1/78 the Council argued that the concept of 'agreement envisaged' presupposed that negotiations are far enough advanced for there to be a preliminary draft text, and that it is necessary for the Court to be able to look at a text of the draft if it is to be able to give its opinion on compatibility. However the Council did not formally challenge the admissibility of the Commission's request for an Advisory Opinion, preferring to argue on the merits in the hope of securing an Opinion in support of its own viewpoint. France, in its written observations to the Court, agreed with the Council. It said that if a request for an Opinion is allowed before the end of negotiations there could be any number of requests and each Opinion could be authoritative only as regards the particular stage at which the request was made. The Court accepted the Commission's argument that it had enough information on the provisions and mechanisms proposed; the subject-matter of the agreement was already known before negotiations began. The Commission had an interest in lodging its request immediately after its disagreement with the Council as regards the question of its powers to negotiate and conclude agreements, the more so as there had been similar uncertainties on several prior agreements. When there is a question of powers to be determined it is clearly in the interests of all states concerned for the question to be clarified as soon as any negotiations have begun. That is, the Court refused to be swayed by the Council's argument, it accepted the difficulty inherent in this type of Advisory Opinion, that it can only state the law on the facts at a particular time, but it did not consider this as a reason for refusing an Opinion.

Finally, the Court has given one ruling under Article 103 Euratom,[62] and this out of all the Court's opinions looks the most like a general Advisory Opinion. The application to the court was made by Belgium which wanted to know whether, in the absence of concurrent participation of the Community, Belgium could adhere to the Convention on the Physical Protection of Nuclear Materials. The Council and the Commission disagreed on this question. Belgium put five detailed questions to the Court; that is, it did not simply ask the Court to decide on the compatibility of the agreement with the Treaty. The Court accepted this; it did not reject Belgium's questions as inadmissible. It said that the Court's examination must take into account all the relevant rules of the Treaty, whether on substance, jurisdiction or procedure.

The ruling it gave was:

> The participation of the Member States in a convention about physical protection such as the Convention at present being negotiated is compatible with the provisions only subject to the condition that (n'est compatible qu'à la condition que) in so far as its own powers and jurisdiction are concerned, the Community as such is a party to the Convention on the same lines as the States . . . . The fulfilment of the obligations entered into under the Convention is to be ensured on the Community's part in the context of the institutional system established by the EAEC Treaty in accordance with the distribution of powers between the Comunity and its Member States.

The Court seems determined to be helpful to the institutions and Member States the Communities in giving its opinions under Articles 95, 103, and 228. Its interpretations of these Articles have been generous. Because of this it has avoided some of the problems potentially involved in the giving of these Advisory Opinions. These problems have been pointed out by Schermers[63] who is extremely suspicious of Advisory Opinions. One of his main worries is that Advisory Opinions detract from the freedom of the Court to rule objectively on specific cases in the future: if the legality of an act is challenged later on new grounds the Court would be hampered in holding it invalid if it had earlier in an Advisory Opinion declared the act valid. Under Articles 95, 103, and 228 the effects of a negative Opinion are clear enough and no particular problems arise: the amendment under Article 95 may not be made, the agreements under Articles 103 and 228 may not enter into force. It is the finding of compatibility that may create difficulties. But, as Schermers points out, the Court has avoided this problem in actions contesting the validity of Community acts by the expedient of holding acts not invalid on the facts before it, rather than pronouncing them valid. A similar course is open to the Court in Advisory Opinions. Only in Case 1/60 on Article 95 EEC does the Court make a straightforward finding that the proposed amendment is compatible with Article 95. In Case 1/75 the Court was asked to decide on the compatibility with the

EEC Treaty of a Draft Understanding, and more particularly on the question whether the Community had the power to conclude the said Understanding and if so whether that power was exclusive. Because the Court was prepared to pronounce on this latter question of competence and because it restricted its answer to this question, finding that 'The Community has the exclusive power to participate in the Understanding on a local cost standard referred to in the request for an Opinion', the Court did not limit its future freedom of action. It did not find that this agreement was compatible with the Treaty but made the much narrower finding that a particular institution had the power to make the agreement. Case 1/78 on Euratom is similar. In neither of these cases did the Court have to pronounce on the compatibility of the substance of the agreement with the Treaty, nor did it appear very willing to do so in Case 1/76.

The significance of the problem of the relationship between an Advisory Opinion and the settlement of later disputes should not be exaggerated. Similar problems could arise with regard to actions under Articles 169, 170, and 177. The International Court of Justice has to live with this problem,[64] as do the European and American Courts of Human Rights.[65] Perhaps one of the reasons why there is no general power on the part of the European Court to give Advisory Opinions is the variety of other procedures and remedies available to the European Court, far greater than those of the International Court of Justice. And the absence of a general power is arguably not a significant limitation of its jurisdiction as far as the behaviour of Member States is concerned because of the scope of the declaratory judgment under Articles 169 and 170 of the EEC Treaty and their equivalents and because of the possibility of a preliminary ruling under Article 177.[66]

(v) INTERIM MEASURES OF PROTECTION

Until recently it remained controversial whether interim measures of protection could be awarded against a Member State in an action under Article 169 or 170 of the EEC Treaty or their equivalents, although there was a large number of decisions by the Court on interim measures against Community organs. For, as discussed above, it seems that the Court is restricted to declaratory relief in its final judgments against Member States. But Article 186 of the EEC Treaty[67] does not impose any limits on the types of cases in which interim measures are permissible. Article 186 provides, 'the Court of Justice may in any case before it prescribe any necessary interim measures'. In most of the earlier actions against Member States such awards were unnecessary as the defendant governments had displayed their willingness to comply with the decision of the Commission. This was not so in Cases 31/77 and 53/77R *Commission* v. *United Kingdom*[68] and 61/77R *Commission* v. *Ireland*[69]. In the former the Commission brought an action under Article 93(2) of the EEC Treaty against the United Kingdom for providing aid to pig producers in violation of Article 92 and in the latter the Commission instituted proceedings under Article 167 of the EEC Treaty concerning fishery conservation measures. Also in Cases 42/82R[70] and 171/83R[71] France denied that it was under an obligation to end its restrictions on the entry of Italian wine or to end its aid to its textile and clothing industry.

Interim measures were ordered against the Member States concerned in all these cases. The Advocate-General in Case 31/77 and 53/77R argued against the Court's being competent to award interim measures against a Member State. He said it was beyond the Court's jurisdiction to order a defendant state to act in a certain way:

> The Court can only address an order to a Community institution or to a natural or legal person, not to a State . . . In view of the immunity of the States and having regard to the system laid down by Article 93 which does not confer on the Court any wider jurisdiction than Article 169, it is not possible to make the leap consisting in directly ordering a Member State to put an end to the grant of a national aid; at the most the Court could only declare the existence of a failure to fulfil an obligation arising from the Treaty, but, even in this case, it would only be for the Member State concerned to draw the consequences of the Court's decision.[72]

But this approach has not been accepted by this Court. In order to preserve the effectiveness of its final judgment the European Court like the International Court exercises a wider jurisdiction so far as remedies are concerned in an interim application than in its final decision. Thus the Court in Case 31/77 did not accept the Advocate-General's reasoning.

Recently the Court was asked to order interim measures against France in an unusual case.[73] The Court had earlier given judgment against France in an Article 169 action for its unlawful restrictions on the import of mutton and lamb. France did not give effect to this judgment so the Commission started proceedings for breach of Article 171 and as part of those proceedings requested as an interim measure that the Court should 'Order the French Republic to desist forthwith from applying any restriction and/or levying any charge on imports of mutton and lamb from the United Kingdom'. The Court in this case refused interim measures.

What approach was taken in these cases by the European Court, and how do these decisions compare with those in the actions for interim measures against Community organs?[74] Four of the cases against Member

States led to orders under Article 186 and such orders were rare in the earlier cases. Apparently before 31/77 and 53/77R the Court had made orders under Article 186 in only a few cases.[75] The cautious attitude of the Court toward measures under Article 186 is clear in Case 25/62R *Plaumann* v. *Commission*.[76] In the main action the applicant was seeking the annulment of a decision addressed to Germany whereby the Commission had refused a request for authorization to suspend in part the customs duties on clementines. It asked as an interim measure for

A declaration that the defendant is required to authorise the Federal Republic of Germany to suspend provisionally to the extent of 3%, subject to security being given, the application of the customs duty in force for clementines . . . for the period from 1 January 1962 to 31 December 1962. [The Court replied that] The applicant is thus asking for more than a mere suspension of the operation of the Decision which it is contesting. It seeks rather to prejudge the results by assuming beyond doubt that these will lead to a decision in its favour in the main action, that is to say, that the Commission will then be required in each case to grant the contested authorisation and moreover that the Federal Republic will avail itself of this authorisation and, indeed, with retroactive effect. It is true that Article 186 of the EEC Treaty does not clearly exclude such measures; nevertheless so far-reaching an interim measure could be justified only by wholly exceptional circumstances and if there were very good reasons for thinking that the party concerned would otherwise suffer serious and irreparable damage.[77]

But in the actions against the United Kingdom and Ireland in two of the cases against France the Court did not take a restrictive view of its powers under Article 186. In Case 61/77R the Irish Government argued that an application for interim measures was inappropriate in the course of proceedings in which the validity of a national law is at issue as it tends to prejudge the main action, and that the power given to the Court by Article 186 is not wide enough to include a power to suspend the operation of a national law which is being contested in the main action. The Court decided to allow interim measures, thus implicitly rejecting the Irish argument.[78] And in Case 42/82R the Court issued an exhaustive and detailed order as to the future conduct by France of its control of the entry of Italian wine.[79] Like the International Court of Justice,[80] the European Court here showed itself willing to go beyond the brief and simple type of order it had made in the two earlier cases to lay down specific and detailed rules for the parties.

In its earliest award of interim measures against a Member State the Court said almost nothing of the conditions for their award: it did not mention even Article 83 of the Rules of Procedure which helps give content to the provisions in Article 185 that 'circumstances require' interim measures the provisions in Article 186 that the Court may grant measures that are 'necessary'. Article 83 provides:

Any request for a stay of execution of an act taken by an institution within the terms of Article 39(2) of the ECSC Treaty, Article 185 of the EEC Treaty and Article 157 of the EAEC Treaty shall be admissible only if the plaintiff has challenged this act in proceedings before the Court. Any request relating to one of the other interim measures referred to in Article 39(3) ECSC, Article 186 EEC and Article 158 EAEC shall be admissible only if it is made by one of the parties in a case before the Court and refers to that case.
The requests referred to in the preceding paragraph shall specify the subject of the dispute, the circumstances giving rise to urgency and the grounds of fact and of law showing prima facie justification for the granting of the interim measure requested.

Nor did the Court discuss the large case-law on interim measures against Community organs. It simply said,

Disregard of the provisions of the final sentence of Article 93, which is the means of safeguarding the machinery for review laid down by that article, interferes with the proper operation of that machinery to such an extent as to be capable by itself of giving rise to the application of Article 186.[81]

However, the Advocate-General in his Opinion,[82] 'having regard to the criteria required by the case law of the Court for the adoption of interim measures', asserted that interim measures should be urgently needed, that the main action should not be manifestly unfounded, and that it was necessary for the Court to examine the possibility of irreparable harm to either party caused by the grant or refusal of interim measures.

In fact the Court apparently has not developed any consistent theory to govern its awards of interim measures in cases against Community organs; the case-law contains many conflicting decisions and it is extremely difficult to deduce any generally applicable principles from these.[83] The factors mentioned by the Advocate-General in Case 31/77 were variously interpreted and different factors were decisive in different cases. And there are differences between the Court's decisions against Member States.

The first two cases are brief and uninformative with no reference to the case-law; Cases 42/82 and 171/83R are longer and contain more developed argument but again do not refer to the case-law except in very general terms.[84] In all four cases—expressly in the last two—the Court considered whether there was a prima facie case on the merits. This was apparently considered as a necessary preliminary condition to be satisfied before other considerations could be taken into account; in this the European Court clearly differs from the practice of the International Court of Justice. This difference cannot be explained solely by reference to the requirements of Article 83 of the Rules of Procedure,[85] however, since in its earlier decisions on interim measures against Community organs it was only in a minority of cases that the existence of a prima facie case on the merits was treated as a decisive preliminary test.[86] It may be that this approach by the

Court in cases against Member States reflects its concern that it should be seen to be considering the interests of member states.

And in all four, as in the cases against Community organs, the Court was concerned to balance the interest involved, to consider whether the harm likely to result from failure to award interim measures would be greater than that from their award. In Case 61/77R the Court took this into account after it had come to its decision that interim measures were justified. It said that although suspension of the measures criticized by the Commission might appear justified in principle, it was appropriate to take into account the consequences for conservation of the proposed abolition of the Irish measures, and therefore deferred its decision on the application so as to give the parties an opportunity to agree upon an alternative solution which might be substituted for the measures forming the subject matter of the proceedings. Also in Case 31/77 the Court was influenced by the fact that the provisional measures sought would not necessarily have irreversible consequences, because if the Commission's decision were annulled in the final judgement the United Kingdom would still be in a position to provide aid retroactively. In this case the Court held that the fact that the Commission had originally tried to remedy the situation without recourse to the Court could not affect the gravity of the United Kingdom's behaviour and thus exclude the application of Article 186. That is, the slowness of the Commission in seeking interim measures from the Court did not prevent their award. This seems slightly to undermine the requirement in article 83 of the Rules of Procedure that interim measures should be urgently needed, and it certainly provides a contrast with the strictness of the Court in some of the earlier cases. In Case 42/82R the Court rejected the French argument that interim measures by allowing free entry of Italian wine into France would threaten public health and might lead to economic and political difficulties and that this damage outweighed the harm to those involved in the export of Italian wine. Finally, in Case 171/83R the Court found that the risk of harm to the common market in textiles and clothing outweighed any possible harm to French undertakings from the grant of interim measures.

But there is a significant difference between the decisions against Ireland and the United Kingdom and that against France in Case 42/82. The major consideration for the Court in the first two cases was clearly the possibility of damage to the Community interest from failure to allow interim measures. The Court did not expressly demand that such harm should be irreparable, but seemed willing to accept that any alleged breach of Community law by a Member State would constitute sufficient harm for the purpose of allowing interim measures. That is, it is clear in both cases that the Court regarded as sufficient the Commission's allegations of harm of a political nature, such as that the authority and effectiveness of the Community was being undermined by the behaviour of the defendant Member State. Therefore the Commission bringing a claim for interim measures against a Member State seemed in a stronger position than an individual or enterprise requesting these against a Community organ, for it is easier to show harm of a political nature to the Community than to produce the more concrete evidence necessary to substantiate an allegation of irreparable material or financial injury.

But the Court did not pursue this approach in Case 42/82R. Here by contrast the Court considered only the harm to Italy threatened by the French restrictions, even though the Commission had based its argument both on political harm to the Community and harm to Italy. In its decisions on interim measures against Community organs the Court demanded that the applicant be able to show the threat of harm to himself: he could not rely on harm that would affect third parties if interim measures were refused. This requirement appears to have been modified in Case 42/82R because of the different interests involved. In the cases against the United Kingdom and Ireland although the parties in their arguments relied on harm to Member States as well as harm to the Community, it was not until the final stage in the latter case that the Court made any reference to this. When the application for interim measures first came before the Court, the Court considered only the possible harm to the Community. It said that Ireland's measures might harm the negotiations on fisheries conservation within the Community, lead to unilateral measures by other Member States, and prejudice the Community position on an international level. After the parties had failed to agree on an alternative regime to that unilaterally introduced by Ireland, the application for interim measures came before the Court again. Now the Court itself considered the possible harm to Member States. It said,

> In view of the advanced stage of the fishing season only an interim measure having immediate effect is capable of preventing irreparable damage to the fishermen of the other Member States . . . since it has emerged at the hearing before the Court that in the particular circumstances the damage caused by the unilateral introduction of the Irish measures primarily affects the interests of the Member States, the measures in question need be suspended only vis-à-vis those States.[87]

Thus it is now unclear whether it is enough for the Commission to show that political harm to the Community would be caused by the defendant state's behaviour or whether it must fulfil the more difficult task of proving material or financial harm to Member States.[88] The Court did not consider this in its fourth decision on interim measures against a Member State, but the Advocate-General argued against making it too easy for the Commission to obtain interim measures against Member States: he said that moral damage was not of a kind to justify interim measures as otherwise any action by the Commission for breach of Article 171 would automatically justify interim measures against the defendant state. There is something in this, though the requirement to balance harm to the Community against possible harm to the defendant state from interim measures and the necessity for a prima facie case would go some way to prevent the award of interim measures against a Member State being quite the matter of course suggested by the Advocate-General. Just as with the International Court of Justice there is uncertainty over the meaning of the requirement that interim measures should be necessary to prevent irreparable harm; it is not clear whether the wide view that any threatened breach of international or Community law necessarily involves irreparable harm or the narrow view that something more is needed will be followed.

In Case 24 and 97/80R the Court for the first time refused to award interim measures against a Member State. The result in this case can probably be explained by the particular circumstances; the Commission was suing France for non-compliance with a judgment of the Court declaring that French restrictions on the import of mutton and lamb violated Community law. As part of its action under Article 171 the Commission requested interim measures. The Court's opinion was not enlightening: it simply summarized the arguments of the parties and then concluded that the purpose of the Commission in seeking interim measures was the same in substance as that of its original action under Article 169 and so the request was not covered by Article 186. It seems from this that awards of interim measures in proceedings for breach of Article 171, although said by the Court to be possible, will in practice not be given.[89] The Court apparently felt that an award of interim measures would not add anything to its earlier judgment under Article 169.[90]

Five cases are of course not enough to generalize from, and anyhow few generalizations are possible here as with the European Court's decisions on interim measures against Community organs and with decisions of the International Court of Justice on interim measures. The European Court in three of its decisions does not provide much in the way of reasoned justification for its award or refusal of interim measures against Member States; in this it resembles the International Court of Justice. Because the European Court has compulsory jurisdiction it does not share the basic problem of the International Court of Justice in a request for interim measures, the necessity to decide whether jurisdiction on the merits is sufficiently likely to make an award of interim measures possible. But this difference may not be of any great practical significance since the International Court of Justice has never in fact refused interim measures on this ground of insufficient likelihood of jurisdiction on the merits. Because of the nature of the remedy involved, similar problems face the International Court of Justice and the European Court; most obviously the need to balance the harm from a refusal of interim measures against that from their award, the question as to what constitutes irreparable harm and the need not to prejudge the merits of the main claim. And similar uncertainties remain in the jurisprudence of the two courts.

However, the European Court has not in its decisions on interim measures, nor in its consideration of its jurisdiction, of Advisory Opinions, and of declaratory judgments, referred to the practice of the International Court of Justice or of other international tribunals. Its references to international law are restricted mainly to questions of state responsibility and do not extend to remedies. It seems, like most other international tribunals, to operate in isolation in its decisions on remedies. And typical also is its lack of any extensive consideration of the question of remedies. But its limited jurisdiction under Articles 169 and 170, its refusal to go beyond a declaratory judgment finding a breach of Community law—whether voluntary or imposed on it by the words of the Treaty—may provide a useful reminder that in international relations the widest jurisdiction to give remedies is not necessarily the most effective.

NOTES

1. Articles 88 and 89 ECSC, 141–3 Euratom.
2. Articles 173–6 EEC, 33–5 ECSC, 146–9 Euratom.
3. See David Davies, Memorial Institute of International Studies, *International Disputes: The Legal Aspects* (1972).
4. See Ch. 4 Section 2.
5. Article 41 ECSC, 150 Euratom.
6. Article 36 ECSC.
7. Articles 95(4) ECSC, 228 EEC, 103 and 104 Euratom. See C. Gray (1983) *ELR* 24. And see section on Advisory Opinions below.
8. D. G. Valentine, *The Court of Justice of the European Communities* (1965), at 9.
9. For a detailed discussion of these procedures see H. G. Schermers, *Judicial Protection in the European Communities* (3rd edn. 1983); H. A. H. Audretsch, *Supervision in European Community Law* (1978).
10. See J. F. MacMahon and M. Akehurst in David Davies, *International Disputes*, op. cit. in n. 3, at 211.
11. UN Charter Article 92.
12. See also Ch. 6.
13. See Schermers, op. cit. in n. 9, at 430.
14. Case 48/71 *Commission* v. *Italy, Re Export Tax on Art Treasures (no. 2)* (1972) CMLR 699; The Commission also started proceedings against France for non-compliance with the Court's judgment in case 24/80 *Re Mutton and Lamb, Commission* v. *France* (1979) ECR 2729, but the case was never decided by the Court.
15. *Commission* v. *Italy* (1969) CMLR 1.

16. *Commission* v. *Italy* (1972) CMLR 699, at 708.
17. Ibid., 706.
18. H. G. Schermers, op. cit. in n. 9, at §429; M. Gaudet in S. M. Schwebel (ed.), *The Effectiveness of International Decisions* (1971) 309; J. Amphoux in W. J. Ganshof van der Meersch (ed.) *Les Novelles—droit des Communautés Européenes* (1969), §1042. But see D. Wyatt (1982) *ELR* 147.
19. (1960) ECR 559.
20. Ibid., 568.
21. Case 314–16/81 and 83/82 *Procureur de la République and Comité National de Défense contre L'Alcoolisme* v. *Waterkeyn* (1982) ECR 4337.
22. It said, 'If the Court finds in proceedings under Articles 169 to 171 of the EEC Treaty that a Member State's legislation is incompatible with the obligations which it has under the Treaty the Courts of that State are bound by virtue of Article 171 to draw the necessary inferences from the judgment of the Court. However, it should be understood that the rights accruing to individuals derive not from that judgment, but from the actual provisions of Community law having direct effect in the internal legal order.'
23. Case 28/81 *Commission* v. *Italy* (1981) ECR 2577.
24. (1979) ECR 2923.
25. D. Wyatt, op. cit. in n. 18.
26. (1973) ECR 101.
27. Op. cit. in n. 18 at 162.
28. See Case 141/78 *France* v. *United Kingdom*, *Sea Fisheries* (1979) ECR 2923.
29. See Ch. 2 Sections 1 and 4.
30. H. Smit and P. E. Herzog, *The Law of the EEC* (1976), §171.04.
31. *Commission* v. *Germany* (1973) ECR 813.
32. See Schermers, op. cit. in n. 9, at §404.
33. *Commission* v. *United Kingdom* (1982) ECR 2601.
34. *Commission* v. *Italy* (1961) ECR 317.
35. Ibid., 325.
36. Case 28/69 *Commission* v. *Italy* (1970) ECR 187; Case 77/69 *Commission* v. *Belgium* (1970) ECR 237; Case 8/70 *Commission* v. *Italy* (1970) ECR 961; Case 79/72 *Commission* v. *Italy* (1973) ECR 667; Case 167/73 *Commission* v. *France* (1974) ECR 359; Case 28/81 *Commission* v. *Italy* (1981) ECR 2577; and the Advocate-General's Opinion in Case 90–91/63 *Commission* v. *Luxembourg and Belgium* (1964) ECR 625.
37. *Commission* v. *Italy* (1973) ECR 101.
38. Ibid., 112.
39. (1963) ICJ Reports 15.
40. (1974) ICJ Reports 253 and 457.
41. See Ch. 2 Section 4, at n. 49.
42. Case 2–3/62 *Commission* v. *Luxembourg and Belgium* (1962) ECR 425; Case 69/77 *Commission* v. *Italy* (1978) ECR 1749.
43. Case 7/61 *Commission* v. *Italy* (1961) ECR 317; Case 7/68 *Commission* v. *Italy* (1968) ECR 423; Case 28/69 *Commission* v. *Italy* (1970) ECR 187; Case 7/71 *Commission* v. *France* (1971) ECR 1003; Advocate-General in Case 2 +

3/62 *Commission* v. *Luxembourg and Belgium* (1962) ECR 436. See discussion by Audretsch, op. cit. in n. 9, at 36.

44. (1979) ECR 419.
45. Audretsch, op. cit. in n. 9, at 40.
46. Case 7/61 *Commission* v. *Italy* (1961) ECR 317; Case 26/69 *Commission* v. *France* (1970) ECR 565; Case 39/72 *Commission* v. *Italy* (1973) ECR 101; Advocate-General in Case 90–91/63 (1964) ECR 635.
47. *Commission* v. *France* (1974) ECR 359.
48. Ibid., 368. See also Advocate-General in Case 95/77 *Commission* v. *Netherlands* (1978) ECR 863.
49. Case 141/78 *France* v. *United Kingdom* (1979) ECR 2923. In this case the Commission actually intervened on the side of France. Rather than themselves bring cases under Article 170 it seems that Member States prefer simply to intervene on the side of the Commission.
50. Articles 41 ECSC, 150 Euratom.
51. Case 26/62 *Van Gend en Loos* (1963) ECR 1.
52. Case 31/69 *Commission* v. *Italy* (1970) ECR 25.
53. *Commission* v. *France* (1971) ECR 1003.
54. (1978) ECR 1307. The Commission also followed this line in Case 128/78 *Commission* v. *United Kingdom* (1979) ECR 419.
55. *Commission* v. *Netherlands* (1978) ECR 863.
56. See P. Pescatore (1961) 2 *HR* 1.
57. A. Barav and F. Burrows in *Division of Powers between the European Communities and their Member States in the Field of External Relations*, Europa Institut of the University of Amsterdam; J. Boulouis (1978) 2 *HR* 343; K. Simmonds (1979) *ICLQ* 644; M. Hardy (1977) *CML Rev.* 561.
58. Opinion 1/59 [1959] ECR 260; Opinion 1/60 [1960] ECR 39; Opinion 1/61 [1961] ECR 243.
59. [1960] ECR 39, at 49.
60. Opinion 1/75, Re the O.E.C.D. Understanding on a local cost standard [1975] ECR 1355, [1976] CMLR 85; Opinion 1/76, Re the draft agreement establishing a European laying up fund for inland waterway vessels [1977] ECR 741, [1977] CMLR 279; Opinion 1/78, Re the International Rubber agreement [1979] ECR 2871, [1979] CMLR 639.
61. *Contra* J. Boulouis (1978) 2 *HR* 343.
62. Ruling 1/78, Re The Draft Convention on the Physical Protection of Nuclear Material, Facilities and Transport [1978] ECR 2151.
63. H. G. Schermers, op. cit. in n. 9, at §530 ff.
64. In its Advisory Opinion on *Application for Review of Judgment no. 158 of the U.N. Administrative Tribunal* (1973) ICJ Reports 166, at 171, the Court said, 'The existence in the background of a dispute the parties to which may be affected as a consequence of the Court's opinion, does not change the advisory nature of the Court's task.'
65. Under the Second Protocol to the European Convention on Human Rights and under Article 64 of the American Convention on Human Rights, on which see T. Buergenthal (1982) *AJ* 231.

66. On the relation between Article 177 and Advisory Opinions see C. D. Gray (1983) *ELR* 24.
67. Articles 39 ECSC and 157 and 158 Euratom. In the text following reference will be made only to the EEC Treaty unless there are material differences between this and the other two Treaties.
68. (1977) ECR 921.
69. (1977) ECR 937 and 1411.
70. (1982) ECR 841.
71. (1983) ECR 2621.
72. Loc. cit. in n. 68, at 934.
73. Case 24 and 97/80R *Commission* v. *France* (1980) ECR 1319.
74. See C. D. Gray (1979) *ELR* 80.
75. Case 160, 161, and 170/73R *Miles Druce and Co. Ltd.* v. *Commission* (1974) ECR 281; Case 109/75R *National Carbonising Co. Ltd* v. *Commission* (1975) ECR 1193. And since the decisions in Cases 31/77 and 53/77R and 61/77 orders under Article 186 in actions against Community organs have been made in only a few more cases—Case 792/79R *Camera Care Ltd.* v. *Commission* (1980) ECR 119 and Case 229 and 228/82R *Ford Werke AG and Ford of Europe Inc.* v. *Commission* (1982) ECR 3091. See also Case 232/81R *Agricola Commerciale Olio S.r.1* v. *Commission* (1981) ECR 2193.
76. (1963) ECR 123.
77. Ibid., 124.
78. The Advocate-General gave express consideration to this question and also rejected the Irish Government view. He said, 'The provision of Article 186 of the EEC Treaty whereby the Court of Justice may in any cases before it prescribe any necessary interim measures is moreover expressed in very general terms and lays down no exceptions for certain types of procedures or measures. It is therefore not evident why Article 186 of the EEC Treaty should not be applicable in proceedings relating to infringements of the Treaty.' (1977) ECR 937, at 953.
79. The Court's order covered the percentage of import consignments that could be analysed by the French, the duration of analyses, and the method for dealing with irregularities in documents. This type of very detailed order by the Court was made also in an order for interim measures under Article 186 against the Commission, Case 229 and 228/82R *Ford Werke AG and Ford of Europe Inc.* v. *Commission* (1982) ECR 3091. It is still too early to say whether these two cases mark a new trend in the jurisprudence of the Court, a new willingness to lay down detailed regulations for the conduct of the parties. In Case 171/83 the Court simply ordered the French Government to refrain from renewal of the contracts under dispute and within one month to suspend performance of those contracts already renewed.
80. As, for example, in the *Anglo-Iranian Oil Company* case (1951) ICJ Reports 89 and the *Fisheries Jurisdiction* cases (1972) ICJ Reports 12 and 30.
81. 31/77 and 53/77R, loc. cit. in n. 68, at 924. According to R. Wainwright (1977) *ELR* 349, this lack of discussion may be attributed to the fact that the procedure adopted by the Commission under Articles 92–4 of the EEC

Treaty (on which see D. Gilmour (1981) *CML Rev.* 63) improved its position in its application for interim measures, for it could show that there had been a binding decision of the Commission ignored by a Member State which had not itself appealed to the Court.

82. (1977) ECR 921, at 928.
83. See Gray, op. cit. in n. 74.
84. However, the Advocates-General do refer to this in their opinions.
85. Anyhow, Article 83 of the Rules provides only that the request shall specify . . . the grounds of fact and of law showing prima facie justification for the granting of the interim measure requested.
86. See Gray, op. cit. in n. 74, at 87.
87. (1977) ECR 1411, at 1414.
88. In Case 171/83R the Court mentioned 'repercussions on markets of other member states' when it was considering the urgency of interim measures, but in its discussion of irreparable harm it spoke only of the effect—apparently material rather than political—on the common market.
89. See T. C. Hartley (1980) *ELR* 363.
90. The one virtue of the brevity of the judgment is that, unlike the Advocate-General, the Court did not expressly accept the unattractive arguments of the French Government. It does not come well from a state already found by a judgment of the Court to be in breach of its obligations to argue that interim measures will weaken the force of the principle of *res judicata*, that judgments against Member States are binding. Nor is the French argument that it will comply with the judgment but that a too early termination of its breach of Community law would cause it irreparable harm very appealing. And the denial that its behaviour will cause irreparable harm to the Community or to the United Kingdom is unconvincing in the light of the earlier decisions of the Court.

4

Special Tribunals

THERE are also various special tribunals with the power to award judicial remedies. Have they—as standing tribunals that have built up a substantial case-law—adopted a systematic approach to remedies and produced coherent general rules on the remedies available and on the assessment of damages? To what extent have they looked to general international law or to municipal law for guidance?

SECTION I

(i) THE EUROPEAN AND AMERICAN COURTS OF HUMAN RIGHTS

(*a*) *Background*

The contrasting enforcement mechanisms established by the European and American Conventions on Human Rights are well known.[1] Under the former, once a claim for breach of the Convention has been declared admissible by the Commission, the claim may be brought before the Court if the respondent state has accepted its jurisdiction.[2] Unless a state party expressly accepts the right of individual petition under Article 25 only states parties may bring claims.[3] This type of action by states parties, like those brought against Member States of the EEC under Articles 169 and 170 of the EEC Treaty,[4] is clearly designed not to protect specific interests of states parties but to secure conformity with the Convention. In fact only the cases brought before the Commission against Greece and against Turkey[5] live up to this ideal of states acting disinterestedly to ensure compliance with the Convention; the other cases[6] show the disadvantages of allowing an *actio popularis* by states even in such a limited form as under the Convention.[7] The American Convention on Human Rights on this question, and generally as regards remedies and enforcement mechanisms, is better designed: it makes interstate proceedings optional[8] and individual petitions compulsory[9] for those states parties that have accepted the jurisdiction of the Court.[10] For individual petitions are vital to make the Convention effective. Under both the European and the American Conventions the individual victim has no standing to bring an action before the Court, but the Commission may take his case to the Court.[11]

Nor does the European Convention contain other provisions that could fill the gap left in the event of a state's refusal to accept individual petitions. In particular the European Convention provisions on the Court's power to give Advisory Opinions are extremely restrictive.[12] Only the Committee of Ministers may request an Opinion, and the requirement that

> Such opinions shall not deal with any question relating to the content or scope of the rights or freedoms defined in Section 1 of the Convention and in the Protocols thereto, or with any other question which the Commission of Ministers might have to consider in consequence of any such proceedings as could be instituted in accordance with the Convention,[13]

makes it difficult to imagine what might be a permissible question to the Court. Clearly this provision was intended to avoid the problems that might arise if the Court could give an Opinion on a question that might later come up in some form in an actual contentious claim. Because the American Convention gives the American Court a much wider advisory jurisdiction[14] than that of the European Court, with the aim of securing the most effective enforcement of the Convention, the American Court has to face these problems. It has considered them in three of its five Advisory Opinions. First, in its Opinion on *Other Treaties*,[15] as part of a very general discussion of the nature and role of Advisory Opinions, the Court said that it would not give an Advisory Opinion if that would interfere with the proper functioning of the Convention system of protection or adversely affect the interests of a victim of human rights violations. In the *Restrictions to the Death Penalty* case[16] the problem was directly before the Court. Guatemala had asked the Court to refuse to give an opinion because the request concerned a dispute between itself and the Commission and it had not accepted the Court's jurisdiction. The Court's response was very similar to that of the International Court of Justice to similar arguments in the *Namibia*[17] and *Western Sahara*[18] cases; it said that the Commission's request was designed to help it perform its functions under the OAS Charter. The advisory jurisdiction provided a parallel system to the contentious cases; it was designed to help states and organs comply with and enforce human rights treaties 'without subjecting them to the formalism and the sanctions associated with the contentious judicial process'. Accordingly it gave an Advisory Opinion.

But the American Court's jurisprudence is still limited to five Advisory Opinions and one individual claim.[19] The European Court of Human Rights has decided more than one hundred individual claims, even though as far as the right to bring claims is concerned the European Convention is once again more restrictive than the American Convention. Under the former it is only the actual victims who may, under Article 25, address a petition to the Commission for possible eventual submission to the Court. There is no *actio popularis* open to individuals. This was reaffirmed by the Commission with apparent satisfaction in Case 8727/79,[20] where they call it 'a concept alien to the system for the protection of human rights and fundamental freedoms set up by the Convention', and by the Court in *Klass*.[21] The Court said that Article 25 did not institute for individuals a kind of *actio popularis* for the interpretation of the Convention. By contrast under the American Convention it is not necessary for the applicant to be a victim. Article 44 provides:

> Any person or group of persons, or any nongovernmental entity legally recognized in one or more member states of the Organization, may lodge petitions with the Commission containing denunciations or complaints of violation of this Convention by a State Party.

Buergenthal interprets this as allowing an *actio popularis*.[22] What is still not clear under the American Convention is whether there must be *a* victim (as Articles 46 and 63 might be taken to imply) even if the claim to the Commission does not have to be brought by him, or whether a claim would be admissible when a law or practice violates the Convention even if no individual has been affected, as is the case with interstate claims under the European Convention.

Although Article 25 of the European Convention requires that the applicant must be a victim, it is now well established that the Court and Commission recognize a wider interest than that of the individual.[23] Convention proceedings are not designed solely for the benefit of injured individuals but rather to secure compliance with its provisions. Thus the Commission may continue with a case before the Court even if the individual applicant wishes to withdraw; in such cases the Court has spoken of its role 'to elucidate, safeguard and develop the Convention obligations'.[24] The Commission has to approve friendly settlements,[25] and it is open to Convention institutions to reformulate the applicant's claim, and to suggest Articles that might have been violated apart from those invoked by the applicant.[26]

(*b*) *Jurisdiction to award remedies*

Under Article 45 of the European Convention, 'The jurisdiction of the Court shall extend to all cases concerning the interpretation and application of the present Convention which the High Contracting Parties or the Commission shall refer to it in accordance with Article 48'. This does not make clear the type of judgment open to the Court. Typically this question is left to be resolved by the jurisprudence of the Court. But the American Convention gives more detailed guidance. Article 63(1) provides:

> If the Court finds that there has been a violation of a right or freedom protected by this Convention, the Court shall rule that the injured party be ensured the enjoyment of his right or freedom that was violated. It shall also rule, if appropriate, that the consequences of the measure or situation that constituted the breach of such right or freedom be remedied and that fair compensation be paid to the injured party.

Buergenthal apparently interprets this as allowing declaratory judgments and damages but not orders for injunctions or specific performance.[27] That is, he accepts that the American Court may determine not only whether there has been a violation of the Convention but also what steps may have to be taken to remedy the violation, but seems not to accept the possibility of the Court ordering states what to do. Article 63(1) is ambiguous and requires clarification by the Court. Whichever interpretation is adopted the American Court's jurisdiction is wider than that of the European Court. For in its judgments on the merits the European Court has limited itself to declaring that there has been a violation of the Convention; it does not go on to declare that there is an obligation on the defendant state to act in a certain way or to take specified measures to remedy the breach. It is not obvious that the Court is legally bound to restrict itself in this way. The International Court of Justice acting under the Optional Clause or under agreements giving it jurisdiction over 'the interpretation and application' of treaties has issued declaratory judgments specifying the obligations of states.[28] But on the other hand the practice of the European Court of Human Rights on this matter is consistent with that of the European Court of Justice under Articles 169 and 170 of the EEC Treaty,[29] and also with the general scheme of the Convention.

Nor does the European Court have the power to issue orders. This question was left open in *Ireland* v. *UK*[30] but was finally resolved in *Marckx*,[31] where the Court held that it had no power to annul or repeal municipal legislative provisions: 'The Court's judgment is essentially declaratory and leaves to the State the choice of means to be utilised in its domestic legal system for performance of its obligation under Article 53.' This limit on the Court's jurisdiction may be confirmed by reference to the many decisions under Article 50 where the Court has held that it is not empowered to direct states parties by issuing orders.[32]

The existence of Article 50 to some extent justifies the generally accepted restrictive interpretation of the Court's jurisdiction to give decisions on the merits under Article 45. For Article 50 provides:

> If the Court finds that a decision or a measure taken by a legal authority or any other authority of a High Contracting Party is completely or partially in conflict with the obligations arising from the present Convention, and if the internal law of the said party allows only partial reparation to be made for the consequences of this decision or measure, the decision of the Court shall, if necessary, afford just satisfaction to the injured party.

It seems implicit in this provision that the European Court in its decision on the merits should only decide whether there has been a violation of the Convention and that it is then for states parties to decide the measures appropriate to comply with their obligations.

The drafting history[33] and wording of Article 50 makes it clear that this was intended as a fallback provision, intended only to fill any gaps left by national legal systems. If the national legal system of the defendant state allows only partial reparation for the breach of the European Convention then the victim may turn to the European Court for relief. Here, as in Articles 13[34] and 26,[35] the secondary place of Convention procedures and remedies in the general scheme of the Convention is clear. But the European Court has not treated Article 50 as a measure of last resort.[36] It has taken a very generous view of the applicability of Article 50 in order to provide speedy reparation for individuals whose rights under the Convention have been violated. It has not generally considered the availability of reparation as a pre-condition for the application of Article 50,[37] rather it has held that Article 50 can be applied whenever the nature of the victim's injury makes *restitutio in integrum* impossible.[38]

(*c*) *Remedies under Article 50*

Under Article 50 the European Court has the power to award 'just satisfaction'. The Convention does not specify what measures are covered by this, nor has the Court given this much explicit attention. In two cases[39] the Court has mentioned international law as governing, or at least as relevant to, the application of Article 50. But it has not turned to international practice for guidance and there are no references to international jurisprudence in its decisions on the application of Article 50. In fact it is doubtful whether international practice could have provided much assistance because traditionally 'satisfaction' has been regarded as a remedy for injury to a *state's* honour and dignity. It has taken the form of a non-pecuniary remedy, such as an order for a salute to the flag of the injured state, or of a declaratory judgment in itself representing just satisfaction, or of pecuniary compensation. But the last is rarely found in arbitral as opposed to diplomatic practice. Nor can international practice on the assessment of damages for injury to individuals afford more guidance. The calculation of compensation for moral injury—the typical injury for victims under the Convention—is necessarily an arbitrary process. Awards for this in arbitral practice are not common or (not surprisingly) consistent.[40] And, as has been shown in Chapters 1 and 2, even on the assessment of damages for material or pecuniary injury there is little uniformity between awards in international arbitral and judicial practice.

Nor has the European Court of Human Rights turned to municipal law for guidance in any systematic way. Both the defendant states and the applicants have occasionally invoked the municipal law of the defendant state, almost invariably on the issue of costs alone.[41] But the Court has consistently refused to accept municipal rules or practice as binding on it. In the *Sunday Times* case the applicants contended that there was no reason to depart from the general English rule that 'costs follow the event', but the Court 'concurs with the Delegates' view that it is not applying a domestic rule if it accepts under Article 50 a claim in respect of costs',[42] and said that under Article 50 the injured party is not entitled to his costs as of right. Also in that case the Commission was doubtful whether an award for costs should cover the cost of services of a salaried solicitor, an employee of the applicant. The government drew the Court's attention to the fact that under English practice at least part of those costs would be recoverable. The Court said that the English practice was not conclusive in the autonomous sphere of Article 50 but accepted its guidance.[43] Again, in *Silver*[44] the Court repeated that 'parallels drawn with domestic practice do not bind the Court, although they may assist it'. The Court has not turned to municipal law for guidance under Article 50 except on this question of costs.

So the European Court on the question of remedies, like the vast majority of arbitral tribunals and the World Court, appears to operate in isolation. Has it evolved any coherent rules on this question?

In its early awards under Article 50 the Court apparently assumed that Article 50 was designed to provide pecuniary compensation for victims of breaches of the European Convention. Thus it simply allowed or refused pecuniary satisfaction.[45] But in *Golder*,[46] in its decision on the merits the Court found that there had been a breach of Articles 6(1) and 8; it then of its own motion and without discussion said that it was of the opinion 'that in the circumstances of the case it is not necessary to afford to the applicant any just satisfaction other than that resulting from the finding of a violation of his rights'.

Again in *Engel*,[47] in addition to making an award of pecuniary compensation for Engel the Court referred to the satisfaction that would result for the applicant from a finding that there had been a violation of the Convention, and the other applicants were given only the satisfaction of this finding. In their separate opinions Judges Ganshof van der Meersch and Evrigenis criticize this:

> It seems to be difficult to accept the proposition that the finding by the Court of a breach of the substantive provisions of the Convention, whilst constituting a condition for the application of Article 50 can at the same time be the consequence in law following from that same provision.[48]

But this convincing criticism was not accepted by the Court in the *Marckx* case. The Commission requested the Court to award the applicants one Belgian franc each as compensation for moral damage. Again the Court held that it was not necessary to afford any just satisfaction other than that resulting from the finding of the violations. This time six judges dissented, saying that an award of one Belgian franc was justified on the basis of the damage suffered and the applicants' interest in being recognized individually as victims of the legal situation brought about by the state. In view of the fact that it was a purely nominal sum that was sought, their insistence on satisfaction beyond a mere declaratory judgment seems rather strange. And since the *Marckx* case it has become clearly established by the jurisprudence of the Court that a finding of a violation may itself constitute just satisfaction under Article 50 for a moral injury. It cannot, however, provide just satisfaction for costs as was argued by the United Kingdom in the *Sunday Times* case. The Court rejected this; it distinguished between damage caused by a violation of the Convention and costs necessarily incurred by the applicant, and said, 'In fact it is difficult to imagine that the finding of a violation could of itself constitute just satisfaction as regards costs.'[49]

The declaratory judgment as satisfaction is familiar from the decision of the International Court of Justice in the *Corfu Channel* case.[50] There it provides a remedy for an injury to a state, not an individual. But it may be, despite the apparent distortion of Article 50, that the finding of a breach is an appropriate remedy for individuals for moral injury under the European Convention. However, the Court does not award this as the only possible remedy for moral injury; it sometimes awards pecuniary compensation instead. So the Court has not avoided the problem of the award of inevitably arbitrary amounts of compensation for moral injury; it seems to compound this arbitrariness by sometimes allowing pecuniary compensation and sometimes refusing it. Nor can any clearly consistent pattern in the Court's decisions be found. It is not possible to predict on the basis of its previous decisions when it will allow pecuniary compensation and when it will not go beyond a mere finding of a violation. If the Court is making an award for material loss it seems it will generally include an element (of unspecified amount) to cover non-pecuniary loss also,[51] but otherwise its approach is unpredictable. The Court has never assumed that there should be compensation for every breach of the Convention. But in some cases it has been willing to assume the existence of moral injury and to award compensation for this.[52] For example, in *Artico*[53] it said of the violation of Article 6(3)(*c*) that 'In all probability he was left with a distressing sensation of isolation, confusion and neglect . . . Mr Artico must have felt defenceless.' It is interesting to contrast this with the much stricter approach in *Corigliano*[54] and *Pakelli*,[55] where the Court refused to assume the existence of any moral injury, and with the approach in cases such as *Silver* and *Campbell and Fell*,[56] where the Court assumed moral injury but said that pecuniary compensation was not justified. Thus in *Silver* the Court said,

> It is true that those applicants who were in custody may have experienced some annoyance and sense of frustration as a result of the restrictions that were

imposed . . . It does not appear, however, that this was of such intensity that it would in itself justify an award of compensation for non-pecuniary damage.[57]

The Court's decision between a mere finding of a violation and the award of pecuniary compensation for a moral injury does not depend on the particular Article violated; that is, on the basis of the Court's jurisprudence it is not possible to predict that a violation of—say—Article 6(1) is more likely to lead to pecuniary compensation than a violation of Article 5(4). The attitude of the defendant government apparently has some impact in that if it does not oppose the award of financial compensation this type of award is more likely to be made,[58] and if it suggests an amount the Court will probably be guided by this.[59] But the converse does not apply; government opposition to pecuniary compensation will not stop the court from making this type of award.[60] On the whole it seems that the Court allows pecuniary compensation for what it regards as serious breaches or for victims with whom it sympathizes, but this does not make for predictability.

When the Court does award pecuniary compensation for moral injury its decisions on the amount inevitably appear arbitrary; such loss is by its nature not capable of precise quantification. And the Court has not attempted to relate its awards to each other; each decision is made in isolation. Nor is this surprising or objectionable: it is difficult to envisage any practicable scale of damages for moral injury. One reflection of this is that applicants often do not quantify their claims for moral injury but leave the assessment of this to the discretion of the Court.[61] Thus in *X and Y* v. *Netherlands*[62] the Court said only that

The damage in question does not lend itself even to an approximate basis of calculation. Assessing it on an equitable basis as is required by Article 50, the Court considers that Miss Y should be afforded just satisfaction which it fixes at 3,000 Dutch Guilders.

This was for a violation of Article 8, for failure of the state to secure respect for the private life of the victim. In *Ringeisen* the applicant received pecuniary compensation for the breach of Article 5(3). The facts that the time spent in detention on remand was deducted from his prison sentence, and that conditions on remand were less severe than in prison, were somehow taken into account.

However, the applicant protested his innocence and certainly felt such excessive detention on remand to be a great injustice. The detention must have been all the more hard to bear in that it inevitably made it much more difficult for him to conclude a composition for the termination of his bankruptcy.

Assessing these various factors the Court considers that Ringeisen should be afforded just satisfaction and fixes at 20,000 DM the overall sum to be paid to him in this regard.[63]

These cases are typical of the approach of the Court.

Awards for material loss (apart from costs and expenses) are less common; in the majority of cases claims for material loss are rejected because the applicant cannot prove injury or that his loss was caused by the breach of the Convention. The Court has consistently taken a strict view of the causation requirement.[64] Thus it has refused to allow compensation for material harm caused by imprisonment when it was not the imprisonment itself that was unlawful but rather (for example) the conduct or length of the trial.[65] But in a few cases[66] the Court has been willing to compensate victims for the loss of an opportunity. For example, in *Goddi* the applicant maintained that if he had had an opportunity of having his defence adequately presented he would have received a lighter sentence. The Court said that it could not accept so categorical an allegation, but agreed that the outcome might possibly have been different if Mr Goddi had had the benefit of a practical and effective defence; accordingly they concluded that 'In the present case such a loss of real opportunities warrants the award of just satisfaction'.[67]

When the European Court awards compensation for material loss it almost invariably combines this with an award for moral injury and makes its award in the form of a lump sum.[68] The process of assessment is not clear. In *Goddi*, where the Court was giving just satisfaction for the loss of opportunities mentioned above and also for 'the non-pecuniary damage which the applicant undoubtedly suffered as a result of the violation of Article 6(3)*c*', it said only,

None of the above elements of damage lends itself to a process of precise calculation. Taking them together on an equitable basis, as is required by Article 50, the Court considers that Mr Goddi should be afforded satisfaction assessed at 5 million lire.[69]

And in *Sporrong and Lönnroth*[70] the Court's lack of concern with methods of assessment is even more apparent. The applicant's right of property under Article 1 of Protocol I had been violated by the Swedish Government's issue of long term expropriation permits and its prohibition on construction. The Court said,

The assessment of the damage suffered presents particular difficulties on this occasion and is thus very problematical. The difficulties turn in part on the technical nature of real-estate matters, the complexity of the calculations made by the experts acting for the applicants and for the Government and the intervening changes in the claims put forward by the injured parties; they arise above all from the virtual impossibility of quantifying even approximately, the loss of opportunities.[71]

The Court rejected both the methods of assessment suggested by the parties, 'but it does not consider that it has to establish another'. This was because the Court limited itself to what it called 'an overall assessment of the factors which it has found to be relevant'; it said simply that 'The damage suffered is made up of a number of elements which cannot be severed and none of which lends itself to a process of precise calculation',[72] and awarded an unexplained lump sum. Nor do those few cases where the Court is making an award for pecuniary loss alone with no element for moral injury show any greater concern with methods of assessment of loss.[73] The approach of the Court to pecuniary awards is impressionistic; it has chosen to give mostly lump sum awards as rough approximation to 'just satisfaction' rather than try to work out and apply rules of international law on the assessment of loss.

The Court's approach to compensation for costs and expenses is hardly more rigorous. Its general rule is that an award to cover the applicant's costs will be made if these are actually, necessarily, and reasonably incurred.[74] Where the amount claimed is not challenged by the Commission or the defendant government it is awarded in full;[75] where the amount is challenged the Court usually awards a 'lump sum assessed on an equitable basis' without detailed explanation.[76] The costs must have been actually incurred by the applicant himself,[77] but a claim for costs will be allowed even where the applicant's lawyer has not yet sent in his bill,[78] on the ground that the applicant is liable to pay those costs. However, in *Dudgeon*[79] it was held that a claim made for fees payable on a contingency basis was not valid, since contingency fees were not acceptable under Northern Ireland law and so Dudgeon was not legally liable for them.

Costs must also have been necessarily incurred. It can be seen from *König*[80] and the *Sunday Times* cases that the Court will not allow costs for extra lawyers or incidental expenses where these are unnecessary. Nor will it reimburse the costs of legal proceedings except where these proceedings are designed to establish or remedy a breach of the Convention.[81] Moreover the Court in the *Sunday Times* case accepted in principle that it could deny costs incurred in advancing extensive submissions which were rejected by the Commission and the Court because these costs were not necessary to the establishment of a breach of the Convention. This was done in *Le Compte, Van Leuven and De Meyere*[82] and in *Campbell and Fell*. In the latter case the Court also refused to award the full amount claimed for the costs of the applicant's barrister on the ground that this was excessive. The costs claimed must be reasonable in amount. In *Neumeister*[83] the Court based its assessment on 'the current rates payable under the scheme for free legal aid operated by the Commission and Delegates of the Commission' and made an award for considerably less than the amount claimed with no more detailed explanation. In *Deweer* the Court simply accepted the amount claimed by the applicant as this was not disputed, actually incurred, and reasonable. This question of the appropriate scale of costs was considered at more length in *König* and the *Sunday Times* case; in both these cases the defendant governments argued that there should be a single standard—the scale established by the Commission for free legal aid—and that claims for costs actually incurred should be rejected if they exceeded the amount available under this scale. However, the Court rejected this argument in *König* and again in the *Sunday Times* case. It distinguished the decision in *Neumeister* where this scale had been accepted saying that the decision in that case stemmed from the fact that Neumeister had not produced any detailed fee notes, unlike *König* and the *Sunday Times*. Moreover, as the Commission had argued, it would be anomalous that applicants who are nationals of countries where justice is less expensive should obtain full indemnification whereas other applicants would have to pay a sometimes considerable balance themselves. But subsequently, in *Young, James and Webster*,[84] the Court issued a warning. It said,

> High costs of litigation may themselves constitute a serious impediment to the effective protection of human rights. It would be wrong for the Court to give encouragement to such a situation in its decisions awarding costs under Article 50. It is important that applicants should not encounter undue financial difficulties in bringing complaints under the Convention and the Court considers that it may expect that lawyers in contracting States will co-operate to this end in the fixing of their fees.

Campbell and Fell shows the result of ignoring this warning.

Under Article 50 then the Court has given pecuniary compensation and has said that the mere finding of a violation may provide just satisfaction. It has not issued orders telling defendant states what to do in order to comply with their obligations and remedy their breaches under the Convention. In the first two cases where it was requested to make an order directed at the defendant state the Court did not decide this question.[85] But in *Le Compte, Van Leuven and De Meyere*, on the basis of the judgment on the merits in *Marckx* the Court assumed that it was not able to give an order in Article 50 proceedings. Applicants have continued to request orders but the Court has not wavered and recently in *McGoff* reaffirmed that 'Its judgments leave to the State concerned the choice of the means to be utilized in its domestic legal system for performance of its obligations under Article 53. The Court is thus not empowered to direct Sweden to take the action requested.'[86] Despite the potentially very wide scope of Article 50 as far as the power to give remedies is concerned, it seems that the European Court of Human Rights does not regard an order as a suitable remedy against a state. And even if the Court does not provide much, if any, guidance to other tribunals on the assessment of compensation, on this question of orders for injunctions or specific performance the approach of the European Court of Human Rights, like that of the European Court of Justice, should guide the International Court of Justice. If the International Court is called on expressly to decide whether it may issue an order to a defendant state in a case where no express provision is made for this, it should adopt the presumption of the other Courts that an order is not a suitable remedy against a state.

NOTES

1. See A. H. Robertson, *Human Rights in Europe* (1977); T. Buergenthal (1982) *AJ* 231; T. Buergenthal, R. Norris, D. Shelton, *Protecting Human Rights in the Americas* (1982).
2. ECHR Article 46.
3. ECHR Article 24.
4. See Ch. 3.
5. ECHR Yearbook, Vol. xii, and Council of Europe Publications for 1983 respectively. See (1986) ILM 308 for the Friendly Settlement of the latter.
6. *Greece* v. *United Kingdom* ECHR Yearbook, ii. 174; *Austria* v. *Italy* ECHR Yearbook, iv. 116, vi. 742; *Ireland* v. *UK* ECHR Ser. A no. 25; *Cyprus* v. *Turkey* ECHR Yearbook, xviii. 82.
7. The possibility of the rejection of abusive claims was accepted in principle in the *First Greek* case (ECHR Yearbook, xi. 730, at 764 and in *Cyprus* v. *Turkey*, Decision 6780/78, Decisions and Reports, ii. 125, at 138.
8. ACHR Article 45.
9. ACHR Article 44.
10. ACHR Article 62.
11. Article 45 ECHR, Article 61 ACHR. See works referred to in n. 1 for a full description of the procedures involved.
12. ECHR Protocol no. 2.
13. Ibid., Article 1(2).
14. ACHR Article 64:

    '1. The member states of the Organization may consult the Court regarding the interpretation of this Convention or of other treaties concerning the protection of human rights in the American states. Within their spheres of competence, the organs listed in Chapter X of the Charter of the Organization of American States, as amended by the Protocol of Buenos Aires, may in like manner consult the Court.

    2. The Court, at the request of a member state of the Organization, may provide that state with opinions regarding the compatibility of any of its domestic laws with the aforesaid international instruments.' See T. Buergenthal (1985) *AJ* 1.
15. (1983) ILM 51.
16. (1984) ILM 320. The Court followed the same approach in its Advisory Opinion concerning *Costa Rican Law for the Practice of Journalism* (1986) ILM 123.

17. 1971 ICJ Reports 16.
18. 1975 ICJ Reports 12.
19. *Viviana Gallardo* (1981) ILM 1057, 1424.
20. Decisions and Reports, xx. 230, at 237.
21. ECHR Ser. A. no. 28, § 30.
22. Loc. cit. in n. 1.
23. R. Higgins (1978) *Rev. hell. DI* 1.
24. The Court has not struck out a case since *de Becker* (ECHR Ser. A no. 4) on this ground, apart from the *Rubinat* case (ECHR Ser. A no. 89), which can be explained by the particular circumstance that another case on the same or very similar facts had already been decided by the Court that day. See, for example, *Ireland* v. *UK* (ECHR Ser. A no. 25) and *Guzzardi* (ECHR Ser. A no. 39).
25. ECHR Articles 28 and 47. But see *Skoogström* (ECHR Ser. A no. 83).
26. See, for example, *Guzzardi*, loc. cit. in n. 24, at § 58; *Foti* (ECHR Ser. A no. 56, § 42).
27. The Court mentioned this question in passing in its Advisory Opinion on *Restrictions to the Death Penalty* (loc. cit. in n. 16), but only quoted the words of Article 63(1). In the light of Buergenthal's strong influence it is probable that his interpretation will prevail.
28. See Ch. 2 Sections 1 and 4.
29. See Ch. 3.
30. ECHR Ser. A no. 25. The Court said, 'The Court does not have to consider in these proceedings whether its functions extend, in certain circumstances, to addressing consequential orders to contracting states. In the present case, the Court finds that the sanctions available to it do not include the power to direct one of those states to institute criminal or disciplinary proceedings in accordance with its domestic law'.
31. ECHR Ser. A no. 31, § 58.
32. See below at n. 85 ff.
33. Article 50 was modelled on provisions such as Article 10 of the 1921 German–Swiss Arbitration and Concilation Treaty (LNTS, xii. 272) which was designed to provide for the situation where a state, because of the requirements of its constitution, is unable to make complete *restitutio in integrum* for a breach of international law. It allows an arbitral tribunal to award pecuniary compensation as a substitute for specific performance or *restitutio in integrum*. See L. F. Gainen (1974) *NYJILP*, 177.
34. This is designed to secure municipal law remedies in each of the states parties for violations of the rights protected by the Convention. See J. Raymond (1980–1) *Human Rights Review* 161.
35. This requires the exhaustion of local remedies for a claim to be admissible by the Commission.
36. See C. D. Gray (1981) *Human Rights Review* 153.
37. Thus in *Luedicke, Belkacem and Koç* (ECHR Ser. A no. 29) the German Government declared before the Court that they would comply with their obligations under the Convention if the Court came to the conclusion that

there had been a violation of the Convention without the necessity for a decision under Article 50 to ensure the execution of the Court's judgment. But the Court was not persuaded by this. Again, in *Eckle* (ECHR Ser. A no. 65) the Court applied Article 50 even though the applicant requested that a decision on this be postponed until he had tried to obtain a domestic remedy. But a domestic remedy may, if not exclude the application of Article 50, nevertheless be taken into account in the assessment of just satisfaction. Compare *Ringeisen* (ECHR Ser. A no. 15) and *Neumeister* (ECHR Ser. A no. 17) and see also *Piersack* (ECHR Ser. A no. 85).

38. See Gray, op. cit. in n. 36, and, most recently, *Eckle*, loc. cit. in n. 37.
39. *Ringeisen* and *Neumeister*, loc. cit. in n. 37.
40. See Ch. 1, at n. 197.
41. *Eckle*, loc. cit. in n. 37; *Silver* (ECHR Ser. A no. 67); *Sporrong and Lönnroth* (ECHR Ser. A no. 88); *Sunday Times* (ECHR Ser. A no. 38).
42. Loc. cit. in n. 41, at §15.
43. Fitzmaurice dissented on this point.
44. Loc. cit. in n. 41.
45. *De Wilde, Ooms and Versyp* (ECHR Ser. A no. 14); *Ringeisen*, loc. cit. in n. 37; *Neumeister*, loc. cit. ibid.
46. ECHR Ser. A no. 18.
47. ECHR Ser. A no. 22.
48. Ibid., at 71.
49. Again Fitzmaurice dissented on this point.
50. (1949) ICJ Reports 4.
51. As, for example, in *Goddi* (ECHR Ser. A no. 76), *Guincho* (ECHR Ser. A no. 81), *Colozza* (ECHR Ser. A no. 89), and *Sporrong and Lönnroth*, loc. cit. in n. 41.
52. As in *Artico* (ECHR Ser. A no. 37), *Van Droogenbroeck* (ECHR Ser. A no. 63), *De Jong, Baljet and Van den Brink* (ECHR Ser. A no. 77).
53. Loc. cit. in n. 52, at §47.
54. ECHR Ser. A no. 57.
55. ECHR Ser. A no. 64.
56. ECHR Ser. A no. 80.
57. Loc. cit. in n. 41, at §10.
58. For example, *Van der Sluijs, Zuiderveld and Klappe* (ECHR Ser. A no. 78), as far as Van der Sluijs was concerned; *De Jong, Baljet and Van den Brink*, loc. cit. in n. 52. Also in some cases the government questioned only the amount claimed, not the award of pecuniary compensation. See, for example, *Goddi*, loc. cit. in n. 51, and *Sporrong and Lönnroth*, loc. cit in n. 41.
59. *Young, James and Webster* (ECHR Ser. A no. 55); *Airey* (ECHR Ser. A no. 41).
60. *Colozza*, loc. cit. in n. 51; *X and Y* v. *Netherlands*, loc. cit. in n. 62.
61. As, for example, in *Guzzardi*, loc. cit. in n. 24; *König* (ECHR Ser. A no. 36); *Colozza*, loc. cit. in n. 51.
62. ECHR Ser. A no. 91, at §40.

63. Loc. cit. in n. 37, at §26.
64. See Gray, op. cit. in n. 36.
65. For example, *Luberti* (ECHR Ser. A no. 75); *Campbell and Fell*, loc. cit. in n. 56; *Sramek* (ECHR Ser. A no. 84).
66. *Artico*, loc. cit. in n. 52; *Goddi*, loc. cit. in n. 51; *Colozza*, loc. cit. in n. 51.
67. Loc. cit. in n. 51, at §35.
68. See cases mentioned in n. 51.
69. §36.
70. Loc. cit. in n. 41.
71. §27.
72. §32.
73. *Foti* (ECHR Ser. A no. 69); *Deweer* (ECHR Ser. A no. 35). It is not clear whether *Ringeisen* and *König* include compensation for pecuniary loss.
74. See *König*, loc. cit. in n. 61; *Deweer*, loc. cit. in n. 73; *Sunday Times*, loc. cit. in n. 42.
75. See, for example, *Sramek*, loc. cit. in n. 65; *McGoff* (ECHR Ser. A no. 83).
76. See, for example, *Piersack*, loc. cit. in n. 37; *Young, James and Webster*, loc. cit. in n. 59.
77. In *Luedicke, Belkacem and Koç* (ECHR Ser. A no. 36) additional fees were claimed by Belkacem's lawyer, but as the claimant himself had received free legal aid he bore no costs himself and suffered no loss capable of being compensated under Article 50 of the Convention. It was Belkacem alone who had the status of an injured party for the purposes of Article 50; his lawyer could not rely on this provision to seek just satisfaction on his own account. See also *Öztürk* (ECHR Ser. A no. 85) and *Van Droogenbroeck*, loc. cit. in n. 52.
78. See *X* v. *United Kingdom* (ECHR Ser. A no. 55) and *Pakelli* (ECHR Ser. A no. 64).
79. ECHR Ser. A no. 59.
80. Loc. cit. in n. 61.
81. Ibid.
82. ECHR Ser. A no. 54.
83. Loc. cit. in n. 37.
84. ECHR Ser. A no. 55, at §15.
85. *Airey*, loc. cit. in n. 59; *Winterwerp* (ECHR Ser. A no. 47).
86. ECHR Ser. A no. 83.

SECTION 2

(i) INTERNATIONAL ADMINISTRATIVE TRIBUNALS

Judicial remedies are also awarded by the administrative tribunals of international organizations for unlawful acts by the organizations against their officials. The United Nations and International Labour Organization tribunals are the best known of the tribunals set up to deal with actions by officials,[1] and their decisions are the most easily accessible.[2] But, as de Vuyst has pointed out,[3] international administrative tribunals do not constitute an interconnected system; they were established as the need arose and their composition, statutes, and rules vary. The call of the United Nations General Assembly in 1978 for the rationalization of the system has not been heeded.[4]

The vital question here is what is the significance of their decisions on judicial remedies in international law. The law they create and apply is generally regarded as a special category, sometimes called the proper law of international organizations, distinct from general international law, although derived from it.[5] Can their decisions make any contribution to the general international law on remedies? As with the courts of human rights discussed in the previous section it must be asked whether international administrative tribunals have looked to international arbitral or judicial practice or to general principles of municipal law, and whether they have, together or separately, produced coherent rules on remedies. Perhaps not surprisingly a study of their large jurisprudence[6] indicates that these specialized tribunals in their generally rather summary discussion of remedies have little of general application or general theoretical importance to impart.

This is partly because the Statutes of the UN and ILO administrative tribunals govern the appropriate remedies for injury to officials. Article 9 of the former provides:

> 1. If the Tribunal finds that the application is well founded, it shall order the rescinding of the decision contested or the specific performance of the obligation involved. At the same time the Tribunal shall fix the amount of compensation to be paid to the applicant for the injury sustained should the Secretary-General, within 30 days of the notification of the judgment, decide, in the interest of the United Nations, that the applicant shall be compensated without further action being taken in his case; provided that such compensation shall not exceed the equivalent of two years' net base salary of the applicant. The Tribunal may, however, in exceptional cases, when it considers justified, order the payment of a higher indemnity. A statement of the reasons for the Tribunal's decision shall accompany each such order.
>
> 2. Should the Tribunal find that the procedure prescribed in the Staff Regulations or Staff Rules has not been observed, it may, at the request of the Secretary-General and prior to the determination of the merits, order the case remanded for institution or correction of the required procedure. Where a case is remanded, the Tribunal may order the payment of compensation, not to exceed the equivalent of 3 months' net base salary, to the applicant for such loss as may have been caused by the procedural delay.
>
> 3. In all applicable cases, compensation shall be fixed by the Tribunal and paid by the United Nations or, as appropriate, by the specialized agency participating under Article 14.

This Article covers all types of claims by officials; it fixes a maximum award which is only to be exceeded in exceptional cases. However, unlike the laws of many Western European states on unfair dismissal, it does not lay down any required minimum payment for cases of unfair dismissal.[7]

Article VIII of the Statute of the International Labour Organization administrative tribunal gives less specific guidance. This says,

> In the cases falling under Article II the Tribunal, if satisfied that the complaint [sc. by the official] was well founded, shall order the rescinding of the decision impugned or the performance of the obligation relied upon. If such rescinding of a decision or execution of an obligation is not possible or advisable the Tribunal shall award the complainant compensation for the injury caused to him.

(ii) RESCISSION AND SPECIFIC PERFORMANCE

Thus the primary remedy under both statutes is rescission or specific performance. However, under the ILO Statute the administrative tribunal has the option to award compensation where the rescinding of a decision or execution of an obligation is not possible or advisable. Under the UN Statute it is for the Secretary-General, rather than the tribunal, to choose between the remedies. And both tribunals frequently award compensation rather than rescission or specific performance. In particular, reinstatement after an unlawful termination or failure to renew is extremely rare.[8] For in many cases specific performance or rescission is impossible, undesirable, or an inadequate remedy. Often restoration of the status quo ante could not be achieved by these remedies; thus where a fixed-term contract has been unlawfully terminated by an international organization and has since expired, rescission of the decision to terminate or an order for the specific performance of the contract would not be effective remedies for the injured official. This was the situation in *Bulsara.*[9] Here the UN tribunal said,

> On the conclusions reached in this case the Tribunal has no alternative as per the language of Article 9 of the Statute of the Administrative Tribunal but to order specific performance of the obligation undertaken by the Respondent, namely to find a suitable assignment for the applicant. However, in view of the fact that the obligation undertaken was circumscribed by a time limit, namely the 'near future', the parties cannot be restored to the status quo ante. The Tribunal therefore holds that compensation in lieu of specific performance is the adequate and proper relief that can be granted to the Applicant.

The ILO tribunal has also decided in several cases, with little or no explanation, that rescission of the unlawful decision would be impossible or inadvisable;[10] and in certain cases it has held that specific performance was, despite Article VIII, outside its jurisdiction.[11]

In the European Communities claims by officials are brought before the European Court of Justice as no special administrative tribunal has yet been established. These actions by officials represent about one half of all cases brought to the Court.[12] The European Court of Justice in this type of action also has available to it a choice of remedies. Actions against the European Communities are governed by Article 215 EEC Treaty (which contains general provisions on breaches of contract and torts by Community organs)[13] or, alternatively, by Article 179 EEC. Remedies under Article 215 are limited to pecuniary compensation, but Article 179 gives the Court unlimited jurisdiction.[14] This provides: 'The Court of Justice shall have jurisdiction in any dispute between the Community and its servants within the limits and under the conditions laid down in the Staff Regulations or the Conditions of Employment.' In practice, as Schermers points out,[15] the cases brought before the Court by officials are typically actions for annulment of unlawful decisions or damages.

Given the express powers of the UN and ILO tribunals to give rescission and specific performance, and given the extensive jurisdiction of the European Court of Justice, there is little of general significance to be derived from their decisions on these remedies as far as general international law is concerned; the former simply provide a particular illustration of the general problem of the limitations of these remedies.[16]

(iii) DAMAGES

Nor are their decisions on damages of any greater general significance. They, like the other tribunals already discussed, appear to function in isolation. They do not look to each other's jurisprudence, they certainly do not apply each other's statutes. In *Goyal*[17] UNESCO argued that the maximum award fixed in the Statute of the UN administrative tribunal should also be observed by the ILO tribunal. But the latter rejected this argument:

> The Tribunal does not agree with this approach. The duty of this Tribunal, as of every other tribunal unless its Statute otherwise provides, is to fix as compensation the sum which appears to it to be equitable in all the circumstances. If any limit be imposed upon an equitable amount, it necessarily means that the sum awarded will be less than the complainant deserves. Doubtless the principle of limitation of liability has been accepted in many systems of law . . . This principle has not, so far as the Tribunal is aware, been generally introduced into the relationship between an employer and his employees. It is far from clear that it governs the relations between the United Nations and its officials, since the Statute of the Administrative Tribunal of the United Nations makes provision for exceptional cases. To the extent to which it does govern such relations, it operates solely by virtue of an express provision in that Statute. Every person, before he becomes an official of the United Nations, in the same way as he can ascertain from the Staff Regulations what will be the conditions of his employment, can ascertain that in the event of its

termination his compensation may be limited. A tribunal without a similar provision in its Statute is not entitled to impose upon an official what would amount in effect to a condition of his employment to which he has not assented.

As with other international tribunals, administrative tribunals do not consider the question of the source of the rules that they apply on the assessment of damages. They do not seem to regard the question as governed by existing rules; rather it is for them to make their own common sense decisions. It has been suggested that they apply general principles of law,[18] but, at least as far as remedies are concerned, there is no express reference to these, and no consideration given to the method of finding these. Thus the tribunals have not, with the exception of *Howrani*[19] and *Keeney*,[20] accepted guidance from municipal legal systems. Several municipal systems make statutory provision for unfair dismissal. For other breaches of contract and for torts the normal remedies apply, but special conditions are attached to unfair dismissal in order to protect the employee's legal interest in his job.[21] In the absence of express reference by these tribunals to municipal law, any explanation of their decisions as based on general principles cannot be more than an *ex post facto* rationalization, a convenient fiction to explain the absence of any express choice of legal system rather than an accurate description of a conscious choice of general principles. Nor do the administrative tribunals refer to international arbitral or judicial practice on the question of remedies.[22]

Predictably the case-law of the different tribunals on the assessment of compensation is not consistent. Each tribunal has its own characteristic approach to this question, but the identity seems to be more one of style than of substance. For there is little by way of theoretical discussion or explanation of their awards by the tribunals. The International Court of Justice in *Application for Review of Judgment No. 158 of the United Nations Administrative Tribunal*[23] does not demand much in the way of reasoned explanation of its award from the UN tribunal. When asked to review the decision in the *Fasla* case the International Court of Justice rejected the allegation that the tribunal had failed to consider the applicant's claim for damages for injury to his professional reputation and career prospects. It held that the extreme paucity of compensation awarded could represent a failure by the tribunal to exercise its jurisdiction only if there were such a discrepancy between the findings of the tribunal and the remedy granted that the award in question could be viewed as going beyond the exercise of reasonable discretion.[24]

Although there are some signs of, or references to, coherent general policies on the assessment of compensation, none of the tribunals routinely refer to earlier decisions or established practices,[25] nor is it a simple matter to deduce general principles from their decisions. Most often when reference is made to a general rule this is done in order to exclude its operation. The dominant impression is one of diversity.[26] Thus, for example, in *Rosescu*[27] the ILO tribunal referred to the purported general rule for assessing compensation for failure to extend an appointment as requiring the calculation of the amount of pay due minus actual or probable outside earnings, but the tribunal then went on to assess the compensation *ex aequo et bono*. Again in *Dicancro*[28] the ILO tribunal mentioned the basis for the assessment of compensation usually employed in cases of non-renewal—the estimation of the value of an expectation—but excluded its application on the particular facts. Nor does the European Court of Justice often refer to its own previous decisions on the assessment of compensation in its actual judgments.[29] The Advocate-General does regularly mention earlier decisions on the calculation of loss, but the Court rarely follows his advice on the question of assessment and often does not even accept his opinion on the merits of staff actions.

(*a*) *Awards ex aequo et bono*

In its early decisions the ILO tribunal, perhaps in recognition of the problem of the source of the rules on the assessment of loss to be applied by it or because of the approximate nature of its calculations, expressly stated that its award of damages was made *ex aequo et bono*.[30] However, the legitimacy of this was questioned before the International Court of Justice in its Advisory Opinion on the *Administrative Tribunal of the International Labour Organization*.[31] The Court held that these decisions were not in fact outside the jurisdiction of the administrative tribunal. It said,

> The Court need not examine the allegation that the validity of the judgments of the Tribunal is vitiated by excess of jurisdiction on the ground that it awarded compensation 'ex aequo et bono'. It will confine itself to stating that in the reasons given by the Tribunal in support of its decision on the merits, the Tribunal said, 'That redress will be ensured ex aequo et bono by the granting to the complainant of the sum set forth below'. It does not appear from the context of the judgment that the Tribunal thereby intended to depart from principles of law. The apparent intention was to say that, as the precise determination of the actual amount to be awarded could not be based on any specific rule of law the Tribunal fixed what the Court, in other circumstances, has described as the true measure of compensation and the reasonable figure of such compensation.[32]

Nevertheless this Opinion appears to have influenced the ILO tribunal, since for a long time it abandoned the practice of making its decisions *ex aequo et bono* and referred only to 'fair' or 'equitable' compensation. It later recovered its nerve and now regularly makes its decisions *ex aequo et bono*.

The UN tribunal expressly referred to the International Court's Opinion in some of its awards and was obviously affected by it. Thus, in *Bulsara*[33] and *Fasla*[34] the tribunal said that its award was 'the true measure of compensation and the reasonable figure of such compensation'. The UN tribunal has in fact never given an award explicitly *ex aequo et bono* except in *Higgins*,[35] where the respondent had expressly consented to this. The European Court of Justice sometimes makes its decisions of compensation 'in equity'[36] and at other times *ex aequo et bono*,[37] but as in the decisions of the ILO tribunal there is no obvious difference of approach between those decisions made *ex aequo et bono* and those not. The latter are not noticeably less obscure or more fully reasoned than the former.

These uncertainties over the law being applied by the UN and ILO tribunals in their assessment of damages and the fact that many of the ILO tribunal's awards and some of those of the European Court of Justice are made *ex aequo et bono* make it unlikely that this international administrative jurisprudence will have anything to contribute to general international law on damages. Nor have these tribunals even succeeded in developing a uniform proper law of international organizations on the assessment of damages since they do not look to each other's decisions for guidance. Accordingly no more than a brief survey of their decisions on damages is needed here.

(*b*) *Assessment of loss*

On the question of causation all the tribunals take the normal approach that only injury directly caused by the illegal act should be compensated and they do so without any extended discussion. Occasionally compensation is refused on the ground that the loss claimed is not caused by the illegal act,[38] and in some cases the amount of compensation is reduced because the behaviour of the applicant has contributed to the loss or because of fault on the part of the applicant,[39] but usually the question of causation is not discussed in these or in other cases.

Some cases on the assessment of compensation for injuries incurred before the decision of the tribunal are straightforward: the calculation of what the applicant would have received if there had been no unlawful action is relatively simple in cases of, for example, the unlawful refusal of a pension or of a salary increase, or of an award of the amount of salary lost up to the time of the tribunal's decision. But decisions on the award of interest—whether as itself providing compensation for delay in payment of money due to the applicant or where interest is given on the award for injury to the claimant—show clearly a lack of consistency between tribunals and even between the decisions of a particular tribunal, the result of flexibility or alternatively of a lack of concern. Most awards of compensation are for lump sums so it is left unclear whether an element for interest is included. In the few cases where interest is awarded that is done mostly without comment or explanation.[40] The European Court of Justice similarly is not concerned to set out its reasoning for its awards of interest.[41] The award of costs by the UN and ILO tribunals is also handled in a pragmatic way: the awards are of round figures, an apparent attempt at swift if rough justice rather than an exact calculation.[42]

But the most difficult question for the tribunals and for the European Court of Justice is the assessment of future losses, of compensation for the damage that will continue after the award. Calculation of the future earnings of employees unfairly dismissed or not renewed in their appointments are inherently speculative. The large mass of decisions by the UN and ILO tribunals do not produce uniform methods or formulas for the calculation of loss. In its earliest cases the ILO tribunal did not distinguish between awards for permanent, probationary, or fixed-term appointments,[43] and even when it later came to do so in most cases there is little, if any, explanation of the amount awarded. In a few cases where the contract of employment unlawfully terminated had only a short period left to run the tribunal has awarded damages covering the full loss of salary until the end of the contract.[44] In cases where the contract was for permanent employment, or where renewal of a fixed-term contract was refused, the tribunal adopted other standards of compensation. No uniform method is apparent: awards are sometimes expressed in terms of years' salary,[45] sometimes as lump sums.[46] Reasoned discussion of the basis of calculation is not offered.

The decisions of the UN administrative tribunal generally contain slightly more detailed discussion of the assessment of damages but, as with the ILO tribunal, the approach is very flexible. The decisions do not reflect a consistent theory as to the appropriate method of calculation. In some, payment of the full amount of salary (minus any indemnities received) until the end of the contract is awarded,[47] in others the chance of outside employment is the decisive consideration,[48] in others the tribunal bases its award on the chance of continued employment in the organization.[49] In many cases the approach adopted for the first time in *Gordon*[50] is followed. Here the tribunal said,

> Whereas the Tribunal has received a further claim for compensation in lieu of reinstatement, the Tribunal, having examined all the facts and the documents in the personnel file, and noting the Applicant's 'high professional competence' as recorded consistently in his reports, the description of his work as 'excellent' and his 'above average' rating in his specialized post, awards $6,000 in lieu of reinstatement.

The factors most commonly considered include the merit of the claimant, his years of service, age, and salary, and the chance of continued or other employment. Consideration of these factors in a way that cannot be clear to observers or contained in a general formula enables the tribunal to arrive at a decision on the appropriate amount of compensation.

The European Court of Justice has only rarely been called on to assess compensation for loss of future salary; the remedy usually requested for unlawful dismissal is annulment. In *Kergall* v. *Assembly*,[51] however, the applicant claimed the difference between the salary he had received from the Assembly and the amount he earned in his new post for the length of time that his contract with the Assembly had left to run. The Court's response in this case is very similar to that of the UN tribunal in, for example, *Dale*.[52] The Court rejected the applicant's claim on the ground that he had only a chance, not a certainty, of renewal. They held that the situation was analogous to one of lawful termination or redundancy, and that damages should be assessed on this basis. Again, in *Luhleich* v. *Euratom*[53] the Commission of Euratom had wrongfully dismissed the applicant. He did not want to return to his former employment with them and so the Court assessed damages. The applicant had not requested a specific amount but had left this to the discretion of the Court which said only, 'In the circumstances of the case it is reasonable to assess the amount of the damage at a sum equivalent to 9 months of the net emoluments received by the applicant at the moment when his dismissal took place.'[54] However, it is not entirely clear whether this represents an award for the loss of future salary, for in addition to his claim under this head the applicant asserted that regardless of the legality of the decision of dismissal he had suffered damage, and requested 3 million BF for material damage and 7 million BF for non-material damage. 'As regards the assessment of these sums the applicant merely states that they are justified by virtue of his age, professional experience and the services which he rendered.' That is, the applicant relies on a list of factors, similar to those on which the UN tribunal ostensibly bases its assessments of damages. The European Court of Justice held that

> In view of the size of the sums claimed such general allegations conform neither with the requirements of Article 18 of the Protocol nor Article 38(1)C of the Rules of Procedure according to which the application must contain at least a brief statement of the grounds on which the application is based,

and that therefore the applicant's claims were inadmissible.

(c) *Moral injury*

Thus the tribunals' assessments of damages for loss of future earnings, probably inevitably, appear somewhat arbitrary. The same is inevitably true of their awards for moral injury. All three tribunals allow compensation for this in cases of unfair dismissal as well as for other wrongful acts. In some of its decisions the ILO tribunal simply takes account of the moral damage and awards a sum which it expressly says covers this and material harm without specifying how much is allowed under each head.[55] In other cases the tribunal makes its awards with no indication whether this is for material or moral harm or for both.[56] Finally, the ILO tribunal sometimes calculates the extent of moral harm separately. Obviously the amount of such an award will be difficult to explain on any rational basis. In *Mauch*[57] the applicant received $1,000 for the moral prejudice caused to him because the Organization had left open to doubt the reasons which had motivated its failure to re-engage him. In *Goyal*[58] damages were awarded for the abrupt and summary manner in which the applicant was suspended. The tribunal said that it would not be right to relate assessment under this head exclusively to the basic salary, for distress and moral prejudice may be as great to a man on a small salary as to a man on a large one, but nevertheless held that the rate of salary affords a guideline and accordingly decided that an award equivalent to six months' salary would be approximately correct. As a final example, in *Dicancro*[59] the applicant received $20,000 for the deep distress caused by a misconceived charge of misconduct not later withdrawn or apologized for. In one case the ILO tribunal recognized that inasmuch as it found the ILO at fault the present judgment was itself a remedy, but also awarded damages for the moral harm suffered.[60]

The UN tribunal has made considerably fewer awards for moral injury. In those decisions which simply list relevant factors to be taken into consideration in assessing compensation in lieu of reinstatement it is not made clear whether the award includes an element to remedy moral harm. There are a very small number of cases where the tribunal has expressly allowed damages for such harm,[61] in others the tribunal has held that the terms of its judgment would constitute sufficient satisfaction for any moral injury suffered by the official.[62] The European Court of Justice similarly sometimes allows pecuniary compensation for moral harm for anxieties, as in *Lachmüller* v. *Commission*[63] and *Fidelaar* v. *Commission*,[64] for wounded feelings, as in *de Bruyn* v. *Assembly*,[65] and for not keeping his personal file in good order in *Ditterich* v. *Commission*.[66] Occasionally purely symbolic damages are allowed.[67] But at other times the Court simply says that a judgment allowing annulment is in itself adequate reparation for moral injury.[68]

The outcome of this section has thus turned out to be essentially negative: to show that the jurisprudence of international administrative tribunals has little of significance to contribute to any general international law of remedies. For these tribunals are not concerned to find, create, or apply general rules, they are not given to general discussion or explanation of their awards on the remedies. This should not necessarily be taken as a criticism; like the European Court of Human Rights it could be said that the UN and ILO tribunals are 'not governed by a specific legal regime but aim at pragmatic solutions in the individual case'.[69] But the danger of this type of approach may be the appearance of inconsistency between like cases. And when considered with other factors such as the specialized nature of the subject matter and the doubt as to the applicable law, the general lack of concern with uniformity in an area where consistency not only within but also between tribunals might have been possible does limit the significance of this jurisprudence.

NOTES

1. They have jurisdiction over claims not only by their own officials but by those also of several other organizations. See B. M. de Vuyst, *Statutes and Rules of Procedure of Internationl Administrative Tribunals* (1981, 2nd ed.).
2. The decisions of the recently established World Bank Administrative Tribunal are also now becoming available. See World Bank Administrative Tribunal Decisions; C. F. Amerasinghe and D. Bellinger, *Main Points in Decisions of the World Bank Administrative Tribunal*; and discussion of the powers of the tribunal by, for example, B. M. de Vuyst (1981–2) *Rev. belge DI* 81; T. Meron (1981) 14 *NYJILP* 1.
3. Op. cit. in n. 1, at (i).
4. GA Resolutions 33/119 and 34/438. See H. G. Schermers, *International Institutional Law* (1980), §565.
5. See C. Parry, *The Sources and Evidences of International Law* (1965), at 25, where he suggests that it might be more satisfactory to label the decisions of international administrative tribunals 'non-municipal law' rather than 'international law'; C. W. Jenks, *The Proper Law of International Organizations* (1962).
6. The question of remedies has been briefly considered by C. W. Jenks, op. cit. in n. 5, at 115; M. Akehurst, *The Law Governing Employment in International Organizations* (1967). And J.-D. Busch (25 *GYBIL* 433) has produced what he calls 'a compilation rather than a deepened analysis of the relevant material'.
7. See *International Encyclopaedia for Labour Law and Industrial Relations*, (ed. R. Blanpain (1977–).
8. Examples are *Abbott* ILO Judgment no. 373; *Go* ILO Judgment no. 631; *Pollicino* ILO Judgment no. 635. For discussion of rescission and specific performance see Akehurst, op. cit. in n. 6, at 19, 193–5; B. C. Koh, *The United Nations Administrative Tribunal* (1966), at 119, 124; Jenks, op. cit. in n. 5, at 106–7.
9. UN Judgment no. 68. See also *Leak* (UN Judgment no. 97), where the tribunal said that as it was no longer possible to restore the situation that would have existed if summary dismissal had never taken place, compensation was the only means of drawing legal inferences from the obligations resulting from the rescission.
10. As in *Garcin* ILO Judgment no. 32; *Gale* ILO Judgment no. 474; *Troncoso* ILO Judgment no. 448; *Azola Blanco and Veliz Garcia* ILO Judgment no. 507.

11. In certain early cases the tribunal held that rescission of an unlawful decision terminating or refusing renewal of an appointent could not alone guarantee reinstatement or renewal. Thus in *Froma* (ILO Judgment no. 22) the tribunal ordered rescission, but went on to say, 'Nevertheless the Tribunal does not have the power to order reinstatement which requires a positive act of the Director General over whom the Tribunal has no hierarchical authority; that in the absence of such a power and unless the Director General should consider himself in a position to reconsider his decision in this matter, the Tribunal is nonetheless competent to order equitable reparation of the damage suffered by the complainant by reason of the measure of which she was the object.'

    This approach was adopted in certain later cases. For example, *Hermann* ILO Judgment no. 133; *Goyal* ILO Judgment no. 136; *Almini* ILO Judgment no. 306. See discussion by Jenks, op. cit in n. 5, at 106–7. But there do not seem to be any more recent examples of this response by the tribunal. Rather it simply refused reinstatement as impossible or inadvisable.
12. H. G. Schermers, *Judicial Protection in the European Communities* (1983, 3rd ed.), at §325.
13. The equivalent articles in the ECSC and Euratom Treaties are Articles 40 and 152 respectively.
14. See reference to this by the European Court of Justice in, for example, *Willame* v. *Commission* Case 12/66 (1967) ECR 153; *Fiehn* v. *Commission* Case 23/69 (1970) ECR 547; *Oberthür* v. *Commission* Case 24/79 (1980) ECR 1743.
15. Op. cit. in n. 12, at §509. See also Akehurst, op. cit. in n. 6, at 195.
16. In contrast, for the European Communities annulment is the normal remedy for unlawful dismissal, and reinstatement by the Community follows without the need for an order by the Court. See Schermers, op. cit. in n. 12, at §325.
17. ILO Judgment no. 176.
18. Akehurst, op. cit.in n. 6, at 72.
19. UN Judgment no. 11.
20. UN Judgment no. 12.
21. See n. 7.
22. Apart from a reference by the ILO tribunal to the ICJ Advisory Opinion referred to below at n. 31 on decisions *ex aequo et bono*.
23. (1973) ICJ Reports 166.
24. Ibid., 196–8.
25. Occasionally such references are misplaced. See Busch, at 443.
26. This is very clear from Busch's useful compilation of decisions.
27. ILO Judgment no. 431.
28. ILO Judgment no. 427. See also *Klee* (UN Judgment no. 242), where the tribunal referred to the formula established in cases of legitimate expectancy of fixed term appointments without specifying exactly what this formula was. Nor is this apparent from the cases. The tribunal in *Klee* rejected the application of the formula in that case since the applicant had a 'clear expectancy of an extension', and surveyed the diverse case-law on comparable facts.

29. However, it is possible that there might be such references in the marginal citations of cases apparently included by the Court in its own transcripts but (very unhelpfully) omitted from the official reports.
30. *Hickel* ILO Judgment no. 5; *Rothbarth* ILO Judgment no. 6; *Duberg* ILO Judgment no. 17; *Froma* ILO Judgment no. 22.
31. (1956) ICJ Reports 77.
32. Ibid., at 100.
33. UN Judgment no. 68.
34. UN Judgment no. 158.
35. UN Judgment no. 92.
36. *Lachmüller* v. *Commission* Case 43, 45, 48/59 (1960) ECR 463; *Fidelaar* v. *Commission* Case 44/59 (1960) ECR 535.
37. *De Bruyn* v. *Assembly* Case 25/60 (1962) ECR 21; *Serio* v. *Commission* Case 62/65 (1966) ECR 561; *Oberthür* v. *Commission* Case 24/79 (1980) ECR 1743.
38. For example, *Mollet* v. *Commission* Case 75/77 (1978) ECR 897. In the UN and ILO tribunals this can be seen mostly in their refusal of material damages, as in *Sita Ram* ILO Judgment no. 367; *Ali Khan* ILO Judgment no. 565; *Elmoznino* UN Judgment no 263; *Naggar* UN Judgment no. 293.
39. For example, *Sergy* v. *Commission* Case 58/76 (1976) ECR 1139; *Babbar* ILO Judgment no. 388; *Firmin* ILO Judgment no. 542; *Perucho* UN Judgment no. 285; *Delano de Stuven*, UN Judgment no. 298.
40. The grant of interest on an award for unlawful injury to an applicant is almost unknown in the jurisprudence of the UN tribunal. In one, perhaps the only, case where this was given, interest at 6 per cent per annum was awarded from the date of the unlawful act (*Roy*, UN Judgment no. 143). Such decisions are slightly more common in the ILO tribunal; the rates of interest vary from the early 4 per cent (*McIntire* ILO Judgment no. 13) to 8 per cent (*Almini* ILO Judgment no. 306) to the more recent 10 per cent (*Maier* ILO Judgment no. 503, *Benyoussef* ILO Judgment no. 595) to 12 per cent (*Azola Blanco* ILO Judgment no. 507) and the interest runs from the date of complaint. Awards for delay are made by both tribunals again at varying rates between 6 per cent and 10 per cent for the ILO tribunal (*Lamadie* ILO Judgment no. 262 and *Usaklilgil* (2) ILO Judgment no. 553), and between 6 per cent and 12 per cent for the UN tribunal (*Dupuy* UN Judgment no. 174 and *Talan* UN Judgment no. 289). There seems to be some attempt to achieve internal consistency (see, for example, *Talan*), but the starting-point for the award of interest varies from the date of complaint to the date of the injury.
41. The European Court of Justice has also in a few cases made awards of interest at rates that have been increased from the early 4 per cent in *Willame* Case 110/63 (1965) ECR 649, to the more recent 6 per cent or 8 per cent. The Advocate-General in the *Pizziolo* Case 785/79 (1983) ECR 1343, at 1353 examined the recent practice and, not very persuasively, said that 6 per cent was the predominant going rate. On the question of the starting date for the award of interest also the Advocates-General seem more concerned to achieve uniformity (see *Jacquemart* Case 114/77 (1978) ECR 1697, at 1713,

and *Pizziolo*, loc. cit. above) than does the Court itself (compare the Court's decisions in *Willame*, *Pizziolo*, and *Mrs P* Case 40/79 (1981) ECR 361).

42. See the discussion of the UN tribunal's approach by the International Court of Justice in the *Application for Review of Judgement No. 158 of the United Nations Administrative Tribunal* (1973) ICJ Reports 166, at 208–12. See also the Dissenting Opinion of Ammoun at 249–51. The UN tribunal apparently began by awarding actual costs. Then in 1950 it issued Policy A/CN.5/R.2 which said that in view of the simplicity of its proceedings the tribunal would not as a general rule grant costs to applicants whose claims have been sustained by the tribunal, but that in exceptional circumstances it would grant costs if these were unavoidable, reasonable in amount, and exceeded the normal expenses of litigation before the tribunal. Despite this policy the tribunal for a long time awarded what seemed to be a fixed amount of $300 before coming more recently to follow its earlier stated policy, as for example in *Powell* UN Judgment no. 237; *Klee* UN Judgment no. 242; *Talan* UN Judgment no. 289. The ILO tribunal has also moved away from the award of fixed amounts to the award of approximations—in hundreds and thousands—of actual costs. For the practice of the European Court of Justice see Schermers, op. cit. in n. 12 at §219 and §704–7, and K. Wolf 11 Europarecht (1976) 7, at 26.
43. See discussion by Busch, op. cit. in n. 6, at 447.
44. *Hickel* ILO Judgment no. 5; *Rothbarth* ILO Judgment no. 6.
45. *Hermann* ILO Judgment no. 133; *Savioli* ILO Judgment no. 346; *Rabozée* ILO Judgment no. 264; *Almini* ILO Judgment no. 306.
46. *Di Giuliomaria* ILO Judgment no. 87; *Diaz Acevedo* ILO Judgment no. 349; *Troncoso* ILO Judgment no. 448; *Halliwell* ILO Judgment no. 415. A good impression of the lack of uniformity can be obtained from Busch, op. cit. in n. 6.
47. *Coll* UN Judgment no. 113; *Witmer* UN Judgment no. 194.
48. *Robinson* UN Judgment no. 15.
49. *Howrani* UN Judgment no. 11, *Klee* UN Judgment no. 242; *Dale* UN Judgment no. 132.
50. UN Judgment no. 29.
51. Case 1/55 (1954–6) ECR 151.
52. Loc. cit. in n. 49.
53. Case 68/63 (1965) ECR 581.
54. Ibid., 605.
55. As in *Froma* ILO Judgment no. 22; *Glatz-Calvin* ILO Judgment no. 127; and *Bambinelli* (2) ILO Judgment no. 676.
56. As in *Garcin* ILO Judgment no. 32; *Saini* ILO Judgment no. 93; *Di Giuliomaria* ILO Judgment no. 87.
57. ILO Judgment no. 27.
58. ILO Judgment no. 136.
59. ILO Judgment no. 427.
60. *Rudin (no. 3)* ILO Judgment no. 630.
61. For example, in *Ogley* UN Judgment no. 215, the applicant was awarded

$1,000 for the uncertainties and harassments to which he had been subjected. See also the list in Busch, op. cit. in n. 6, at 443.

62. As in *Detiere* UN Judgment no. 36, *Champetier* UN Judgment no. 171, but apparently not since then.
63. Cases 43, 45, and 48/59 (1960) ECR 463.
64. Case 44/59 (1960) ECR 535.
65. Case 25/60 (1962) ECR 21.
66. Case 207/81 (1983) ECR 1359.
67. *Mrs V* v. *Commission* Case 18/78 (1979) ECR 2093.
68. Case 18 and 35/65 *Gutmann* v. *Commission* (1966) ECR 103; Case 53/72 *Guillot* v. *Commission* (1974) ECR 1; Case 59 and 129/80 *Turner* v. *Commission* (1981) ECR 1883.
69. Busch, op. cit. in n. 6, at 464.

5

National Claims Commissions, the Iran/United States Claims Tribunal, and International Commercial Arbitration

SECTION I

TRADITIONAL interstate arbitration has declined but there remain various alternative procedures and partial substitutes (apart from the role of international organizations): lump sum settlements and national claims commissions, and international commercial arbitration between states and corporations. This chapter will examine whether national claims commissions and international commercial arbitral tribunals are capable of making any contribution to the development of an international law of judicial remedies and will consider the nature of any such contribution.

(i) LUMP SUM SETTLEMENTS

These have been defined as follows:

> A lump sum settlement involves an agreement arrived at by diplomatic negotiations between governments to settle outstanding claims by the payment of a given sum without resorting to international adjudication. Such a settlement permits the state receiving the lump sum to distribute the fund thus acquired among claimants who may be entitled thereto pursuant to domestic procedure.[1]

Over 130 of these settlements have been made since the Second World War. Detailed discussion of lump sum settlements and of the decisions of national claims commissions established to distribute the lump sum is not necessary here, for these topics have been considered at length in many books in the Procedural Aspects of International Law series.[2] The history of these settlements is now familiar; they have been used since 1802 as an alternative to international adjudication. Before the Second World War the choice between these two methods of settling international claims was apparently not influenced by the type or number of claims involved, but subsequently these two factors were among those that led states to use lump sum settlements rather than international adjudication. The latter is politically unacceptable to many states; the large number of claims arising from war and from nationalizations made a quick method of settling international claims desirable; a lump sum settlement does not necessarily involve the assignment or admission of liability under international law.

It is the last factor that has contributed greatly to the controversy over the significance of this treaty practice in international law. In only six agreements is there an express admission of responsibility, and these were all made by Japan to settle war claims against her.[3] In the other settlements no mention of international liability is made, save that it may be expressly excluded.

Most of the lump sum settlements concern the payment of compensation for nationalization. In theory a nationalization may constitute a violation of international law if, for example, it is discriminatory or arbitrary. It has also been argued that non-payment of compensation makes nationalization unlawful. Whatever the force of this argument, and in spite of the decision of the International Court of Justice in the *Chorzów Factory* case,[4] where it said that a different measure of compensation from that for a lawful expropriation should be paid for an unlawful expropriation, the lawfulness or otherwise of an expropriation was not mentioned in any of these lump sum settlements. The next most common subject of lump sum settlement is war claims. Here again it is not clear whether these claims were based on breaches of international law. Many of the agreements were designed to fulfil obligations under the 1947 Peace Treaties, and it is generally accepted that these Treaties allow claims that would not be covered by traditional customary international law.[5] Third, many lump sum settlements provide for creditor claims. In the past the national states of creditors have not generally espoused such claims but have left it to organizations such as the Council for the Protection of Foreign Bondholders to protect creditors' interests.[6] Finally there is a small number of other types of claims. These include the settlement of claims against Germany for Nazi persecution,[7] various agreements settling the consequences for creditors of the absorption of Lithuania, Latvia, and Estonia into the USSR,[8] an agreement between Panama and the United States on compensation for injuries and losses to United States citizens caused by a riot and fire,[9] and an agreement between Great Britain and Indonesia on compensation for damage to the British embassy.[10] Liability is not admitted in any of these agreements and in some it is expressly excluded. In many it is doubtful whether international responsibility is involved.

Therefore the question of the legal significance of all these lump sum settlements is not a simple one, nor one that can be disposed of here. Discussion has centred on nationalization to the exclusion of the other types of lump sum settlement; in particular writers have differed as to whether this treaty practice has helped to create a new rule of international law that only partial compensation, or something less than 'prompt, adequate and effective' compensation, is due for nationalization. It is notorious that the

International Court of Justice in the *Barcelona Traction* case took the view that lump sum settlements are each *sui generis* and may not be relied on as creating customary international law.[11] And more recently the arbitrator in *Aminoil*[12] also adopted this approach.

Even if they have contributed to changes in the customary international law on compensation for nationalization, certain problems remain. It is not clear—and perhaps of no great practical importance except for arbitration tribunals—whether the lump sum settlements on compensation for nationalization can have any relevance to compensation for unlawful takings, or only for lawful takings. Indeed there is almost as much controversy over the right to nationalize—the requirement of a public purpose, the prohibition of arbitrary or discriminatory takings, the effect of stabilization clauses—as there is over compensation. And since the division between lawful and unlawful takings is not clear the continued viability of the distinction suggested by the Court in the *Chorzów Factory* case,[13] the distinction between the assessment of compensation for lawful takings and of damages for unlawful takings must be problematical, even for tribunals.[14]

(ii) NATIONAL CLAIMS COMMISSIONS

But here what is important is that doubts over the legal significance of lump sum settlements also affect the question of the role of national claims commissions in the development of the international law of remedies. Under lump sum settlements the distribution of the lump sum was generally[15] left to the claimant state; some of these established national claims commissions for this purpose. The decisions of the pre-Second World War national claims commissions were apparently made in accordance with customary international law.[16] But now it is only the United States Foreign Compensation Settlement Commission that is expressly directed under its enabling Act to make its decisions according to the provisions of the relevant lump sum agreement and to 'the applicable principles of international law, justice and equity'. And it is only the United States FCSC that publishes its decisions. The British Foreign Compensation Commission has to apply the governing Order in Council and no express guidance as to the applicable law is given to the French Commissions. Lillich and his associates have claimed that the decisions of these national claims commissions have contributed to the development of international law,[17] but Lillich himself acknowledges that there are difficulties in this. He refers to the unilateral nature of the decisions, the danger of divergence between commissions, the absence of a true adjudicatory process, and the possible underlying psychological bias of a national commission.[18] And in practice these factors considerably diminish any international significance that the decisions may have. The inaccessibility of the decisions other than those of the United States FCSC necessarily limits their possible impact. More importantly their unilateral nature, even if applying international law, means that their contribution to the development of international law can only be on a level with that to be made by municipal courts. The decisions themselves are brief and not generally fully reasoned on the question of the assessment of damages. There is little reference to international arbitral or judicial practice even by the United States FCSC. And not only are there basic inconsistencies between the various national commissions on the assessment of damages[19] (on the questions of lost profits, interest, and valuation methods), but even within the United States FCSC there is no one consistent approach; this can be seen clearly from the varying decisions on the assessment of compensation for expropriation.[20]

(iii) IRAN–UNITED STATES CLAIMS TRIBUNAL

In contrast the Iran–United States Claims Tribunal marks a new departure. In their Claims Agreement[21] the United States and Iran provided for the establishment of a claims tribunal. Although this was to be an international tribunal,[22] it would be far from the traditional arbitral tribunal.[23] The tribunal has jurisdiction over claims by nationals of one party against the other party and over intergovernmental claims; it is to decide claims that 'arise out of debts, contracts (including transactions which are the subject of letters of credit or bank guarantees), expropriations or other measures affecting property'.[24] Over 4,000 claims have been submitted, and Lillich, abandoning his previous caution, has called it, 'the most significant international arbitration in history'.[25] But that was in 1982 and now seems an overdrawn description; the jurisprudence of the tribunal to date has little of importance to contribute to the development of international law in general and on the assessment of damages in particular.[26]

There are various reasons for this disappointing result. First, many or most of the claims so far disposed of by the tribunal were not international claims at all. Under the Claims Agreement, Article V:

> The Tribunal shall decide all cases on the basis of respect for law, applying such choice of law rules and principles of commercial and international law as the Tribunal determines to be applicable, taking into account relevant usages of the trade, contract provisions and changed circumstances.

In most decisions—and a majority of these are on debt and contract claims, not normally the basis for claims under international law—the tribunal has not specified the law it is applying. In some the separate or dissenting opinion refers directly or indirectly to international law but this alone can not be conclusive.[27] The tribunal's flexible approach may be seen clearly in *CMI International, Inc.* v. *Iran*;[28] this case is unusual for its express consideration of the question of the applicable law. The case concerned a contract and the claimant argued that the proper law was that of Idaho. The tribunal did 'not believe it is rigidly tied to the laws of the contract, at least insofar as the assessment of damages is concerned,' and went on to discuss Article V as follows:

It is difficult to conceive of a choice of law provision that would give the Tribunal greater freedom in determining case by case the law relevant to the issues before it. Such freedom is consistent with, and perhaps almost essential to, the scope of the tasks confronting the Tribunal, which include not only claims of a commercial nature such as the one involved in the present case, but also claims involving alleged expropriations or other public acts, claims between the two governments, certain claims between banking institutions and issues of interpretation and implementation of the Algiers Declarations.

Thus the Tribunal may often find it necessary to interpret and apply treaties, customary international law, general principles of law and national laws, 'taking into account relevant usages of the trade, contract provisions and changed circumstances,' as Article V directs.[29]

With respect to the assessment of damages the tribunal held that its main task was 'to determine what are the losses suffered by the claimant and to award compensation'. It said that its search was for justice and equity—even in cases where, arguably, relevant national laws might be designed to further other goals—and finally preferred to analyse the damages question in accordance with the general principles of law, rather than by reference to the Uniform Commercial Code as incorporated in the statute law of Idaho. The tribunal was apparently referring to general principles of municipal law; it made only a brief reference to writers on comparative municipal law and in the end awarded a lump sum with very little explanation.

Despite its distinctly cavalier attitude to normal conflicts rules, the tribunal did here specify the applicable law. And there are a few other cases where the tribunal expressly decided this question.[30] But the law chosen is very rarely public international law, or even general principles of law. In fact the *American International Group Inc* v. *Iran*[31] remains alone among the reported cases as a clear instance of the application of public international law by the tribunal; and even here the tribunal simply assumes that the applicable law is public international law and does not expressly consider the question.

Even if we look not only to this case, but also to those other cases which might conceivably be regarded as expropriation cases subject to international law[32] (even in the absence of any express pronouncement or implicit indication to this effect by the tribunal) there is little guidance on the question of remedies and in particular on the assessment of damages. Part of the explanation for this lies in the approach of the tribunal; this is just one instance of the general problem that the tribunal's decisions are very brief and far from fully reasoned. As Stein has said, 'The Tribunal's treatment of the issues presented to it [is] so laconic, uninformative and unexplained that it forces us to consider directly the limits on the role of law in the Tribunal's decision.'[33] Another factor that reduces the significance of the tribunal's pronouncements on the assessment of damages is that these are sometimes the result of a compromise. Thus in *American International Group Inc* v. *Iran* itself Arbitrator Mosk in his Concurring Opinion said that he concurred in the award in order that a majority could be formed.[34]

> This Award represents a 'compromise solution' in which I have joined so that some award could be issued . . . I recognize that the value of the Claimants' nationalized interest in Iran America cannot be established with precision. I believe, however, that there are justifications for an Award of damages higher than that provided by the Tribunal in this case. Moreover, the Tribunal should have discussed more fully in its Award certain issues such as the applicability of the US–Iran Treaty of Amity, the time at which the payment of compensation was required and the standard of compensation utilized.

Perhaps not surprisingly the resulting compromise does not appear a very fruitful source for future development of the international law of remedies. The decision, like so many others, appears an isolated one. For on the assessment of compensation the tribunal makes no reference to municipal or international jurisprudence and its decision is an unusual one. The tribunal decided that it could not be held that the nationalization was by itself unlawful as there was not sufficient evidence before the tribunal to show that the nationalization was not carried out for a public purpose or was discriminatory. But 'it is a general principle of public international law that even in a case of lawful nationalization the former owner of the nationalized property is normally entitled to compensation for the value of the property taken'. That is, the tribunal found that the taking was lawful. The fact that compensation had not been made 'within any period after the date of nationalization that would be considered legally required' did not itself make the taking unlawful, but compensation for the lawful nationalization would have to be paid. The issues before the tribunal were the standard of compensation to be applied and the date payment was due.

The tribunal's decision is consistent with the *Chorzów Factory* case[35] in its decision that the appropriate date for the assessment of the value of an undertaking that had been lawfully nationalized was the date of the taking. But what is unusual about the decision, and done without any comment, is that the tribunal's assessment of the amount to be awarded included an element for loss of future profits although the taking was lawful.[36] This follows the approach in the *Aminoil* arbitration[37] to be discussed in the next section. It does not seem consistent with the reasoning of the Permanent Court of International Justice in the *Chorzów Factory* case; there the Court distinguished between lawful and unlawful takings. The latter alone were to be compensated by the monetary equivalent of *restitutio in integrum*. The former were limited to the value of the undertaking at the moment of dispossession, plus interest to the day of payment. It is implicit in this—and necessary if the Court's suggested distinction is to have any substance—that the Court did not contemplate that the value of the undertaking lawfully taken should include an element for lost profits. There must be some uncertainty about this given the brevity of the Court's discussion; the precise differences between compensation for lawful and for unlawful takings must remain speculative. What is clear is that both in this *American International Group Inc* v. *Iran* case and in the *Aminoil* case the tribunals were not concerned with any possible difference; they did not discuss this point nor mention the *Chorzów Factory* case.

In *American International Group Inc* v. *Iran* the claimants contended that the nationalization was a violation of international law, that 'just' compensation equal to the 'full value' of their interest in the nationalized corporation was due, and that for the purposes of determining this the company's value must be measured as a going concern, including such elements as future business prospects and good will. They claimed $39,010,000. The respondents argued first that modern developments in international law in United Nations and settlement practice had created a new standard of partial compensation. Alternatively, they said that if full compensation was due it would be inappropriate to value the property as a going concern. Rather compensation should be made for 'actual worth of assets owned on the date of nationalization' without consideration of such elements as goodwill or loss of future profits. The appropriate measure of compensation was net book value, or 'assets minus liability without consequential damages'.

The tribunal, without comment except to the effect that the net book value is used mainly for liquidation purposes, rejected this method and held that the appropriate method was to value the company as a going concern, taking into account not only the net book value of its assets but also such elements as goodwill and likely future profitability, had the company been allowed to continue its business under its former management. But it rejected the value produced by the claimants' experts as too high. Their appraisals had not sufficiently considered changes in general social and economic conditions in Iran, or their likely duration. They did not account for the effects of Iranian taxes on net profitability, changes in the company's financial position before nationalization were not reflected in the valuation, and, finally, the company had been conducting its business for only four years and such a short period must be deemed to provide an insufficient basis for projecting future profits. Accordingly the tribunal with no further explanation said that the higher and lower limits of the range within which the value of the company could reasonably be assumed to lie were wide apart, and that it would therefore have to make an approximation of that value, taking into account all relevant circumstances. It came up with a figure of $10 million plus interest at 8.5 per cent. Apart from its problematical adoption of going concern value as the appropriate standard of compensation for even lawful takings,[38] there is little of assistance here for other tribunals concerned with the assessment of damages.[39] Nor do other decisions of the tribunal in expropriation cases[40] or in cases where the tribunal refers to general principles of law[41] or even in cases where the Concurring Opinion refers to international law[42] provide any more assistance. Despite—or rather, perhaps, because of—the vast number of claims the Iran–US Tribunal has to date had little to contribute on the question of remedies in international law.[43]

NOTES

1. E. D. Re (1964) *ASIL* 39, at 40.
2. Edited by R. B. Lillich.
3. R. B. Lillich and B. H. Weston, *International Claims: Their Settlement by Lump Sum Agreements* (1975), Vol. ii, Treaties nos. 30, 44, 46, 73, 114, and 115.
4. PCIJ Ser. A no. 17, at 47.
5. R. B. Lillich and G. A. Christenson, *International Claims: Their Preparation and Presentation* (1962), at 66. Indeed it is perhaps not possible to speak of customary international law in this area: each peace treaty may be regarded as a special case; claims arising from war have been dealt with only according to peace treaties. See, for example, G. G. Fitzmaurice (1948) 2 *HR* 259.
6. See R. B. Lillich and B. H. Weston, *International Claims: Their Settlement by Lump Sum Agreements* (1975), Vol. i, at 186; (1975) *United States Digest* p 485; 8 Whiteman *Digest*, 93; Annual Reports of the Council for the Protection of Foreign Bondholders.
7. See Lillich, op. cit. in n. 3, Treaties nos. 64, 71, 96, 99, B2.
8. Ibid., Treaties nos. 48, 51, 66, 91, 94.
9. Ibid., Treaty no. 11.
10. Ibid., Treaty no. 116.
11. (1970) ICJ Reports 4 and 40. See criticism of this view by R. B. Lillich (1971) *AJ* 522 and in *International Claims: Their Settlement by Lump Sum Agreements* (1975).
12. (1982) ILM 976. And see Section 2 below.
13. pp. 46–7.
14. See Section 2 below, at n. 57.
15. Apart from the Iran–US Settlement. See below at n. 21.

16. See R. R. Wilson (1942) *AJ* 56; R. B. Lillich, *International Claims: Their Adjudication by National Commissions* (1962), 71–5.
17. Perhaps the most extreme claims are made by B. H. Weston who writes, 'replacing in importance the contributions of the pre-war ad hoc international claims commissions, the jurisprudence that emerges from these modern-day decisions reflects probably more accurately than anything else the norms of state responsibility that do now in fact prevail between investing and taking nations'. B. H. Weston, *International Claims: Post War French Practice* (1971), at p. x.
18. R. B. Lillich, op. cit. in n. 16, at 104.
19. See the accounts in R. B. Lillich, *International Claims: Post War British Practice* (1967), at Ch. 6; R. B. Lillich, *International Claims: Their Adjudication by National Commissions* (1962); B. H. Weston, op. cit. in n. 17; R. B. Lillich and B. H. Weston, *International Claims: Contemporary European Practice* (1982); A. Drucker (1955) *AJ* 477; R. B. Lillich (ed.), *The Valuation of Nationalized Property in International Law* (1972–5).
20. See R. B. Lillich (ed.), *The Valuation of Nationalized Property in International Law* (1972–5), at i. 95 (Lillich), 117 (S. Freidberg and B. B. Lockwood); R. B. Lillich, *International Claims: Post War British Practice*, Ch. 6; B. H. Weston, *International Claims: Post War French Practice* (1971), at 30–3, 178–82.
21. (1981) ILM 230.
22. Consisting of nine arbitrators: 3 American, 3 Iranian, 3 European, to sit in 3 separate chambers except when a decision of the full tribunal was desirable on an important question of law or procedure.
23. Which is why I have chosen to deal with it here rather than in Chapter 1. On the special nature of the tribunal see, for example, D. R. Robinson (1983) *Int. Lawyer* 661; J. M. Selby and D. P. Stewart (1984) *Int. Lawyer* 211; S. H. Amin (1983) *ICLQ* 750.
24. Claims Agreement Article II.
25. R. B. Lillich (1982) *ASIL* 5.
26. Iran–United States Claims Tribunal Reports.
27. As for example, in Case A/1 (1 Iran–US CTR 189); *Grimm* v. *Iran* (2 Iran–US CTR 78); *Dallal* v. *Iran* (3 Iran–US CTR 10).
28. 4 Iran–US CTR 263. See also *Isaiah* v. *Bank Mellat* (2 Iran–US CTR 232).
29. 4 Iran–US CTR 263, at 267–8.
30. For example *White Westinghouse International Co* v. *Bank Sepah-Iran* (1 Iran–US CTR 169); *Rexnord Inc* v. *Iran* (2 Iran–US CTR 6).
31. 4 Iran–US CTR 96 (1984) ILM 1; *INA Cpn* v. *Iran* (1986) AJ 181 must now be added; this case has not yet been reported in full. It contains a discussion of the international law standard of compensation for lawful expropriation.
32. *Dames and Moore* v. *Iran* (4 Iran–US CTR 212); *Starrett Housing Corporation* v. *Iran* (4 Iran–US CTR 122).
33. T. L. Stein (1984) *AJ* 1, at 2.
34. 4 Iran–US CTR 96, at 111–12. See also *Starrett Housing Corporation* v. *Iran*, Concurring Opinion of Arbitrator Holtzmann, loc. cit. in n. 32, at 159.

35. See Ch. 2 Section 3, at n. 9.
36. See also *INA Cpn* v. *Iran*, loc. cit. in n. 31. Here the tribunal said that the international law on large scale lawful nationalizations had undergone reappraisal and that maybe the 'full' or 'adequate' standard of compensation had been undermined. But this was a case of a small capital investment and here international law demanded compensation in an amount equal to the fair market value of the investment. Compare *Questech Inc* v. *Ministry of National Defence* (1986) AJ 362.
37. See Section 2, at n. 57.
38. This was followed in *INA Cpn* v. *Iran*. The tribunal rejected Iran's arguments for net book value and based its award on the purchase price of the investment.
39. The Concurring Opinions of Arbitrator Mosk in this case and Arbitrator Aldrich in *ITT Industries Inc* v. *Iran* (2 Iran–US CTR 348) (the propriety of making this latter Concurring Opinion where there had been an award on agreed terms is very doubtful. See note by Iranian Arbitrator Shafeiei, at 356.) provide more detailed discussion. These Opinions largely support the claimants' positions and represent what might be called the traditional Western view.
40. In *Starrett Housing Corporation* v. *Iran* (4 Iran–US CTR 122) at the interlocutory stage the tribunal again made no distinction between lawful and unlawful takings; it simply decided to refer the question of compensation to an expert and requested him to estimate the value of the undertaking at the date of taking, 'considering as he deems appropriate the discounted cash flow method'. The United States Arbitrator Holtzmann in his Concurring Opinion criticized the decision for the inadequacy of the terms of reference imposed on the expert. He said it was unfortunate that the tribunal had not provided any analysis or discussion of the standards of international law, and criticized the tribunal for making special mention of the discounted cash flow method without knowing whether this method normally used for valuing a going concern with a long expectancy of business would be equally appropriate for a short-term project.
41. In *Isaiah* v. *Bank Mellat* (loc. cit. in n. 28) it is interesting that the tribunal refused to award interest on the award for the amount of a dishonoured cheque because the respondent had tried to ensure that the cheque be paid, but it is not clear what legal system, if any, produced this result. In *CMI International Inc* v. *Iran* (4 Iran–US CTR 263) the tribunal, searching for justice and equity (having rejected the claimant's argument that it was entitled to damages on the basis that it was a 'lost volume' seller, as a seller whose capacity to sell exceeded the available market), dealt in a very summary fashion with the assessment of lost profits under general principles of law. It is not clear how it arrived at the amount awarded, a lump sum including interest.
42. In *R. N. Pomeroy* v. *Iran* (2 Iran–US CTR 372) the tribunal awarded a lump sum for amounts due but not paid under a contract for services. In *Dames and Moore* v. *Iran* (loc. cit. in n. 32) the tribunal said that because of gaps in the

evidence and difficulties in quantifying the amount due for property expropriated, it was justified in estimating the value at the date of the taking. In both these cases an award of interest was made, 10% in the latter, unspecified in the former. In neither case was the rate discussed. The tribunal has not been consistent in its awards of interest and their award is often objected to in principle by the Iranian arbitrators. See, for example, the 'Opinion' of Judge Sani in *Granite State Machine Co. Inc.* v. *Iran* (1 Iran–US CTR 442, at 452); *Rexnord Inc* v. *Iran* (2 Iran–US CTR 14, at 27); *Dames and Moore* v. *Iran*, Request for reconsideration by Iranian Agent ((1984) AJ 240).

43. But see now *Phelps Dodge Corp. and OPIC* v. *Iran* (1986) ILM 619 and *SEDCO Inc.* v. *Iran* (1986) ILM 629 which appeared too late for inclusion in this book.

SECTION 2

(i) INTERNATIONAL COMMERCIAL ARBITRATION

THE vast mass of international commercial arbitration does not concern us here; most decisions are not published, nor made on the basis of public international law. But certain recent decisions are exceptional in both these respects.[1] These are cases about state contracts, contracts between states or state agencies and foreign enterprises, governed at least in part by international law or general principles of law. These decisions have attracted extensive academic discussion, but as the already large volume of writing on internationalized state contracts continually expands it seems that the number of such contracts is actually decreasing; their day is nearly over.[2] Nevertheless there is much of interest for the international law of remedies in these recent arbitration decisions, *BP* v. *Libya*, *Topco* v. *Libya*, *Liamco* v. *Libya*, and *Aminoil* v. *Kuwait*.[3]

(*a*) *Applicable law*

In certain earlier cases on state contracts where there was no express choice of law clause in the contract itself the arbitrators had turned to the general principles of law. The idea of the internationalization of contracts developed with cases like the *Lena Goldfields* arbitration,[4] *Petroleum Development* v. *Abu Dhabi*,[5] and *Sapphire International Petroleum* v. *NIOC*.[6] With the exception of *Aramco* v. *Saudi Arabia*,[7] where the arbitrator found that public international law was one of the sources of the law to be applied on the merits of the case, the arbitrators referred to the general principles of law rather than to public international law.[8] In three more recent cases decided under the auspices of the International Centre for the Settlement of Investment Disputes,[9] *AGIP* v. *Congo*, *Benvenuti and Bonfant* v. *Congo*, and *Amco Asia Cpn* v. *Indonesia*,[10] it was international law that applied. In the first the parties had chosen, as the proper law of the contract, 'Congolese law supplemented if necessary by any principles of international law'. In the other two cases there was no express choice of law so Article 42(1) of the ICSID Convention applied; this requires the tribunal to apply 'the law of the Contracting State party to the dispute as well as such rules of international law as may be applicable'. But on the question of remedies the tribunal in *AGIP* v. *Congo* turned exclusively to Congolese (in fact French) law and in *Benvenuti and Bonfant* v. *Congo* the assessment of damages was determined, with the parties' agreement, *ex aequo et bono*. So there is nothing in these cases of direct relevance for the international law of remedies, though their failure to turn to international law on the question of remedies may be significant.

However, in *Amco Asia Cpn* v. *Indonesia* the tribunal turned not only to Indonesian law but also to international law on the question of compensation for an unjustified revocation of a licence to invest. It found that

> The full compensation of prejudice, by awarding to the injured party the damnum emergens and the lucrum cessans is a principle common to the main systems of municipal law, and therefore, a general principle of law which may be considered as a source of international law,

and confirmed this by reference to international judicial decisions and awards.[11] It also held that only direct and foreseeable prejudice should be compensated. But its actual assessment of damages was brief and made without reference to other cases or state practice. The tribunal regarded the debate on the appropriate standard of compensation for expropriation as irrelevant to its decision because Indonesia had not claimed that its action was a nationalization. Thus its award should be seen in the context of earlier decisions on possible methods of assessing damages for breach of contract but because of its brevity it does not add much to these.

The tribunal held simply that compensation should be made for the going concern value of the enterprise in which the claimant was no longer allowed to invest. It said that there were several methods of calculating this and that the most appropriate method in the circumstances was the net present value of the business.[12] The currency of the award was to be US dollars; this was decided without reference to any earlier decisions but simply on the basis of the particular facts of the case. The original investment had been made in dollars and the relevant Indonesian law allowed the repatriation of capital and earnings. When it came to the question of interest the tribunal without explanation abandoned international law and decided that Indonesian law applied and, finally, on the question of costs, the tribunal ordered each party to bear its own cost without mention of any governing law. Thus the tribunal used international law as a source of the basic rules of full compensation and of directness and foreseeability but did not look to it for any more detailed guidance. The particular relationship between the parties was the most important factor in the tribunal's assessment of compensation.

In the *BP*, *Topco*, *Liamco*, and *Aminoil* cases international law had a larger role than in the ICSID cases. In the first three the parties had provided that

> The Concession shall be governed by and interpreted in accordance with the principles of the law of Libya common to the principle of international law, and in the absence of such common principles then by and in accordance with the general principles of law including such of those principles as may have been applied by international tribunals.

The arbitrators applied this in different ways when they came to the question of remedies. In *BP* v. *Libya* Lagergren was unable to find that there existed principles of the law of Libya common to principles of international law pursuant to which the BP concession was still valid and subsisting and the remedy of *restitutio in integrum* available to the claimant.[13] He reached this conclusion on the basis that he could not come to any certain conclusion as to the position of Libyan law on the material available, but he nevertheless proceeded to consider international law in some detail before going on to apply general principles of law. In *Topco* Dupuy found that there were principles common to Libyan and international law on the question of remedies,[14] and that these required *restitutio in integrum* in this case. In *Liamco* Mahmassani found that although Libyan and international law agreed on the impossibility of *restitutio in integrum* in the circumstances of the case, there were not any common principles on the assessment of compensation so that on this question it was necessary to apply general principles of law.[15] In *Aminoil* Article III of the arbitration agreement provided:

> The law governing the substantive issues between the Parties shall be determined by the Tribunal, having regard to the quality of the parties, the transnational character of their relations and the principles of law and practice prevailing in the modern world.

The tribunal said that the determination of the applicable law had not caused them any difficulty; but they did not make any clear statement as to what this should be. They said that it could hardly be contested that the law of Kuwait applies to many matters over which it is the law most directly involved but that 'this conclusion does not carry any all-embracing consequences with it' because established public international law is necessarily a part of the law of Kuwait, and in their turn the general principles of international law are part of public international law. Article III brings out the wealth and fertility of the set of legal rules that the tribunal is called upon to apply. The tribunal concluded that 'the different sources of the law thus to be applied are not—at least in the present case—in contradiction with one another'.[16] When the arbitrators came to consider the question of indemnification they found that it was principally international law that should be applied.[17]

To summarize, in their decisions on remedies the arbitrator in *BP* applied general principles of law to the questions both of restitution and of compensation, in *Topco* the question of remedies was governed by Libyan law and international law, in *Liamco* the question of the availability of restitution was governed by Libyan and international law but that of compensation was dealt with in accordance with general principles of law, and in *Aminoil* the applicable law on indemnification was international law.

This question of the governing law of state contracts remains controversial, for writers are divided on the question of the relationship between public international law and general principles of law in this context.[18] Some argue that general principles of law are capable of constituting a separate legal system,[19] while others deny this and insist that a reference to general principles of law can be no more than a reference to public international law designed to import the latter as the governing law.[20] These arguments are generally conducted in terms of principle, especially by those saying that general principles can be a source but not a system of law and, forty years from the start of this particular controversy, there is no sign of its resolution, although it may be overtaken by events.[21]

But these arguments and the different choices of law by arbitrators do raise a potentially important question mentioned briefly in Chapter 1: whether or not general principles of law are capable of constituting a separate legal system, what difference, if any, does it make to the results of an arbitration whether the arbitrator applies public international law or general principles of law to the question of remedies? What is the relation between decisions based on public international law and those based on general principles? Because, although general principles of law are part of public international law, in theory there is a possibility of conflict between the two on the question of remedies. In practice the diversity of the case-law of international arbitral and judicial tribunals on judicial remedies on the one hand and on the other the inherent flexibility of general principles and the lack of rigour in the approach of tribunals to these[22] mean that the possibility of consistent results from either source and hence of conflict between the two must be remote.

The small number of cases between states and foreign enterprises where general principles of law are applied does not provide clear answers to these questions nor indeed to the question whether general principles of law or international jurisprudence is a better source of rules on remedies for tribunals. Nor is the basic question of the relation between the two discussed by the tribunals.

What is clear from the early cases on state contracts is that in those cases governed by general principles of law the only authorities referred to by the arbitrators, apart from one brief reference in *Sapphire* v. *NIOC*,[23] are those of municipal law. In contrast the *Aramco* case, decided in part on the basis of public international law, contains no references to municipal law. On the question of his power to issue a declaratory judgment the arbitrator relied on international law textbooks and rulings of the Permanent Court of International Justice and its successor.

Of the more recent cases two involve recourse to general principles, *BP* v. *Libya* and *Liamco* v. *Libya*. But here the choice of law clause expressly provided that the tribunal should apply 'the general principles of law including such of those principles as may have been applied by international tribunals'. This apparently combines municipal law principles with the jurisprudence of international tribunals and requires the arbitrator to consider both. But there is some ambiguity here. One of the fundamental problems with general principles of law is the lack of any agreement as to their source or nature; there is no agreement whether they are exclusively principles of municipal law or whether they include principles of international law. Thus here it is unclear whether the reference to 'such of those principles as may have been applied by international tribunals' means only those decisions which mention general principles of municipal law or whether it covers any general rules that may be derived from international jurisprudence. And if the latter is the better interpretation, then how are the two to be combined?

These questions were raised in *BP* v. *Libya* when the tribunal turned to general principles in order to decide whether *restitutio in integrum* was available.[24] The claimant argued that 'general principles of law, including such of those principles as may have been applied by international tribunals' includes a reference to public international law. But the arbitrator did not decide this question. He said only that if the claimant's argument were correct then under public international law *restitutio in integrum* would not be available. He then made the opposite assumption: he said that it was arguable that the choice of law clause meant only principles of municipal law and on this assumption he examined various systems of municipal law and concluded that they produced disparate results. He did not decide between the two arguments. In *Liamco* the arbitrator did not discuss this question when he applied general principles on the assessment of compensation.[25] He simply stated that 'One of these general principles of law is Equity, which is commonly and unanimously recognized as a supplementary source of law in Libyan law, Islamic law and international law', and went on to assess equitable compensation. This clearly supports an interpretation of the choice of law clause that covers international law, but it is not clear whether such an interpretation would be justified if the choice of law clause referred simply to 'general principles of law' without mention of international tribunals.

(*b*) *Available remedies*

Thus on the questions of the source and nature of general principles of law, of their relation to public international law, in particular on the question of remedies, there is little illumination in the arbitrations on state contracts. As regards the content of general principles on the question of remedies, some interesting points arise from the cases, but the material is limited. For most of the cases on state contracts, even including those where there was no express decision by the tribunal on the applicable law but only passing references to general principles, have led to declaratory judgments,[26] usually not going beyond interpretations of the parties' obligations under the contract.[27] Few awards of damages were made.[28] There is no unequivocal example of an order for specific performance or *restitutio in integrum*. Even in the *Greek Telephone Company* case[29] (where the arbitrator made no express choice of law but referred in his decision to Greek and French law, 'general rules', and 'general principles') the government was given the choice between specific performance and compensation. The contribution of these decisions based on general principles of law to the question of remedies will be discussed and compared with that of the cases based on public international law later in this section.

For in *Liamco* v. *Libya* and *BP v. Libya*, although the actual decision on the particular remedy appropriate was made on the basis of general principles, the awards include extensive discussion of remedies in public international law. These cases and *Topco* v. *Libya* provide a marked contrast to earlier interstate arbitration in their detailed discussion of previous jurisprudence,[30] though they differ on the significance to be attributed to it. Part of the explanation for this may be that the arbitrators were anxious to sell their decisions to the defendant government and so to make the awards as persuasive as possible. For in all these arbitrations Libya refused to appear and put its case before the tribunal. It is interesting that in *Aminoil* v. *Kuwait*, where the defendant government participated fully in the proceedings, there are noticeably fewer references to earlier cases, and none on the question of the assessment of compensation.

But all these references to authority are far from producing agreement on the question of remedies. Although the cases concern very similar facts the decisions are not consistent; there are striking conflicts between the arbitrators' conclusions. As was described above it was the arbitrators' conflicting interpretations of Libyan and international law that resulted in their different determinations of the applicable law. In *Topco* the arbitrator held that Libyan and international law agreed that *restitutio in integrum* was the proper remedy; in *BP* it was found that Libyan law and international law did not have common principles on the availability of restitution; finally, in *Liamco* the arbitrator said Libyan and international law agreed that *restitutio in integrum* was not a proper remedy.

These differences highlight dramatically the uncertainties of international law on remedies. And in these cases the difficulties in arriving at uniform rules are compounded by the fact that the subject matter is expropriation. For the differences between writers and between states on this question are notorious and apparently irreconcilable; and these differences on substance directly influence decisions on appropriate remedies. Here, as elsewhere, questions of substantive law cannot be clearly separated from questions of remedies. Whether *restitutio in integrum* and specific performance are available remedies depends on the arbitrator's view on the relation between the rule *pacta sunt servanda* and the right of permanent sovereignty over natural resources. If the former prevails, as in *Topco*, restitution and specific performance may be ordered; if the latter, as in *Liamco*, the only remedy can be compensation.

In their examination of these interrelated questions most of the arbitrators do not look solely to prior arbitral and judicial practice but also to state practice for guidance. Unusually in comparison with earlier tribunals, when considering the question of remedies—on the question of the appropriate remedy and the standard of compensation—the arbitrators examine general state practice on expropriation. Thus in *BP* the arbitrator used state practice to support his conclusion that restitution would not be a suitable remedy, and in *Liamco* and *Aminoil* state practice on the question of methods and standards of compensation was considered. *Topco* is the partial exception: on the question of the right to nationalize the arbitrator did refer to state practice, but when it came to remedies he decided that *restitutio in integrum* was the proper remedy solely on the basis of the decisions of tribunals, states' claims to tribunals, and the views of writers.[31] Even on this basis his decision is open to criticism,[32] and his failure to consider state practice on remedies is serious in the light of the widely held conviction that the comparatively early tribunal decisions on expropriation are some way from modern state practice.

It is obvious that there is fundamental disagreement on the remedies available for expropriation, and on whether *restitutio in integrum* and specific performance are the primary remedies or possible remedies, and in what circumstances. This question of appropriate remedies depends in part on the prior question whether the expropriation is lawful or unlawful. Some of the problems in assessing the significance of the collection of decisions on state contracts arise not simply from their differences on the question of available remedies but from their approaches to this prior question of the legality of the expropriation. For in theory the lawfulness or otherwise of an expropriation could affect first the remedies available and second the standard of compensation.[33] As far as the former is concerned, it can be only for illegal takings that restitution and/or specific performance are possible remedies. In *BP* and *Topco* the taking was expressly held to be illegal, in *Aminoil* the taking was legal,[34] but in *Liamco* this issue was apparently deliberately left unresolved by the arbitrator. Liamco's claim that the taking was unlawful and *restitutio in integrum* was therefore the proper remedy was rejected by the tribunal without any explicit pronouncement on the question of legality; the question whether compensation is a condition or merely a consequence of a lawful taking was not decided. The arbitrator never expressly chose between the two alternative bases for the assessment of compensation put forward by Liamco, he did not make it clear whether he was assessing compensation for an unlawful taking or merely for a failure to pay compensation for a lawful taking.[35]

What, then, do these cases have to say on the question which remedies are available to tribunals under international law? Restitution and specific performance will be considered first. As was described above, out of the earlier state contract cases only the *Greek Telephone Company* case (not unambiguously a decision based on general principles of law) involved an order for specific performance, and even here the defendant government was given the alternative of paying compensation. Technically, of course, the remedies of *restitutio in integrum* and specific performance are distinct but, in cases of breach of state contracts, complementary. But the arbitrators in *BP* and *Topco* tended to run the two together; they do not mention their separate functions. Thus in *BP* the arbitrator discussed the precedents for restitution in international law, and those for specific performance in Libyan law. His brief justification was that

> Generally speaking, however, it is probably true to say that the discussion about restitutio in integrum in public international law and that concerning specific performance in the field of the general principles of law, in fact have reference to the same problem.[36]

Again in *Topco* the claimant company asked that Libya should be held to perform the Deeds of Concession and fulfil their terms. The arbitrator considered both restitution and specific performance in Libyan law as if they were interchangeable, in international law he mentioned only *restitutio in integrum*. He concluded that *restitutio in integrum* was available and made an order in the terms requested by *Topco*, an order resembling specific performance rather than *restitutio in integrum*.

More serious than this running together of specific performance and *restitutio in integrum*, the arbitrators in *BP* and *Topco* confuse these remedies with declaratory judgments. They do this because they fail, or choose not, to distinguish the question of the continued existence of the contract after its breach by Libya from the question of the remedies to be awarded.

In *BP* the claimant company had asked the Court to make eight declarations as follows:

1. The Libyan Nationalization Law of 7 December 1971 and the subsequent implementation thereof were each a breach of the obligations of the Libyan Government owed to the Claimant under the Concession Agreement and so remain;
2. The said breaches were and are ineffective to terminate the Concession Agreement, which remains in law valid and subsisting;
3. The Claimant is entitled to elect, at any time so long as the Respondent's breach continues, to treat the Concession Agreement as at an end;
4. The Claimant is entitled to be restored to the full enjoyment of its rights under the Concession Agreement;
5. The Claimant is the owner of its share of any crude oil extracted from the area of the Concession Agreement after as well as before 7 December 1971 and of all installations and other physical assets, and the Libyan Government has no right to any such oil, installations or physical assets, which it can enjoy or transfer to any third party;
6. Performance of the Claimant's obligations under the Concession Agreement is suspended for so long as the Libyan Government remains in breach thereof; and
7. The Claimant is entitled to damages in respect of the interference by the Libyan Government with the Claimant's enjoyment of its rights under the Concession Agreement. If the Claimant does not exercise its rights under Declaration (3) above, then it is entitled to damages accruing up to the date of the final award herein. If the Claimant does exercise the rights under Declaration (3) above, it is entitled to all damages arising from the wrongful act of the Libyan Government.
8. The Claimant further respectfully requests the Sole Arbitrator to reserve for a subsequent stage of the proceedings the assessment of the damages due under Declaration (7) above.

That is, BP had requested purely declaratory relief. It is true that these declarations would have made it quite clear what behaviour was required from the Libyan Government; although the award that was sought was not in form an order for specific performance or *restitutio in integrum*, in substance the requested declaratory judgment was similar to these remedies. This substantial similarity does not, however, justify the interpretation by the arbitrator of the claimant's request. He said,

It may be argued that the Claimant does not in fact ask for an order of restitutio in integrum but merely for a declaratory statement as to its legal position under the BP concession and with respect to certain property and that the issue of whether restitution in kind is an available remedy therefore is not presented. Such a distinction . . . may be relevant for a proper understanding of the decisions of international tribunals . . . The tribunal holds, however, that no such distinction should be made. If it is found that the Claimant is entitled to be restored to the full enjoyment of its rights under the BP Concession, and is the owner of the oil and the assets referred to, then the Claimant is entitled to an order for specific performance or, alternatively, a declaratory award of entitlement to specific performance.[37]

The arbitrator went on to treat the two separate questions of the continued existence of the concession and the remedies available as one question; he made his answer to the former question of the continuation of the concession depend not on rules concerning the consequences of a breach of a concession but rather on the availability of the remedies of specific performance and *restitutio in integrum*.

Having refused to allow the distinction between a declaratory judgment and an order by a tribunal in his interpretation of the claimant's application, the arbitrator then relied on this distinction in his examination of international arbitral practice to help him reach his conclusion that specific performance and *restitutio in integrum* were not remedies of public international law available at the option of the party suffering a wrongful breach by a co-contracting party. Because these remedies were not available he held that he could not declare that the BP concession continued in force. This confusion first of declaratory judgments with specific performance and *restitutio in integrum*, and second of the continued existence of a contract with the question of the availability of specific performance and *restitutio in integrum*, has been strongly criticized by writers and led BP to appeal for the reopening of the arbitration on the ground of the partial invalidity of the award.[38] There are also signs in *Liamco* of a similar, though less serious, running together of declaratory judgments, specific performance, and *restitutio in integrum*. Liamco in addition to its request for an order by the tribunal that Libya should perform its obligations under the contract also asked for a declaration that Libya's nationalization was unlawful and not entitled to international recognition, and that Libya did not have title to oil extracted from Liamco's concessions. The arbitrator refused to make this declaration for the same reason that he had refused to order restitution, that it was not consistent with state sovereignty and the right to nationalize. But he did not stop with that unexceptionable statement; he went on to say that the arguments in favour of making the declaration were 'faced with the same practical impossibility of enforcement as that of the remedy of restitutio in integrum . . . Any Declaratory Award as requested would be practically unenforceable.'[39] Here again the arbitrator ran together both the question of the consequences of Libya's actions and that of remedies, and also the remedies of *restitutio in integrum* and the declaratory judgment.

This confusion of remedies, perhaps not surprising in view of the unsystematic development of this subject by earlier tribunals, is nevertheless disappointing in these cases with their more than usually extended discussions of remedies in international law. It provides another, particularly striking instance of the generally desultory and unmethodical approach to the question of remedies.

(c) *Restitutio in integrum and Specific Performance*

In *Topco* alone was an award of *restitutio in integrum* made; the arbitrator found that this was the primary remedy in international law. He did so on the basis of a brief survey of earlier judicial and arbitral decisions. He took the wide view of the significance of the *Chorzów Factory* case,[40] mentioned *El Salvador* v. *Nicaragua*,[41] and also invoked the extremely doubtful cases of *Martini*,[42] *Mavrommatis (Jerusalem) Concessions*,[43] and the *Temple of Preah Vihear*.[44] Otherwise he relied only on claims by states and writings of publicists. This limited and partial survey of authority is much less convincing than the more detailed and rigorous survey by the arbitrator in *BP* v. *Libya*. The latter started by stressing that his inquiry would be limited to the general field of economic interests and especially to long-term contracts of a commercial or industrial character and property and other assets employed in industrial undertakings. For, as he pointed out, the relevant issues may be fundamentally different in other contexts such as disputes concerning sovereignty over territory.[45] And unlike the arbitrator in *Topco* he examined current state practice and not just the decisions of tribunals. On the latter he disagreed with the reasoning in *Topco* on the central question of the significance of the *Chorzów Factory* case: he regarded the Permanent Court's pronouncement on *restitutio in integrum* as *obiter*, and the case as one where express provision had been made for this remedy in a treaty. He went on to reject the *Martini* case as an example of *restitutio in integrum*. He gave separate consideration to those cases where express provision was made for *restitutio in integrum*, and to cases on state contracts, and to claims by states. His conclusion was:

> The survey of cases and other relevant materials presented above demonstrates that there is no explicit support for the proposition that specific performance, and even less so restitutio in integrum, are remedies of public international law available at the option of a party suffering a wrongful breach by a co-contracting party.[46]

He then turned to general principles of law since he had not been able to find principles of the law of Libya common to principles of international law pursuant to which the BP concession was still valid and the remedy of *restitutio in integrum* available to the claimant. Nor did general principles of law support the claim for *restitutio in integrum*. Not only was there a clear difference of approach between Anglo-American law and German law, but, more important, the principles even of those systems of law which recognize the most far-reaching rights for an innocent party to demand specific performance, are principles of ordinary commercial law. It is probably not desirable that these principles should be stretched to apply to long-term concessions like that of BP. Also 'the fact that the State is the respondent party is one which cannot be overlooked': remedies of specific performance and restitution in kind normally are unavailable against governmental authorities under public contracts. His final conclusion was that 'the principal remedy under public international law in regard to matters of essentially economic significance is damages'.

Even in *Topco* the arbitrator had accepted that *restitutio in integrum* should not be awarded where there was an absolute impossibility of envisaging specific performance, or when an irreversible situation had been created. It did not seem to him on the facts of the case that that was so here. He accordingly ordered the Libyan Government to perform its contracts and, as directed by the arbitration agreement, set a time limit for the implementation of his decision. However, he apparently understood that this left the defendant government with a choice—either to carry out the decision within the time limit or to pay as damages the monetary equivalent of specific performance.[47] This is merely implicit in the final declarations made by the tribunal where the arbitrator reserved the question of further proceedings if the award were not to be implemented within the time limit.

The arbitrator in *Liamco* adopted as his starting-point a similar position to that taken in *Topco*—that under Libyan law and international law obligations were to be performed in kind where that was possible.[48] But his reasoning and conclusions are a long way from those of *Topco*. From this starting-point he went on to say that in international law, *restitutio in integrum* was conditioned by the possibility of performance, and consequently hindered by its impossibility. 'Such impossibility is in fact most usual in the international field.' He invoked various arguments against the award of *restitutio in integrum*: that it is an intolerable interference in internal sovereignty, that it militates against the respect due for the sovereignty of the nationalizing state, that there is no sufficient authority for the fact (*sic*) that nationalization in breach of a concession is an internationally unlawful act for which the remedy is restitution, and that it presupposes the cancellation of the nationalization measures at issue, and such cancellation also violates the sovereignty of the nationalizing state. For these reasons, he said, Liamco had admitted implicitly the impossibility of restitution in kind, and requested the tribunal to award remedies in lieu of restoration to its rights in Libya.

Thus although the starting-point in *Liamco* resembles the conclusion in *Topco* that *restitutio in integrum* is the primary remedy in international law, in *Liamco* this looks like lip-service. The arbitrator had failed unequivocally to decide the prior question of the legality of the nationalization and there is little indication that he regarded *restitutio in integrum* as a real option. His repeated insistence on the impossibility of *restitutio in integrum* in cases of nationalization is very different from the attitude in *Topco* and leads to an end result close to that in *BP*, that *restitutio in integrum* is not available for nationalization. So only in *Topco* does the arbitrator award the order for performance of the contract requested by the claimant, and even here the possibility of an award of damages in lieu is left open. On the basis of these cases, and bearing in mind the failure of the arbitrator in *Topco* to refer to state practice on *restitutio in integrum* in the area of state contracts, it now seems in practical terms unconvincing to assert that *restitutio in integrum* is the primary remedy in cases of nationalization, and extremely doubtful that it is even an available remedy.

(*d*) *Declaratory Judgments*

As was described above, the arbitrators in *BP* and *Liamco* treated the claimants' requests for declaratory judgments on the effects of the expropriations as essentially requests for *restitutio in integrum* and accordingly rejected those requests for the same reasons that they refused *restitutio in integrum*. But in *BP* the arbitrator did make the declarations requested by the claimant that the Libyan Nationalization Law and its implementation were a breach of the obligations of the respondent and that the claimant was entitled to damages arising from the wrongful act of the respondent. The arbitrator clearly envisaged the continuation of the proceedings in order to determine the amount of damages. But to some extent this declaratory judgment finding a breach of international law and an obligation to pay damages itself provided a remedy for the claimant for the breach of international law suffered by it.

Aramco v. *Saudi Arabia*[49] is a similar case. Here the tribunal discussed its power to give a purely declaratory judgment on the question, among others, 'Is Article 4 of the agreement between the Government and Mr A. S. Onassis . . . in conflict with the Aramco Concession Agreement?' This request goes beyond those made in the cases on state contracts governed by the general principles of law;[50] it does not simply ask for an interpretation of the contract but comes near to requesting a declaration that there has been a breach, if not of international law, then of an internationalized contract. The tribunal looked to international authorities for guidance, found that it had the power to make such an award, and gave the declaration requested. This type of declaration (and to a lesser extent that in *BP*) makes clear to the parties their respective rights and obligations but nevertheless remains distinct from *restitutio in integrum*, and their identification by the arbitrator in *BP* is unfortunate.

(*e*) *Damages*

In *BP* the arbitrator merely declared that there was an obligation on the respondent to pay damages; he postponed their actual assessment. In

Liamco and *Aminoil*, and earlier in *Lena Goldfields* and *Sapphire*, damages were awarded. There are some interesting similarities between the decisions and indications of the path of future development but there is little by way of consistent or clear guidance on actual methods of assessment.

In the *Lena Goldfields Arbitration*,[51] which was governed by the general principles of law, the tribunal chose to assess the loss of the claimant company on the basis of the unjust enrichment of the respondent. But the significance of this as a precedent is somewhat diminished by the fact that the tribunal itself said that this method produced the same result as the assessment of damages according to ordinary legal principles; it is not clear whether it would have been equally acceptable if this had not been so. The method is controversial in international law and is not widely accepted as a general principle. Its application was rejected by the arbitrator in *Liamco*.[52] In *Sapphire International Petroleum* v. *NIOC*,[53] another case governed by 'the principles of law generally recognized by civilized nations', the arbitrator was expressly given the power to award damages by the arbitration agreement. His starting-point was that

> According to the generally held view the object of damages is to place the party to whom they are awarded in the same pecuniary position that they would have been in if the contract had been performed in the manner provided for by the parties at the time of its conclusion.

He referred to French legislation and writers and Anglo-American textbooks to support the award of both *damnum emergens* and *lucrum cessans*. As regards the former the assessment was straightforward.[54] The assessment of damages for lost profits, however, caused some difficulty for the claimant could not show the exact extent of this loss but only that it had suffered the loss of an opportunity. Again the arbitrator referred to French and Anglo-American law to justify in principle the award of compensation for loss of an opportunity. Because the amount could not be established exactly an award was made *ex aequo et bono* to cover lost profits.

Both *Lena Goldfields* and *Sapphire* were clearly awards of damages for unlawful takings. *Topco* and *BP* were also cases of unlawful takings but they both postponed any assessment of damages and did not discuss standards of compensation or methods of assessment.[55] In *Aminoil* and *Liamco* damages were actually awarded. The general significance, however, of these two cases is problematical. For in *Aminoil* the compensation was for a lawful taking and in *Liamco* the question of the legality of the taking was left open. It is far from certain whether the reasoning and methods of assessment of these awards could apply to cases of unlawful takings, or only to cases of lawful takings, or whether the same rules could apply to both. Traditionally the *Chorzów Factory* case[56] has been cited as authority for the proposition that there is a distinction between the methods of assessing compensation for lawful and unlawful takings. But the exact content of this distinction was not made clear in the *Chorzów Factory* case, nor have writers been able to illuminate its significance.[57] In *Liamco* the distinction is almost totally obscured. The arbitrator examined the authorities both on unlawful and on lawful takings. He pointed out the difficulties with both but did not himself make it clear if he was following either line of authority or if any distinction between the two approaches survived. And in *Aminoil* compensation was assessed for what was said to be a lawful taking. It is not clear from the award whether its general approach and methods of assessment should be restricted to lawful takings or whether they are intended to have a wider application. In this regard it is interesting that Fitzmaurice in his Separate Opinion[58] disagreed with the award's holding that the taking was lawful but nevertheless was prepared to accept the operative part of the award on the assessment of compensation. For him any theoretical difference in the standard of compensation or the method of assessment between lawful and unlawful takings was not significant. These cases, and the recent decision of the Iran–US Claims Tribunal in *American International Group Inc.* v. *Iran*[59] leave unclear whether any distinction as to the amount of compensation is to be made between lawful and unlawful takings. Their general significance is therefore indeterminate, the more so because in both *Liamco* and *Aminoil* the assessment of compensation was calculated very much on the basis of the particular facts and relationships of the case.

In both the discussion of the assessment of compensation is lengthy. In *Liamco* most of this is taken up by an examination of arbitral precedents and state practice, whereas in *Aminoil* the discussion centres more directly on methods of assessment. But in both the actual method of assessment employed is obscure, and the relation of the reasoning to the particular figures arrived at is for the most part not clear so that any guidance to be derived from these cases must come from the general statements of the arbitrators. For in *Liamco* the arbitrator's consideration of arbitral and state practice leads him to the conclusion that international law is unsettled. When he turns to general principles of law he simply says that it is reasonable and just to adopt the formula of equitable compensation and goes on to make lump sum awards without explanation of the amounts. In *Aminoil* the tribunal does discuss the question of the method of assessment to be adopted, but the nature of the method chosen makes its application to particular facts unpredictable. The tribunal, after a discussion of developments in the field of expropriation inside and outside the United Nations, abandons the search for a single standard or method of calculating compensation, a chimera that has been obsessively pursued by many scholars. It says, 'The determination of the amount of an award of "appropriate" compensation is better carried out by means of an enquiry into all the circumstances relevant to the particular concrete case, than through abstract theoretical discussion.'[60] Here the fact that Kuwait welcomes foreign investment is crucial; it means that there is no room for rules of compensation that would make nonsense of foreign investment. For central to the tribunal's approach to indemnification is the notion of the legitimate expectations of the parties. These expectations arise from their particular relationship; in every long-term contract economic calculations, the weighing up of rights and obligations, of chances and risks, constitute the contractual equilibrium. Clearly the assessment of compensation on such a basis as the legitimate expectations arising from the contractual equilibrium will be a flexible process; such a process of calculation cannot be precise or predictable.

Although in both cases the assessment of *damnum emergens*, of compensation for the loss of the claimant company's plant, was relatively straightforward,[61] on the question of lost profits there was little certainty even on issues of principle, let alone on the actual methods of assessment. In *Liamco* the claimant put forward alternative claims, one on the basis that the taking was lawful, the other on the basis that it was unlawful. It argued that on either basis compensation for lost profits was due and that

> The key to the computation of money damages to which it is entitled should be the reliance on the size of the concession reserves, and then the calculation of such damages by finding the profits which would have been realised by the extraction and sale of these reserves from the effective date of expropriation over the life of the concession.[62]

But the arbitrator found that the international law on compensation for lost profits was uncertain. Although there were cases on wrongful nationalization where lost profits had been compensated the arbitrator remarked that these precedents were already old and had been given before the recent evolution of the concept of the right of nationalization. And as for lawful takings the arbitrator challenged the claimant's argument made on the basis that there were precedents for the compensation of lost profits and that elements to cover this head were included in lump sum settlements. He said that international legal theory and practice were not in agreement on one general uniform rule in this respect and invoked notorious instances of partial compensation. Because the question of lost profits was controversial in international law he turned to general principles of law, and based his award on the general principle of equitable compensation.

Even if the discussion in *Aminoil* may be taken to be of some general significance in international law and not just limited to the particular facts or to lawful takings, there is little here to clarify the position on lost profits.

Aminoil had proposed two possible methods for the assessment of its loss: first it claimed the total of the anticipated profits to the natural termination of the concession, discounted at an annual rate of interest and minus those assets that were to revert to the government on termination. Alternatively it claimed the total of the anticipated profits counted and discounted over a limited period but taking countervailing account of the value of its assets. The tribunal said that both these methods were acceptable in principle, preferably taken in combination. Thus it appeared to accept in principle that in this case compensation for lost profits was payable. It went on to criticize some of the assumptions underlying Aminoil's claims: the assessment of future losses should not be made only on the basis of the relationship between the parties as it was in 1961, and the claimant's projections of the future of the petroleum industries were not acceptable. For the parties in their relations and negotiations had not worked on these but on a different conception, that of the reasonable rate of return. And it was to be on this basis of the reasonable rate of return that the tribunal was to make its assessment.[63] This finding and the later decision by the tribunal to make separate appraisals of the value on the one hand of the undertaking itself as a source of profit, and on the other of the totality of the assets[64] apparently reflect a willingness to compensate for lost profits. But, as with *Liamco*, when it comes to the actual calculation the method of assessment is not clear, even to the extent that Mann argues that, despite the earlier passages in its reasoning, no compensation for lost profits is given.[65] In the absence of express explanation by the tribunal it is not possible to say whether he is right or not, whether the award covers lost profits and in what measure. For in its section headed 'The Figures' the tribunal to a large extent simply accepts the Joint Report of the experts of the parties on questions of quantum. Where there are differences between the accounting firms the tribunal has taken the mean of the two totals indicated.[66] When the tribunal considered the amounts due to Aminoil, first for the various components of the undertaking separately considered, and secondly for the undertaking itself as a going concern, it simply accepted the Joint Report as furnishing acceptable indications concerning the assets other than fixed assets. For fixed assets it took the depreciated replacement value and rejected net book value as inappropriate.[67] It did not specify the amount to be awarded under these two heads. There is no explanation of the calculation by which it arrived at its award. All the tribunal says is,

> In consequence, taking that basis [sc. depreciated replacement value] for the fixed assets, taking the order of value indicated in the Joint Report for the non-fixed assets, and taking into account the legitimate expectations of the concessionaire, the Tribunal comes to the conclusion that at the date of 19 September, 1977, a sum estimated at $206,041,000 represented the reasonably appraised value of what constituted the object of the takeover.[68]

The process by which this figure was arrived at is impenetrable.

In both cases the tribunal refused to meet the companies' claims in full, in both cases the tribunal also rejected the respondent governments' arguments (made before the tribunal in *Aminoil*, in public statements in *Liamco*) that the appropriate measure of compensation was net book value. In *Liamco* the arbitrator briefly dismissed the opposing claims of the government and the company as 'irreconcilable, unacceptable extremes'.[69] In *Aminoil* the tribunal devoted more attention to the arguments for net book value but dismissed them as supported neither by practice nor by *opinio juris*.[70] This agreement between the two decisions is significant. It seems that net book value is not established in international law as the appropriate standard of compensation even in cases of lawful expropriation.

But if we look to these decisions for positive rather than negative guidance on the assessment of compensation and in particular on the question of lost profits, basic issues of principle are left unresolved. In *Liamco* the arbitrator found that international law is unsettled on the question of compensation for lost profits in cases of expropriation. When he turned to general principles of law he apparently accepted that the principle of equitable compensation did allow such compensation, at any rate when the loss was direct and certain,[71] but he did not discuss the extent of this compensation or the method of its assessment. And in *Aminoil*, as we have seen, the tribunal in its reasoning ostensibly conceded the possibility of compensation for lost profits but in its actual assessment did not make clear the amount, if any, to be allowed under this head in its assessment of the undertaking as a going concern. Thus on the basic issues whether there is a distinction between lawful and unlawful takings so far as compensation is concerned, the extent of compensation for lost profits and the method of assessing this, these decisions reflect the wider uncertainty. It seems that these tribunals have chosen, probably wisely, not to attempt to legislate on these questions. In both the result is a compromise between the position of the claimant and that of the government concerned. The tribunals seem concerned to produce an acceptable result rather than to settle definitively the applicable rules of law.[72] This is particularly marked in *Aminoil* and in this case alone out of the recent oil arbitrations the respondent government did comply with the tribunal's award. All this means that in these cases, like those of the Iran–United States Claims Tribunal, the role of law in the decision making of the tribunal is open to question. Whether the award was made on the basis of the general principle of unjust enrichment as in *Lena Goldfields*, or of equitable compensation as in *Liamco*, or *ex aequo et bono* as in *Sapphire*, or on the basis of the legitimate expectations of the parties as in *Aminoil*, the tribunals were not concerned to make clear their process of assessment. And writers are divided as to whether *Liamco* and, especially, *Aminoil* represent a promising way forward for the future or a regrettable aberration. For some they are to be welcomed for their abandonment of the unworkable *restitutio in integrum*, for their pragmatic approach to the question of compensation, and for their willingness to base their assessment on the particular relationship of the parties rather than vainly search for general rules.[73] For others they are deplored as an abandonment of law and legal rules.[74]

NOTES

1. *BP* v. *Libya* 53 ILR 297; *Topco* v. *Libya* 53 ILR 389; *Liamco* v. *Libya* (1981) ILM 1; *Aminoil* v. *Kuwait* (1982) ILM 976; *AGIP* v. *Congo* (1982) ILM 726; *Benvenuti and Bonfant* v. *Congo* (1982) ILM 740; *Amco Asia Cpn* v. *Indonesia* (1985) ILM 1022. See discussion by P. B. Gann (1985) 23 *Col. JTL* 615; G. Delaume (1981) *AJ* 784; R. B. von Mehren and P. N. Kourides (1981) *AJ* 476; P. Rambaud (1980) *AFDI* 274; A. Varma (1979–80) *Col. JTL* 259; A. A. Fatouros (1980) *AJ* 134; R. C. A. White (1981) *ICLQ* 1; C. Greenwood (1982) *BYBIL* 27; P.-Y. Tschanz (1984) *Int. Lawyer* 245; F. A. Mann (1983) *BYBIL* 213.
2. See G. Delaume, op. cit. in n. 1.
3. Loc. cit. in n. 1.
4. (1929–30) 5 AD 3, 426.
5. 18 ILR 144.
6. 35 ILR 136.
7. 27 ILR 117.
8. For a list of other arbitration decisions on state contracts see *BP* v. *Libya*, at 343; and J. G. Wetter and S. M. Schwebel (1964) *BYBIL* 183. Certain of these cases (*Alsing* v. *Greece*, *Petroleum Development* v. *Qatar*, *Qatar* v. *International Marine Oil Co.*, and perhaps also the *Greek Telephone Co.* case) are also sometimes said to be governed by the general principles of law but their status is rather less clear than that of those referred to above.
9. Established under the Convention on the Settlement of Investment Disputes between States and Nationals of Other States (1965) ILM 524. On its establishment, jurisdiction, and functioning see the ICSID annual reports. Also J. K. Ryans and J. C. Baker (1976) *J World TL* 65.
10. Loc. cit. in n. 1. Strictly *Amco Asia Cpn* v. *Indonesia* is a case involving not a state contract but a 'sui generis legal relationship comparable to a contract'.
11. The tribunal referred to the *Chorzów Factory* case, *Lena Goldfields*, *Shufeldt*, *Sapphire*, *Norwegian Shipowners* claims and the *Lighthouses* arbitration (1985) ILM 1037.
12. 'Based on a reasonable projection of the foreseeable net cash flow during the period to be considered, said net cash flow being then discounted in order to take into account the assessment of the damages at the date of the prejudice, while in the normal course of events, the cash flow would have been spread on the whole period of operation of the business.' (1985) ILM 1037.
13. 53 ILR 297, at 348.

14. 53 ILR 389, at 507.
15. (1981) ILM p. 1, at 76.
16. (1982) ILM p. 976, at 1000.
17. Ibid., at 1032.
18. See, for example, R. Y. Jennings (1961) *BYBIL* 156; J. D. M. Lew, *Applicable Law in International Commercial Arbitration* (1978).
19. For example, A. McNair (1957) *BYBIL* 1; P. C. Jessup, *Transnational Law* (1956); H. Pazarci (1975) *RGDIP* 354.
20. The most forceful proponent of this argument is F. A. Mann (1944) *BYBIL* 11, (1959) *BYBIL* 34; (1960) *AJ* 572; and (1975) *Rev. belge DI* 562.
21. See n. 2.
22. On the unsystematic approach of tribunals to general principles see, for example, F. A. Mann (1957) *BYBIL* 20, R. B. Schlesinger (1957) *AJ* 734.
23. 35 ILR 136, at 185 there is a reference to the practice of international arbitral tribunals as discussed by A. Hauriou (1924) *RGDIP* 203 on the award of damages for lost profits. In the event the tribunal assessed lost profits *ex aequo et bono*.
24. p. 348.
25. p. 507. The arbitrator had also referred to general principles earlier when analysing the choice of law clause. At 37 he says, 'These general principles are usually embodied in most recognized legal systems, and particularly in Libyan legislation, including its modern codes and Islamic law. They are applied by municipal courts and are mainly referred to in international and arbitral case-law. They, thus, form a compendium of legal precepts and maxims, universally accepted in theory and practice.'
26. As in *Ruler of Qatar* v. *International Marine Oil Co. Ltd* (20 ILR 534); *Petroleum Development* v. *Abu Dhabi* (loc. cit. in n. 5); *Aramco* v. *Saudi Arabia* (loc. cit. in n. 7).
27. On *Aramco* see below at n. 49. The arbitrator in *BP* v. *Libya* referred to the *Greek Utility* cases (Wetter and Schwebel, op. cit. in n. 8) and the *Beyrouth Water* case ((1954) ICJ Pleadings, *Électricité de Beyrouth Company* case, 423) as establishing in extensive detail the precise rights and obligations of the parties in specific terms. Here again there is doubt as to the status in international law of these decisions.
28. Such awards were made in *Lena Goldfields* arbitration (loc. cit. in n. 4) and *Sapphire International Petroleum* v. *NIOC* (loc. cit. in n. 6).
29. Wetter and Schwebel, op. cit. in n. 8.
30. See Ch. 1 above.
31. In *Liamco* the arbitrator's rejection of *restitutio in integrum* as a possible remedy on the facts was rather cursory but was nevertheless justified in part on the ground of the prevalent international practice (1981 ILM 1, at 63).
32. See, for example, Varma, Fatouros, and Greenwood, op. cit. in n. 1.
33. See below at n. 57. See also above at Ch. 1, at n. 233, Ch. 2 Section 3, at n. 10, and Section 1 of this chapter at n. 13.
34. But see the Separate Opinion of Fitzmaurice at (1982) ILM 1043.
35. Certain writers have assumed that the taking was unlawful (Greenwood, op.

cit. in n. 1; von Mehren and Kourides, op. cit. ibid.) but it seems to me that the ambiguities of the award make such a conclusion unwarranted. See discussion by Rambaud, op. cit. in n. 1.

36. p. 351.
37. p. 330.
38. p. 358.
39. p. 65. See criticism by von Mehren and Kourides, op. cit. in n. 1.
40. PCIJ Ser. A no. 17.
41. (1917) AJ 674.
42. 2 RIAA 975. See discussion in Ch. 1, at n. 52.
43. PCIJ Ser. A no. 5. See discussion in Ch. 2 Section 1, at n. 34.
44. (1962) ICJ Reports 6. *Restitutio in integrum* was not requested in this case.
45. For this reason he found that the *Temple of Preah Vihear* case was not relevant to the case before him.
46. p. 347.
47. p. 509.
48. p. 63.
49. Loc. cit. in n. 7.
50. But see n. 27.
51. Loc. cit. in n. 4.
52. pp. 80–1. The arbitrator said that in favour of the unjust enrichment evaluation was the fact that it was realistic as it represented the actual profit that had been or would be realized by the respondent. 'Nevertheless, it is also undeniable that the bases of this evaluation constitute a discharge of contract, and a frustration of the intention of the contracting parties. Moreover they do not take into consideration the great initial expenses and risks taken by LIAMCO in their pioneer works and subsequent activities.'
53. Loc. cit. in n. 6.
54. The arbitrator allowed compensation for expenses incurred in the performance of the contract but refused it for expenses incurred in making the contract, since positive and negative damages should not be combined. As to the amount, he accepted the accounts of the claimant's experts.
55. See criticism by D. W. Bowett (1978) *CLJ* 5.
56. Loc. cit. in n. 40, at 46–7.
57. See, for example, G. M. White, *Nationalisation of Foreign Property* (1961); M. H. Mendelson (1985) *AJ* 414; A. A. Fatouros, *Government Guarantees to Foreign Investors* (1962), at 307; Bin Cheng (1959) *Transactions of the Grotius Society* 267.
58. Loc. cit. in n. 34.
59. 4 Iran–US CTR 96 (1984) ILM 1. See Section 1 of this chapter, at n. 35.
60. p. 1033.
61. In *Liamco* the loss of the physical plant and equipment was assessed on the basis of the market value at the time of the taking. The arbitrator accepted the claimant's evidence as to the amount. In *Aminoil* the fixed assets were compensated at the depreciated replacement value.
62. p. 78.

63. The tribunal stressed that it was necessary to allow for the fact that, when the concession was over, there was no need to provide a profit margin to provide for risks or continuing investment in that project.
64. On the method of valuing the physical assets the tribunal said that it was not possible to lay down any absolute rule. On the facts it said that the assets should be valued at the date of transfer taking account of depreciation and inflation. Net book value was not a suitable standard of compensation except in cases of recent investment where the original cost would not be far from the replacement cost. It was necessary to bear in mind both that for the state mineral resources were a non-renewable asset and should be regarded as capital and that for the company there was a need to reconstitute in real terms the capital value of its investment.
65. Op. cit. in n. 1.
66. It did this to settle the claims against *Aminoil*.
67. See n. 64 and 70.
68. p. 1042.
69. p. 75.
70. pp. 1035–7. Compare the initial acceptance and later rejection of this standard by the United States FCSC as described by R. B. Lillich (ed.), *The Valuation of Nationalized Property in International Law* (1972–5), at 95, 117.
71. He apparently allowed compensation for lost profits, though to an unspecified extent, for the Raguba field but rejected them for the Mabruk field as not certain and direct.
72. This can be seen also in their awards of interest. In *Liamco* this was decided on the basis of Libyan law and accordingly was awarded at the rate of 5 per cent per annum from the date of the award. In *Aminoil* the tribunal said only that in order to establish what was due in 1982 (the date of the award) 'Account must be taken both of a reasonable rate of interest, which could be put at 7.5%, and of a level of inflation which the Tribunal fixes at an overall rate of 10%—that is to say at a total annual increase of 17.5% in the amount due, over the amount due for the preceding year.' This combination of interest and inflation has been criticized as possible double recovery by D. W. Bowett (1983) 2 *HR* 169, at 202.
73. See, for example, Rambaud, op. cit. in n. 1; Tschanz, op. cit. ibid.
74. See, for example, Mann, op. cit. in n. 1.

6

Scope and Future Development of Judicial Remedies

THE question of the limits on what can be expected from and achieved by the use of judicial remedies in international law has not received much attention. Writers have confined themselves to discussions of the political restrictions on the use of judicial settlement of disputes in international law; even discussion of the future role of the International Court of Justice tends not to include any examination of the use of judicial remedies. However, any proposal to extend the use of judicial settlement to new areas, and any discussion of its present role, must take account of the limitations of judicial remedies. Because judicial remedies are almost invariably retrospective, limited in the extent to which they can modify the status quo, dependent on a finding of state responsibility and the product of a bilateral process, their role is necessarily restricted.

This is not the place for a full discussion of the inadequacy of the imposition of state responsibility as a means of dealing with problems such as polluting and ultra-hazardous activities. Because the existence or content of rules of customary international law in these areas is controversial, and because anyway detailed regulation is necessary, states have begun to make treaties to deal with these problems. On the whole these treaties do not rely on the imposition of state responsibility. For where co-operation in preventing injury is more important than any subsequent remedy, where there is injury to areas beyond national jurisdiction or to states' interests not clearly protected by international law, bilateral claims do not provide an economically efficient or effective response.[1] Writers have accordingly considered the possibility of a wider responsibility owed by states to the international community as a whole.[2]

Nor is this the place for a full discussion of the question of standing to request a judicial remedy in international law; one familiar type of proposal designed to increase the work and influence of the International Court of Justice is based on the extension of the right to bring contentious cases and request Advisory Opinions. But some of the suggestions that have been made for overcoming the limits on the role of state responsibility and recent developments in this area will now be considered in the light of their possible impact on judicial remedies.

(i) ACTIO POPULARIS AND JUDICIAL REMEDIES: STANDING IN THE WORLD COURT

In the European Communities a Member State may bring an action for a declaration by the European Court of Justice that another Member State is in breach of its obligations under Community law without having to show a direct legal interest apart from the general interest in the observance of Community law. Similarly a Member State may intervene in an action by the Commission against another Member State without having to prove it is directly affected by the breach.

In contrast the International Court of Justice has not yet made this step; the idea of a general right to secure the observance of international law is not established. This is another limitation on the declaratory judgment in the jurisprudence of the World Court: the International Court of Justice and its predecessor have not allowed *locus standi* to states except where they could show that they were directly affected by the actions of the defendant state. The *Wimbledon* case,[3] however, shows a generous approach by the Court to this question. The British, French, Italian, and Japanese Governments instituted proceedings asking the Court to declare that,

> 1. The German authorities . . . were wrong in refusing free access to the Kiel canal to the steamship 'Wimbledon';
> 2. The German government is under an obligation to make good the prejudice sustained as a result of this action by the said vessel.

The Court said, 'The first question to be considered is whether proceedings could be instituted by the four Governments above mentioned in the terms of the Application filed', for only the French Government was seeking damages on behalf of a company of its nationality.

> The Court has no doubt that it can take cognizance of the application instituting proceedings in the form in which it has been submitted. It will suffice to observe for the purposes of this case that each of the four Applicant Powers has a clear interest in the execution of the provisions relating to the Kiel Canal, since they all possess fleets and merchant vessels flying their respective flags. They are therefore, even though they may be unable to adduce a prejudice to any pecuniary interest, covered by the terms of Article 386, Paragraph 1 of which is as follows:
>
> 'In the event of violation of any of the conditions of Articles 380 to 386, or of disputes as to the interpretation of these articles, any interested Power can appeal to the jurisdiction instituted for the purpose by the League of Nations.'[4]

Thus a generous interpretation of 'any interested Power' was given by the Court in this case; the applicant states did not have to show any actual harm to their interests, nor any definite immediate threat to these interests. It was enough that they had fleets and merchant vessels flying their flags.

This was a case of states suing another for breach of a treaty to which they were all parties; the question whether the type of interest possessed by the claimant states in this case would be enough to support an action for a breach of customary international law was left open.

This generous approach was continued in the first stage of the *South West Africa* case.[5] Ethiopia and Liberia brought an action against South Africa for breach of its obligations under the Mandate for South West Africa. South Africa contested the jurisdiction of the International Court of Justice on several grounds including the argument that

> The conflict or disagreement alleged by the governments of Ethiopia and Liberia to exist between them and the government of the Republic of South Africa is by reason of its nature and content not a 'dispute' as envisaged in Article 7 of the Mandate for South West Africa, more particularly in that no material interests of the governments of Ethiopia and/or Liberia or of their nationals are involved therein or affected thereby.

This and the other arguments of South Africa against the jurisdiction of the Court were rejected. The Court held that it had jurisdiction under Article 7 of the Mandate, which provided:

> The Mandatory agrees that, if any dispute whatever should arise between the Mandatory and another Member of the League of Nations relating to the interpretation or the application of the provisions of the Mandate, such dispute, if it cannot be settled by negotiation, shall be submitted to the Permanent Court of International Justice provided for by Article 14 of the Covenant of the League of Nations.

In its interpretation of this provision the Court went even further than had its predecessor in the *Wimbledon* case on the question of *locus standi* of claimant states. There states parties to a treaty had been allowed to bring a claim against another party for its breach even though no definite injury or threat of injury to themselves or their nationals had been shown. Now Article 7 of the Mandate, to which Ethiopia and Liberia were not themselves direct parties, was held itself to give them the right to bring a claim against the Mandatory without it being necessary for them to show that their own or their nationals' interests were affected by South Africa's behaviour. The Court said,

> For the manifest scope and purport of the provisions of this Article indicate that the Members of the League were understood to have a legal right or interest in the observation by the Mandatory of its obligations both toward the inhabitants of the Mandated territory and toward the League of Nations and its Members.[6]

But this apparent acceptance of the possibility of an *actio popularis* for a declaratory judgment was abandoned by the Court in the second phase of its judgment.[7] In a very controversial and much criticized decision the Court reopened the question of *locus standi*; it said that this had not been settled by the Court's decision on its jurisdiction. Ignoring its discussion of the question whether the claimant states had sufficient legal interest to bring their case before the Court in its earlier decision, the Court now said that

To hold that the parties in any given case belong to the category of State specified in the clause [sc. the jurisdictional clause]—that the dispute has the specified character—and the forum is the one specified—is not the same thing as finding the existence of a legal right or interest relative to the merits of the claim.[8]

This question of the existence of a legal right or interest was one on the merits of the case for it to decide now. The Court canvassed a series of arguments to support the view that individual Member States of the League of Nations had their own individual rights to call for the performance even of those provisions of the Mandates in which they had no material interest, and rejected them all. Finally it considered the force of Article 7(2) of the Mandate and the argument that this conferred on Member States a substantive right to claim from the Mandatory the carrying out of the Mandate. The Court in contrast to its earlier liberal approach now said,

It would be remarkable if this were the case, if so important a right having such potentially far reaching consequences . . . had been created indirectly and in so casual and almost incidental a fashion by an ordinary jurisdictional clause lacking . . . in any of the special features that might give it the effect claimed—and which would certainly be requisite in order to achieve that effect.[9]

Here there was no special language, no clear indication that it was intended to give Member States of the League a substantive right to bring claims, nor was Article 7 comparable to the jurisdictional clauses of the Minorities Treaties which clearly gave states members of the Council of the League, a body with supervisory functions over the performance of the Minorities Treaties, the right to bring claims against states in breach of their obligations. Finally, the possible argument that the proper functioning of the Mandates system required the existence of a right on the part of individual Member States of the League of Nations to bring claims against Mandatories in breach of their obligations before the International Court was also dismissed.

The argument amounts to a plea that the Court should allow the equivalent of an actio popularis, or right resident in any member of a community to take legal action in vindication of a public interest. But although a right of this kind may be known to certain municipal systems of law, it is not known to international law as it stands at present: nor is the court able to regard it as imported by the general principles of law referred to in Article 38(1)*c* of its statute.[10]

Thus, although the Court recognized, without any reference to the *Wimbledon* case, that a state might be able to bring a claim for breach of a treaty to which it was a party even if its own interests were not directly affected by the breach, in general it took a restrictive view of the right to bring actions before the International Court. A right for a state not within the above category—the *Wimbledon* category—to bring a claim would not be lightly inferred from a jurisdictional clause of the type in the *South West Africa* case; according to the Court in this case a clear indication that such a right was intended must be present. It seems even more unlikely that a state would be able to bring a claim for a breach of customary international law that did not directly affect its own interests.

Apart from dicta in the *Barcelona Traction* case[11] that

> An essential distinction should be drawn between the obligations of a State towards the international community as a whole, and those arising vis-à-vis another state in the field of diplomatic protection. By their very nature the former are the concern of all States. In view of the importance of the rights involved all States can be held to have a legal interest in their protection; they are obligations erga omnes,

there has not been any advance from this position by the International Court of Justice.[12] So there does not seem to be adequate justification for Judge Schwebel's argument in his Dissenting Opinion in the Court's decision on Nicaragua's request for interim measures;[13] he goes too far when he suggests that the holding in the *South West Africa* case has been 'decisively displaced' by the Court's judgment in *Barcelona Traction*[14] and his conclusion that

> The United States has, in the specific term of Barcelona Traction, 'a legal interest' in the performance by Nicaragua of its fundamental international obligations; even if it is not immediately and directly affected by the breaches of international law which it attributes to Nicaragua, the United States 'should therefore be considered justified in invoking the responsibility' of Nicaragua as the state which, the United States maintains, is at root responsible for the internationally unlawful acts which are at issue in this case,

remains controversial.

And the Court's decisions on applications to intervene in contentious actions have (unlike those of the European Court of Justice which is untroubled by lack of compulsory jurisdiction) also been restrictive.[15]

So problems which do not involve any direct injury to a particular state but rather affect the international community as a whole cannot be dealt with by means of bilateral claims for a declaratory judgment. In the absence of an *actio popularis* such problems, and in particular regimes laying down rules for areas such as the deep sea-bed[16] or outer space[17] declared to be the common heritage of mankind will depend on organizational mechanisms of enforcement. For in so far as the concept of responsibility to the international community as a whole is a reality this is through the functioning of international organizations rather than any formal judicial procedure. International organizations provide a partial substitute for the lack of any general action on behalf of the world community and also for the lack of compulsory judicial settlement.[18]

(ii) INTERNATIONAL CRIMES AND JUDICIAL REMEDIES

The inadequacy of the traditional bilateral procedure as a deterrent against breaches of international law and as a mechanism for dealing with such breaches has led some writers to advocate the development not only of an action on behalf of the international community, but also of the international criminal responsibility of states.[19] They reject the idea that the only possible consequence of a breach of international law is the duty to make reparation. Clearly there are enormous problems with the transfer of the concept of criminal responsibility from municipal to international law. But it is possible to argue that the ideas of guilt and punishment have a place in state practice. Those General Assembly and Security Council resolutions that condemn the behaviour of states could be said to constitute punishment by disgrace, a means of declaring international criminal responsibility. An injured state may seek such a resolution as a remedy for itself; the resolution represents the response of the international community to the unlawful behaviour of states.

The organs of the League of Nations were less ready than their counterparts in the United Nations to pass such resolutions condemning the activities of Member States, perhaps because the idea of an international organization to deal with the fundamental problem of maintaining peace was new and so its organs were hesitant to risk causing offence and thus weakening the influence of the League. Anyhow there are very few unequivocal condemnations of state conduct by the League of Nations.[20] The United Nations General Assembly and Security Council were more ready to pass such resolutions, few at first and then an increasing number.[21] To a very limited extent these resolutions, representing the reaction of the international community to events, make up for the lack of compulsory third party settlement of disputes and for the limitations of bilateral claims, and also for the lack of an international legislature.[22]

These resolutions often state that certain activities are contrary to international law, or a breach of the United Nations Charter or of some other treaty, or of earlier resolutions of the political organs of the United Nations. The majority of them call on the offending state to alter its behaviour so as to comply with international law and also to restore the previously existing situation. Thus the Security Council and General Assembly often call for the withdrawal of troops from a state invaded in violation of international law or occupied illegally.[23] The Security Council has called for the release of prisoners[24] and the return of property[25] unlawfully taken. Also the Security Council and General Assembly have declared measures to be illegal and invalid.[26]

Most of the condemnations by the political organs of the United Nations are for the unlawful use of force, violations of territorial integrity, colonialism, and apartheid. Some condemnations are expressed in general terms unrelated to the behaviour of any particular state, such as General Assembly Resolution 1514 on the right to self-determination, which condemns alien subjugation of states, General Assembly Resolution 3514 condemning the corrupt practices of transnational and other corporations,[27] General Assembly Resolution 2714 against the violation of human rights,[28] General Assembly Resolution 2674 condemning aggressive wars, and General Assembly Resolution 3452 rejecting the use of torture.[29] Other resolutions refer to specific behaviour of a particular state. Rhodesia, South Africa, Portugal, and Israel are the states most often subjected to censure by the United Nations organs. Recently regional organizations have begun to follow the United Nations practice of issuing condemnations.[30]

Occasionally the resolutions go further than condemnation and demand that the offending state should pay reparation to its victim. This goes beyond punishment by disgrace and represents an attempt to extract a remedy from the wrongdoer. Such resolutions are uncommon; none were passed by the organs of the League of Nations. The question of demanding reparation was first considered by the United Nations Security Council in 1955.[31] The Security Council passed a resolution condemning Israel for its violation of the cease-fire, the armistice, and the United Nations Charter, but did not attach a demand for reparation. The representatives of the United Kingdom, France, and the USA discussed this issue: they all agreed that compensation was due for injury but France said that the Security Council was not the organ best equipped or legally competent to arrange for fair compensation in this instance.

In 1964 the Security Council actually demanded the payment of compensation for the first time. They deplored the incidents caused by the army of the Republic of Vietnam's invasion of Cambodia and requested that just and fair compensation should be offered to Cambodia.[32] A few similar demands by the Security Council and, after 1974, by the General Assembly followed this.[33] There is no evidence that any of these resolutions were ever acted on. The response of the President of Guinea to Security Council Resolution 290 shows the limits of such demands. He declined the offer made by the Secretary-General to send officials to help assess the damage caused by Portugal. He said that the moral and material damage could not be expressed in monetary terms especially as the aggressor persisted in denying the offence; the only reparation acceptable to Guinea would be the immediate independence of Angola, Mozambique, and Guinea.[34] The future conduct of the wrongdoing state is often more important to its victim than any award of compensation for past unlawful action. These brief demands for reparation for damage caused by unlawful actions do not convey much information about the nature of the reparation envisaged. It is not clear how the compensation is to be calculated; it is not obvious why reparation is demanded in some cases but not others. Certainly such requests are exceptional.

It might be argued that the activities—invasions, occupations, the practice of apartheid, colonialism, and the violation of human rights—that have been condemned by the political organs of the United Nations amount to international crimes. The two main elements involved in the suggested international criminal liability of states are, first, the idea that certain breaches of international law are particularly serious with the result that, second, responsibility to the international community as a whole is involved, for the interests affected are wider than those involved in injury to a particular state. But the concept of international criminal responsibility is not yet firmly established in international law, and when the International Law Commission in their current work on state responsibility accepted Article 19 on International Crimes they were engaged in progressive development rather than codification of the law:

Article 19—*International Crimes and International Delicts*

1. An act of a state which constitutes a breach of an international obligation is an internationally wrongful act, regardless of the subject matter of the obligation breached.

2. An internationally wrongful act which results from the breach by a state of an international obligation so essential for the protection of fundamental interests of the international community that its breach is recognised as a crime by that community as a whole, constitutes an international crime.

3. Subject to paragraph 2, and on the basis of the rules of international law in force, an international crime may result, inter alia from:

(*a*) a serious breach of an international obligation of essential importance for the maintenance of international peace and security, such as that prohibiting aggression;
(*b*) a serious breach of an international obligation of essential importance for safeguarding the right of self-determination of peoples, such as that prohibiting the establishment or maintenance by force of colonial domination;
(*c*) a serious breach on a widespread scale of an international obligation of essential importance for safeguarding the human being, such as those prohibiting slavery, genocide and apartheid;
(*d*) a serious breach of an international obligation of essential importance for the safeguarding and preservation of the human environment, such as those prohibiting massive pollution of the atmosphere or of the seas.

4. Any internationally wrongful act which is not an international crime in accordance with paragraph 2 constitutes an international delict.[35]

Apart from the obvious problems over the substantive definition, over which activities are to constitute international crimes,[36] the most important practical problem is the implementation of this Article. How are such provisions to be given any practical effect? The International Law Commission is now working on this as part of the second part of its draft on the 'content, form and degrees of international responsibility', but progress is slow. The present draft Articles do not mention judicial proceedings as a possible response to international crime, and so are not concerned with judicial remedies. Questions as to whether an international crime should give a right to any state to bring an *actio popularis* for a declaratory judgment, and whether an international crime may create an obligation to pay punitive damages to injured states, are not resolved. For the International Law Commission in its consideration of the content, form, and degrees of international responsibility has understandably distinguished international judicial decisions (an exceptional response to alleged breaches of international law) from general state practice, and concerned itself with drawing up rules for the latter. [37] The Rapporteur has found that international judicial decisions are not of much relevance for an understanding of general state practice, of non-judicial responses to breaches of international law. He has also stated that the role of the Commission is not to provide guidance to international tribunals.[38]

Thus draft Article 6 sets out the obligations of states when an international crime has been committed: obligations not to recognize, not to help, and to use United Nations procedures where applicable.[39] Because not exhaustive Article 6 leaves open the possibility of special judicial remedies as a response to international crimes, but this possibility, like that of implementing a general regime for international crimes, appears very remote. There is little sign at present of state acceptance of, or enthusiasm for, international criminal responsibility. In fact it is not clear what the International Law Commission's proposals would add to existing United Nations procedures, and it is this question of the relationship between the two that is one of the main objects of concern of those members of the Commission not happy with the idea of creating a category of 'international crimes'.

It is interesting to compare Article 19 with the work of the International Law Commission on 'International liability for injurious consequences arising out of acts not prohibited by international law'. Whereas the former envisages international criminal responsibility for 'a serious breach of an international obligation of essential importance for the safeguarding and preservation of the human environment, such as those prohibiting massive pollution of the atmospheres or of the seas', the latter proposes to deal with polluting activities by co-operation and as a last resort by imposing liability for harm caused by what are recognized as lawful activities.[40] Of course there is no necessary conflict between the two but state practice in this area suggests that the latter is the more constructive and fruitful approach.

(iii) MUNICIPAL LAW REMEDIES FOR BREACHES OF INTERNATIONAL LAW

Better established than the international criminal responsibilty of states is the international criminal responsibility of individuals;[41] under customary international law any state may exercise jurisdiction over an individual charged with slavery, piracy, war crimes, or crimes against humanity. More recently treaties have been made to bind contracting states either to prosecute or to extradite those allegedly guilty of offences such as hijacking and attacks on diplomats when found on their territory.[42] This method of turning to municipal law mechanisms and remedies to deal with breaches of international law, of imposing municipal criminal liability on an individual rather than attempting to impose international responsibility on his state or to establish an international criminal tribunal, may be seen also in treaties on polluting and ultra-hazardous activities. Thus the 1954 Convention for the Prevention of the Pollution of the Sea by Oil[43] (entered into force 26 July 1958) prohibits the discharge of oil within specified areas and says that the flag state is to make contravention of this prohibition an offence under its own law. Two Conventions on dumping, The London Convention on the Prevention of Marine Pollution by Dumping of Wastes and Other Matter (entered into force 30 August 1975), Article VII, and the Oslo Convention for the Prevention of Marine Pollution by Dumping from Ships and Aircraft[44] (entered into force 7 April 1974), Article XIV, say that parties must take appropriate measures to prevent and punish conduct in breach of the Convention. The 1973 IMCO Convention for the Prevention of Pollution from Ships[45] (entered into force 2 October 1983) and the Paris Convention for the Prevention of Marine Pollution from Land-based Sources[46] (entered into force 6 May 1978) contain similar provisions. Two of these Treaties dealing with polluting activities include more detailed directions as to the type of punishment required. The 1954 Convention for the Prevention of the Pollution of the Sea by Oil, Article VI, says that penalties should be 'Adequate in severity to discourage any such unlawful discharge and shall not be less than penalties which may be imposed under the law of that territory in respect of the same infringements within the territorial sea'. The 1973 IMCO Convention, Article 4(4), is similar: 'Penalties specified under the law of a party pursuant to the present Article shall be adequate in severity to discourage violations of the present convention and shall be equally severe irrespective of where the violations occur', but the possibility of different states imposing sanctions of different degrees of severity remains. Finally the 1982 UN Law of the Sea Convention apparently also provides for the imposition of criminal liability by states in order to protect and preserve the marine environment.[47]

Treaties also provide for the imposition of civil liability under municipal law: several treaties on aviation, nuclear and maritime activities, and the utilization of river basins require that states parties ensure a municipal remedy for damage caused by certain defined activities. These treaties create uniform regimes; their implementation is left to states parties. The Preamble to the Paris Convention on Third Party Liability in the Field of Nuclear Energy[48] (entered into force 1 April 1968) reflects this aim. The states parties are 'convinced of the need for unifying the basic rules applying in the various countries to the liability incurred for such damage', but it is possible, even probable, that the interpretation and application by the states parties of the provisions of these treaties will vary.[49]

In the field of maritime pollution the 1969 International Convention on Civil Liability for Oil Pollution Damage[50] (entered into force 19 June 1975) states that the owner of a ship shall be responsible in municipal law for oil pollution produced by spillage from his ship, which causes damage on the territory of a contracting state. This responsibility is strict. This is a common feature of the treaties which provide for municipal law liability for polluting and ultra-hazardous activities, and obviously a practical necessity, as proof of fault would often be extremely difficult or impossible. It is not just deliberately caused pollution or other harm which these conventions are designed to control. The various conventions allow certain defences to the imposition of strict liability; the extent of these is not uniform in all the conventions.

The 1971 Convention on the Establishment of an International Fund for Compensation for Oil Pollution Damage[51] (entered into force 16 October 1978) was designed to supplement the Civil Liability Convention, 'Considering that this regime does not afford full compensation for victims of oil pollution damage in all cases while it imposes an additional financial burden on shipowners'. Accordingly it provided that oil cargo owners should bear part of the economic consequences of oil pollution damage resulting from the escape or discharge of oil carried in bulk at sea by ships. The 1976 London Convention on Civil Liability for Oil Pollution Damage from Offshore Operations[52] (not yet in force) provides that the operator of an offshore facility shall be strictly liable under municipal law for damage covered by the Convention. The Tanker Owners Voluntary Agreement on Liability for Oil Pollution (TOVALOP),[53] the Contract Regarding an Interim Supplement to Tanker Liability for Oil Pollution (CRISTAL),[54] and the Offshore Pollution Liability Agreement (OPOL)[55] supplement these Conventions. These are all contracts subject to English law. TOVALOP is an agreement between tanker owners that they will clear up spills caused by their ships or compensate governments for the clean-up expenses they incur as a result of such spills. In CRISTAL the cargo owners set up a fund to reimburse the expenses of clean-up operations by tanker owners and to compensate victims who would otherwise receive only inadequate compensation. Finally, according to OPOL, the operators of offshore facilities used for the exploration or production of oil and gas agree to compensate the victims of pollution and also the state which incurs costs for taking remedial measures.[56]

Article 235(2) of the 1982 UN Convention on the Law of the Sea, which deals with maritime pollution also, requires contracting states to make provision for the imposition of municipal liability:

> States shall ensure that recourse is available in accordance with their legal systems for prompt and adequate compensation or other relief in respect of damage caused by pollution of the marine environment by natural or juridical persons under their jurisdiction.

The multilateral Conventions on nuclear activities also provide for municipal liability as the main mechanism for enforcing obligations under the Conventions.[57] Under the Vienna Convention on Civil Liability for Nuclear Damage[58] and the Paris Convention on Third Party Liability in the Field of Nuclear Energy the operator of a nuclear installation is liable under municipal law for damage caused by a nuclear incident. Also the United States has concluded a series of agreements governing the entry of the Nuclear Ship Savannah into foreign waters in which it is stipulated that the United States will be liable under the law of the port state for damage caused by the NS Savannah.[59] West Germany has made a similar set of treaties on the Nuclear Ship Otto Hahn.[60] A final example of a treaty providing for municipal law liability is the 1974 Nordic Environment Protection Convention[61] (entered into force 5 October 1976). According to this agreement between Denmark, Finland, Norway, and Sweden, anyone in the territory of a contracting state affected by a nuisance caused by environmentally harmful activities in another contracting state has the right to institute proceedings in a court of that state.

Many of the common characteristics of these Treaties providing for municipal liability may be explained by the requirements of the insurance industry. Thus liability is channelled to one person to make it clear who should insure against the risks involved.[62] Also liability is limited. Under the 1969 Civil Liability Convention, fault on the part of the shipowner may prevent his relying on this limitation of liability, but other conventions do not follow this approach. Another common feature is the requirement that the person potentially liable for damage should maintain insurance or some other form of financial security to cover his liability.[63] All these treaties make express provision as to which courts are to have jurisdiction to decide on and assess liability. These provisions are not uniform.[64]

Thus several treaties require the imposition of municipal liability, civil or criminal, for breach of their terms or of regulations drawn up by states in accordance with the treaty. That is, municipal law procedures are used to enforce acceptable standards and modes of behaviour. The treaties create a uniform regime, binding on states parties under international law, and it is left to the parties to implement the regime under their own legal systems. Such treaties, designed to unify various municipal law rules, are well established in civil aviation and marine transport. Now the interesting development of increasing resort to such treaties to enforce international law standards may be observed. The adoption by international arbitral tribunals of municipal law remedies was discussed earlier; here a different policy may be seen. States have chosen to provide for remedies for behaviour made unlawful by treaties and for harm caused by activities defined by treaty at the municipal rather than at the international level.

(iv) REPARATION FOR INJURIES CAUSED BY LAWFUL ACTIVITIES

For states have on the whole, despite the famous Principles 21 and 22 of the Stockholm Declaration,[65] chosen not to deal with ultra-hazardous and polluting activities by the imposition of state responsibility.[66] And out of the many recent treaties establishing regimes to deal with these activities, the 1972 Convention on International Liability for Damage caused by Space Objects[67] (entered into force 1 September 1972) remains exceptional in its detailed provisions on state responsibility. Often treaties, bilateral and multilateral, provide only or mainly for co-operation in the control of pollution.[68] Such treaties do not contain any provisions on international responsibility or compensation for polluting activities; they aim at the prevention of harm through the improvement of each state's knowledge of the problem and co-operative efforts to cut down pollution. Some treaties require the imposition of municipal liability as described above. Those treaties that do provide for international responsibility generally do so in a single article[69] or simply reserve the possibility of international responsibility.[70]

In fact in the outer space and nuclear Treaties liability is incurred only when certain defined activities cause harm; the activity itself is not unlawful. The International Law Commission is accordingly now working on a draft set of rules on international liability for injúrious consequences arising out of acts not prohibited by international law as a separate project from its work on state responsibility.[71] But there is a wide division of opinion among writers as to the desirability of this approach and the members of the Commission are themselves divided on whether the project is worthwhile. The future of this project is uncertain: the scope of the draft articles and their ultimate status have still to be determined. There are those who argue that the principles of strict liability provide the appropriate means to deal with ultra-hazardous and polluting activities and that the International Law Commission approach is fundamentally misconceived, even a dangerous threat to the regime of state responsibility.[72] But in so far as the existence of a general principle of strict liability in this area is not universally accepted, and as the emphasis in the practice of states appears to be on co-operation rather than the imposition of strict liability, it may be that they are fighting a losing battle.

However, the International Law Commission approach does raise several important questions concerning remedies. The scheme at present put forward by the Special Rapporteur envisages the payment of reparation as a last resort arising only when the other provisions have not prevented the occurrence of harm.[73] Sections 4–7 govern assessment of compensation; these are very flexible guidelines: everything depends on their interpretation and application in a particular situation.[74] Several members of the Commission have expressed reservations over these provisions;[75] one member has doubted whether they would be viable in the absence of specific provision for a dispute settlement mechanism.[76]

These draft provisions are apparently intended to serve as guidelines both for states parties involved in negotiating a settlement and for a third party authorized to make recommendations or decisions on compensation. They certainly represent a marked departure from the traditional rules, such as they are, evolved by judicial and arbitral bodies, on the assessment of damages. The influence of McDougal is clear; the reparation due 'shall be ascertained in accordance with the shared expectations of the States concerned', 'account shall be taken of the reasonableness of the conduct of the parties'; account may also be taken of listed 'relevant factors'. These provisions have been attacked for not providing objective standards. But this is an area where objective standards and perhaps even general principles seem to be illusory goals. The attempt to balance interests, despite the obvious difficulties involved, is more likely to produce economically efficient and/or socially just results (and—more important—results acceptable to the states involved) than the simple imposition of strict liability with a consequent duty to pay damages assessed according to traditional rules.[77] But the implementation of any new set of guidelines to supplement existing rules on the assessment of damages by more flexible rules on compensation for harm caused by lawful activities is hardly an immediate possibility.

Thus recent developments, particularly in the area of polluting and ultra-hazardous activities, highlight the limitations of the imposition of state responsibility and of traditional judicial remedies. Most of the discussion in this chapter of possible responses to these limitations may seem of limited practical importance: apart from the move by states to municipal as opposed to international judicial remedies other suggested responses—the creation of an *actio popularis*, of international criminal responsibility, of liability for injurious consequences of lawful acts—still appear only remote possibilities. And a large part of the explanation for this lies in a relative lack of concern over mechanisms for implementing possible new regimes; the treatment of judicial remedies is one symptom of this lack of concern. For the question of what role, if any, they are to play has been largely ignored. But if new mechanisms to supplement that of traditional state responsibility are to be evolved the question of judicial remedies should not be left as an afterthought. Their relationship with the rules governing general state practice must be worked out; if there are fundamental changes in the law of state responsibility it does not seem possible that judicial remedies will remain unaffected.

NOTES

1. See K. B. Hoffman (1976) *ICLQ* 509. An indication of the inadequacy of state responsibility as a means of dealing with polluting activities may also be found in the International Law Commission's attempt to draw up rules on 'International liability for injurious consequences arising out of acts not prohibited by International law'. See ILC Yearbooks from 1980.
2. See, for example, P. C. Jessup (1946) *Col. LR* 903; R. Y. Jennings (1967) 2 *HR* 323, at 511.
3. PCIJ Ser. A no. 1.
4. Ibid., 20.
5. (1962) ICJ Reports 319.
6. Ibid., 343.
7. (1966) ICJ Reports 4.
8. Ibid., 37.
9. Ibid., 38.
10. Ibid., 47.
11. (1970) ICJ Reports 4, at 32.
12. The question of *locus standi* was raised again in the *Nuclear Tests* cases (1974) ICJ Reports 253 and 457. One of the Australian claims was that 'The interference with ships and aircraft on the high seas and in the superjacent airspace, and the pollution of the high seas by radio-active fallout, constitute infringements of the freedom of the high seas'. However, the Court, because of its decision that there was no longer a dispute in existence and therefore no need for it to give a judgment, did not have to discuss this point. It did not have to decide whether a state could bring a claim for breach of customary inter-

national law—in this case the infringement of the freedom of the high seas—without showing harm to its own interests or those of its nationals.

13. (1984) ICJ Reports 4, at 190.
14. Nor does the passage in the 1976 ILC Yearbook, Vol. ii, Part I, 28–54 provide unequivocal support for his position as he claims. For the Rapporteur, Ago, says, 'The position taken in the judgment on the *Barcelona Traction* case is perhaps still too isolated to permit the conclusion that a definite new trend in international judicial decisions has emerged.'
15. See the application by Malta for permission to intervene in the *Tunisia/Libya* case (1981) ICJ Reports 4 and the application by Italy in the *Libya/Malta* case (1984) ICJ Reports 3.
16. Article 136 of the 1982 United Nations Convention on the Law of the Sea declares that the deep sea-bed is the common heritage of mankind. But neither Article 139 on 'Responsibility to ensure compliance and liability for damage' nor Article 187 on the jurisdiction of the sea-bed disputes chamber make any clear provision for an *actio popularis*. There is, however, a provision for Advisory Opinions in Article 191. Moreover, one of the functions of the Sea-bed Authority is to 'exercise such control over activities in the Area as is necessary for the purpose of securing compliance with the relevant provisions of this Part . . . States Parties shall assist the Authority by taking all measures necessary to ensure such compliance in accordance with Article 139.' There is no comparable body set up to regulate the High Seas, another area beyond national jurisdiction. In Part VII of the Convention which deals with the High Seas there is no mention of any responsibility owed to the international community. But Part XII on the Protection and Preservation of the Marine Environment contains provisions on the prevention of pollution generally and on enforcement measures open to interested states to secure compliance with the rules in this Part of the Convention. However, the absence of an international body such as the Sea-bed Authority means that the protection given to the community interest, rather than that of any particular state, is less strong.
17. The Treaty on Principles governing the Activities of States in the Exploration and use of Outer Space including the Moon and other celestial bodies (1967) ILM 386 (entered into force 10.10.67) provides in Article 1, 'The exploration and use of outer space, including the moon and other celestial bodies shall be carried out for the benefit and in the interests of all countries, irrespective of their degree of economic or scientific development and shall be the province of all mankind.' However, here again there is no specific provision for the protection of the community interest. Thus the statements quoted above that certain areas are the common heritage of mankind are not supported by provisions enabling states other than those directly harmed by breaches of international law concerning these areas to obtain judicial remedies against the wrongdoing state.
18. See, for example, M. Lachs in K. Venkata Raman (ed.), *Dispute Settlement through the United Nations* (1977), at 283.
19. See especially the work of the International Law Commission: R. Ago (1976)

ILC Yearbook, Vol. ii, Part I, 24; F. V. García-Amador (1954) *ILC Yearbook*, ii. 24. See *contra* Q. Wright (1974–5) *Virg. JIL* 561; P. M. Dupuy (1980) *RGDIP* 449.

20. The Assembly of the League made a statement on 24 Feb. 1933 that Japan had violated the Covenant by its aggressive occupation of Chinese territory. The Council of the League passed a resolution on 17 Apr. 1935 condemning the actions of Germany in rearming itself in breach of its treaty obligations. Finally the Council condemned attacks on Spanish merchant ships by Germany and Italy as morally repugnant and a violation of the Nyon agreement on 29 May 1937. See F. P. Walters, *A History of the League of Nations* (1952), at 494, 609–12, 726 respectively.
21. By 1960 there had been a significant increase in the number of these resolutions. There has been no large variation in this number since then.
22. Obviously it would be unjustified to regard such decision-making by the General Assembly (or by the Security Council) as a purely judicial process, but the need for the state proposing or supporting a resolution to justify its position and secure support from other states means that legal considerations play an important part in the decision-making. That is, although it should not be inferred from the absence of condemnation by the Security Council and General Assembly that certain behaviour is permissible under international law—for it is notorious that it is political factors that determine whether a particular state is to be condemned or not—where a state's activities are condemned then this condemnation will be legally justifiable. See O. Schachter (1964) *AJ* 960; R. Higgins (1970) *AJ* 1.
23. For example, the Security Council has called on Belgium to withdraw its troops from the Congo: (1960) UN Yearbook 97. Security Council Resolution 268 requests Portugal to withdraw its troops after an unlawful attack on Zambia: (1969) UN Monthly Chronicle no. 8, p. 34. Security Council Resolution 264 demands an end to the presence of South African troops in Namibia: (1969) UN Monthly Chronicle, no. 4, p. 3. The General Assembly made the same demand in Resolution 2871. General Assembly resolutions up to Resolution 3049 have been collected by D. J. Djonovich in *United Nations Resolutions*, Ser. 1. Accordingly references for General Assembly resolutions will be given only for later resolutions. The General Assembly in Resolution 31/106D also condemned Israel's continued occupation of Arab territories and called for its withdrawal: (1977) UN Monthly Chronicle, no. 1, p. 20.
24. As in Resolution 317 which deplores the fact that Israel has not yet given effect to the Security Council's strong desire that Syrian and Lebanese military and security personnel abducted by Israelis should be released as soon as possible, and calls on Israel for their return: (1972) UN Monthly Chronicle, no. 8, p. 3. See also (1948–9) UN Yearbook 216 and 217.
25. For example, in 1970 it asked Portugal to release the Guinea civilian plane and barge it had taken: (1970) UN Monthly Chronicle, no. 1, p. 28.
26. For example, the General Assembly in Resolution 2652 declared illegal measures by the racist regime in Rhodesia to deprive people of their legitimate rights and entrench the policies of apartheid: (1971) UN Monthly

Chronicle, no. 1, p. 52. The General Assembly and Security Council have passed a number of resolutions saying that Israeli measures in Jerusalem were invalid, or null and void. See General Assembly Resolution 2253, Security Council Resolution 252 (1968) UN Monthly Chronicle, no. 6, p. 3, General Assembly Resolution 3525, (1976) UN Monthly Chronicle, no. 1, p. 30. On the domestic effect of resolutions see C. C. Schreuer, *Decisions of International Institutions before Domestic Courts* (1981).

27. (1976) ILM 180.
28. (1971) UN Monthly Chronicle, no. 1, p. 81.
29. (1976) UN Monthly Chronicle, no. 1, p. 55.
30. Thus the Organization of African Unity has condemned South Africa's policy of apartheid, the attitude of the United Kingdom towards Rhodesia, and NATO's gift of aid to Portugal. The Organization of American States has condemned the Dominican Government for its violation of a treaty, and also the ties which Cuba has established with the Sino-Soviet bloc in contravention of the principles of the OAS Charter. See L. L. Randolph, *Third Party Settlement of Disputes in Theory and Practice* (1973), at 39[a] and 42[a]
31. Whiteman *Digest*, xii. 164. The question was next discussed by the Security Council in 1960 in the context of the Eichmann case: (1960) UN Yearbook 196. See also Whiteman *Digest*, v. 208. The Security Council declared that the transfer of Eichmann from the Argentine was a violation of its territorial sovereignty and incompatible with the United Nations Charter. It requested Israel to make appropriate reparation in accordance with the United Nations Charter and the rules of international law. The Israeli foreign minister replied that his government had apologized for the violation of Argentine law and denied that there had been a violation of Argentine sovereignty. With regard to the request for appropriate reparation, he said that Israel's expression of regret was adequate. The representative of the USSR raised the question of whether Israel should be requested to make reparation in the more concrete form of handing back the illegally seized Eichmann. The representatives of France, the United Kingdom, and the USA agreed that the Argentine had received appropriate satisfaction from the debate in the Security Council, Israel's expression of regret, and the adoption of the resolution. The return of Eichmann was not necessary. Argentina and Israel finally issued a joint statement on 3 Aug. 1960 resolving 'to view as settled the incident which was caused in consequence of the action of the citizens of Israel, which violated the basic rights of the state of Argentina'. Argentina thus tacitly dropped its claim for any reparation beyond this admission of responsibility by Israel.
32. (1964) UN Yearbook 145.
33. In 1969 the Security Council again suggested the payment of reparation. In Resolution 262 they condemned Israel's attack on Beirut airport as a violation of the cease-fire agreement and of the United Nations Charter and said that Lebanon was entitled to appropriate redress for the destruction it suffered: (1969) UN Monthly Chronicle, no. 1, p. 3. In Resolution 290 the Security Council condemned Portugal for its attack on Guinea and demanded full compensation by Portugal for the extensive damage to life and property

caused by armed attack and invasion. They requested the Secretary-General to assist the Government of Guinea in the assessment of the extent of the damage involved: (1971) UN Monthly Chronicle, no. 1, p. 3. In 1976, the Security Council deplored South Africa's invasion of Angola and called on South Africa to meet the just claims of Angola for full compensation for the damage and destruction inflicted on its state and for the restoration of the equipment and materials the invading forces had seized: (1976) UN Monthly Chronicle, no. 4, p. 5. Finally in 1981 the Security Council demanded the payment of reparation by Israel for its attack on the Iraqi nuclear reactor: (1981) ILM 963.

It was not until 1974 that the General Assembly in Resolution 3240C requested reparation: (1974) UN Monthly Chronicle, no. 11, p. 63. It said that Israel was responsible for the destruction and devastation of an Arab town in breach of the Geneva Convention, and requested the establishment of a special committee to survey the destruction and assess the nature, extent, and value of the damage. In Resolution 32/9 the General Assembly held that South Africa was liable to pay reparation to Namibia for the damage caused by its illegal occupation of the territory of Namibia and its acts of aggression against the Namibian people since the termination of the Mandate in accordance with General Assembly Resolution 2145: (1977) UN Monthly Chronicle, no. 11, p. 83.

34. (1971) UN Monthly Chronicle, no. 1, p. 18.
35. (1976) ILC Yearbook, Vol. ii, Part II, p. 117.
36. On this see, for example, P. M. Dupuy (1980) *RGDIP* 449.
37. See (1981) ILC Yearbook, Vol. ii, Part I, p. 79, at 83.
38. See (1981) ILC Yearbook, i. 124.
39. Article 6 provides:

'1. An internationally wrongful act of a State, which constitutes an international crime, entails an obligation for every other state: (*a*) not to recognize as legal the situation created by such act; and (*b*) not to render aid or assistance to the author State in maintaining the situation created by such act; and (*c*) to join other States in affording mutual assistance in carrying out the obligations under (*a*) and (*b*).

2. Unless otherwise provided for by an applicable rule of international law, the performance of the obligations mentioned in paragraph 1 is subject *mutatis mutandis* to the procedures embodied in the United Nations Charter with respect to the maintenance of international peace and security.

3. Subject to Article 103 of the United Nations Charter, in the event of a conflict between the obligations of a State under paragraphs 1 and 2 above, and its rights and obligations under any other rule of international law, the obligations under the present article shall prevail.' (1982) ILC Yearbook, i. 199. The Special Rapporteur has now replaced this by draft Article 14 ((1984) ILC Yearbook, i. 20) which is essentially unchanged.

40. See ILC Yearbooks from 1980.
41. But problems similar to those with the international criminal responsibility of states have arisen for the International Law Commission in its work on the

draft Code of Offences against the Peace and Security of Mankind. (See ILC Yearbooks from 1983.) The International Law Commission was originally asked to draft this code in 1947 but went 'from enthusiasm to hesitation to procrastination'. At the request of the General Assembly it has now returned to the topic. One of the many difficulties facing the Commission is the problem of harmonizing its work on this topic with that on Article 19 on the international criminal responsibility of states. Another is the question of implementation. The Commission's request for guidance from the General Assembly as to whether its mandate extended to the preparation of a statute providing for an international criminal jurisdiction did not receive a specific reply (see (1984) ILC Yearbook, i. 5).

42. For example, there are three conventions dealing with the problem of attacks on aircraft: the 1963 Tokyo Convention on Offences and Certain Other Acts Committed on Board Aircraft (entered into force 4 Dec. 1969): (1962–3) ILM 104; the 1970 Hague Convention for the Suppression of the Unlawful Seizure of Aircraft (entered into force 14 Oct. 1971): (1971) ILM 133; and the 1971 Montreal Convention for the Suppression of Unlawful Acts against the Safety of Civil Aviation (entered into force 26 Jan. 1971): (1971) ILM 1151. See discussion by E. McWhinney, *The Illegal Diversion of Aircraft and International Law* (1975); A. Abramovsky (1974) *Col. JTL* 381 and (1975) *Col. JTL* 451; C. S. Thomas and M. J. Kirby (1973) *ICLQ* 163. See also the Convention on the Prevention and Punishment of Crimes against Internationally Protected Persons (entered into force 20 Feb. 1977): (1974) ILM 41; and discussion by L. M. Bloomfield and G. Fitzgerald, *Crimes against Internationally Protected Persons: Prevention and Punishment* (1975); C. L. Rozakis (1974) *ICLQ* 32, and M. C. Wood (1974) *ICLQ* 791; the Convention on the Suppression and Punishment of the Crime of Apartheid (entered into force 18 July 1976): (1974) ILM 50; the Convention on Torture as an International Crime (not yet in force); (1980) ILM 647; the *Convention on the Physical Protection of Nuclear Material* (not yet in force): (1979) ILM 1419.

43. (1970) ILM 1.

44. (1972) ILM 262.

45. (1973) ILM 1319.

46. (1974) ILM 352.

47. Part XII (1982) ILM 1261, at 1308.

48. (1961) AJ 1082; Supplement in (1962) ILM 685.

49. Thus the rules of the Warsaw Convention for the Unification of Rules relating to International Carriage by Air, Cmd. 4284, are not applied uniformly by the courts of the different contracting states. R. H. Mankiewicz has described how international conventions for the unification of private law tend to become disunified by the decisions of national courts: (1972) *ICLQ* 718. See also J. A. Cabranes (1966) *ICLQ* 660; A. Kean (1970) *ICLQ* 124.

50. (1970) ILM 45, revised in 1976 Protocol: (1977) ILM 617. New proposals for revision in (1984) ILM 177.

51. (1972) ILM 284, revised in 1976 Protocol: (1977) ILM 621. New proposals for revision in (1984) ILM 195.

52. (1977) ILM 1450. See B. A. Dubais (1977) 9 *JMLC* 61.
53. (1969) ILM 497.
54. (1971) ILM 137.
55. (1974) ILM 1409.
56. See G. L. Becker (1974) 5 *JMLC* 609 for a detailed discussion of TOVALOP and CRISTAL.
57. Even though the degree of state involvement in nuclear activities is not obviously less than that in operations in outer space, and for the latter international responsibility of the state is provided for in the 1967 Outer Space Treaty: (1967) ILM 386. See below at n. 67.
58. (1963) ILM 727.
59. See D. C. Piper in *De lege pactorum*, *Essays in Honour of R. R. Wilson* (1970), 233 for a detailed discussion of these agreements.
60. See B. Rüster and B. Simma (eds.), *International Protection of the Environment* (1975), i. 482.
61. (1974) ILM 591.
62. In the 1969 Civil Liability Convention it is the shipowner who is liable, partly because the registered owner is perhaps the easiest person to identify of those involved in the carriage of oil by sea. In the 1976 London Convention on Civil Liability for Oil Pollution Damage from Offshore Operations and in the conventions on nuclear activities it is the operator of the installations who is liable.
63. It is left to the national state of such a person to specify the type and terms of this security. Thus in the 1969 Civil Liability Convention, Article VII says that a ship registered in a state party to the Convention is obliged to maintain insurance or other financial security to cover its liability of the type and on the terms specified by the competent public authorities, and it must obtain a certificate from its state of registration that it has complied with this. The Paris, Brussels, and Vienna Conventions on nuclear activities contain similar provisions. Under the Supplement to the Paris Convention, Article 3, if the operator is not able to provide adequate security then public funds will be used for this purpose. Likewise the Vienna Convention, Article 7, says that the installation state is to ensure payment of compensation to the extent that the insurance available is inadequate. The 1976 London Convention differs from the other agreements in its provisions on the question of security. It is not possible at present to obtain insurance to cover the amount set under this convention for the limit of liability. Therefore the convention stipulates a minimum insurance requirement. The controlling state (that is, the state with jurisdiction over the offshore operations) has the power to specify the amount of security it requires, and this may be above the minimum set by the convention, as well as the type and terms of the security.
64. In the 1969 Civil Liability Convention it is the courts of the state where damage occurred that may exercise jurisdiction (see *The Times*, 13 Nov. 1978 on the Amoco Cadiz). The Fund Convention also accepts this where such a state is party to both the Civil Liability Convention and the Fund Convention. Where it is a party to the former only, then it is the courts of the state of

the fund headquarters that have jurisdiction. Of the nuclear conventions, the Vienna Convention, Article II, assigns competence to the courts of the state where damage is suffered, or if this is outside state territory then jurisdiction rests with the courts of the state of the installation. Under the Brussels Convention relating to Civil Liability in the Field of Maritime Carriage of Nuclear material (entered into force 15 July 1975): (1972) ILM 277, the claimant has the right to choose the court in which he will bring his action. The Paris Convention provides jurisdiction for the courts competent in accordance with the law of the contracting state in whose territory the installation causing the harm is situated. The Savannah agreements give jurisdiction to the state of the port where damage is suffered. The 1976 London Convention allows a choice as to which courts are to have jurisdiction: it may be either those of the state where damage occurs or else those of the state which controls the offshore installation.

65. The Stockholm Declaration made at the end of the 1972 United Nations Conference on the Human Environment ((1972) ILM 1416) apparently seeks to establish the principle of international responsibility for transboundary pollution. Principle 21 lays down that 'States have in accordance with the Charter of the United Nations and the principles of international law the sovereign right to exploit their own resources pursuant to their own environmental policies and the responsibility to ensure that activities within their jurisdiction or control do not cause damage to the environment of other states or of areas beyond the limits of national jurisdiction'. Principle 22 continues, 'States shall co-operate to develop further the international law regarding liability and compensation for the victims of pollution and other environmental damage caused by activities within the jurisdiction or control of states to areas beyond their jurisdiction'. Probably this should be construed as a statement of aspiration rather than of existing law.

66. This is not the place for a lengthy consideration of the question of the role of state responsibility in polluting and ultra-hazardous activities, but what is particularly striking from a study of state practice is the lack of instances of payment of damages for polluting activities on the basis of state responsibility in customary international law. States choose to deal with the problem by making treaties or, increasingly, by co-operating with other states to work out satisfactory regimes. There are apparently no clear instances of one state acknowledging that it has incurred liability under customary international law for injury caused to another state by polluting or ultra-hazardous activity conducted on its territory or by its nationals. Although the recent claim by Canada against the USSR for six million dollars for damage caused by a nuclear-powered satellite in 1978 was based not only on the Convention on International Liability for Damage caused by Space Objects but also on 'general principles of international law', it is not clear that the Russian payment of three million dollars represents an acknowledgement that the latter basis of claim was well founded. See the claim at (1979) ILM p.899, the settlement at (1981) ILM 689, and C. Q. Christol (1980) *AJ* 346. In the case of the Torrey Canyon ((1970) ILM 633), compensation was paid to the French and

British Governments by the shipowners, not by any state. The issue of the international responsibility of flag states was not raised. See also the Sedco blow-out ((1983) ILM 580). The United States Government paid compensation to Japan for injury caused to a group of islands and their fishing industry by the Marshall Islands nuclear test, but they made it clear that this did not constitute an admission of international liability but was merely an *ex gratia* payment (237 UNTS 197). Similarly certain Swiss farmers were compensated for damage resulting from air pollution caused by a factory in German territory (H. Smets in *The Avoidance and Settlement of International Environmental Disputes* (1974)) and in 1974 Liberia paid compensation to Japan for Japanese fishermen injured by pollution from a Liberian tanker ((1975) RGDIP 842). No doubt there are other similar cases not widely reported. Nor does international arbitral practice give much guidance on the question whether there is international responsibility for polluting and ultra-hazardous activities. The two cases most often relied on by writers as support for their assertion of the existence of international responsibility for polluting activities—the *Trail Smelter* arbitration (3 RIAA 1905) and the *Corfu Channel* case ((1949) ICJ Reports 4)—are not convincing precedents. See A. P. Rubin (1970–1) *Oregon LR* 259. It is doubtful whether it is possible or desirable to extrapolate from the rules of state responsibility for injury to a foreign national by a state within its own territory a rule imposing responsibility on a state for injury caused by an activity within its territory to a foreign national outside its territory or to the interests of another state. See K. B. Hoffman (1976) *ICLQ* 509. A similar objection applies to any attempt to derive a rule prohibiting harmful transboundary pollution from the rules governing the activities of armed bands. See *contra* I. Brownlie (1973) *Int. Rel.* 240.

67. (1972) AJ 702; see C. Q. Christol (1980) *AJ* 346.
68. For example, the Bonn Agreement for Co-operation in dealing with the Pollution of the North Sea by Oil (entered into force 9 Aug. 1969): (1970) ILM 359; The Agreement between the United States and Germany on Co-operation in Environmental Matters: (1974) ILM 598; The Convention for the Protection of the Mediterranean Sea against Pollution (entered into force 12 Feb. 1978): (1976) ILM 290.
69. The London Convention on the Prevention of Marine Pollution by Dumping of Wastes and Other Matter (entered into force 30 Aug. 1975), Article X: (1972) ILM 1294 and (1979) ILM 516; The Convention for the Protection of the Mediterranean Sea against Pollution (entered into force 12 Feb. 1978), Article XII: (1976) ILM 290; The Convention on the Protection of the Marine Environment of the Baltic Sea (entered into force 3 May 1980), Article 17: (1974) ILM 544. Article 235 of the UN Convention on the Law of the Sea (not yet in force): (1982) ILM 1261, definitely refers to international responsibility for activities which violate Part XII of the Convention which deals with the Protection and Preservation of the Marine Environment. This says, 'States are responsible for the fulfilment of their international obligations concerning the protection and preservation of the marine environment. They shall be liable in accordance with the international law'.

However, it is recognized that the law on this area is still not fully developed. Paragraph 3 adds, 'With the objective of assuring prompt and adequate compensation in respect of all damage caused by pollution of the marine environment, States shall co-operate in the implementation of existing international law and the further development of international law relating to responsibility and liability for the assessment of and compensation for damage and the settlement of related disputes, as well as, where appropriate, development of criteria and procedures for payment of adequate compensation such as compulsory insurance or compensation funds.' See also the Final Act of the Conference of Plenipotentiaries on the Protection and Development of the Marine Environment of the Wider Caribbean Region, Article 14: (1983) ILM 22; Convention for Co-operation in the Protection and Development of the Marine and Coastal Environment of the West and Central African Region, Article 15: (1981) ILM 729; Agreement governing the Activities of States on the Moon and other Celestial Bodies, Articles 14 and 18: (1979) ILM 1434.

70. Two of the treaties on nuclear activities expressly reserve the possibility of international responsibility: The 1963 Vienna Convention on Civil Liability for Nuclear Damage (entered into force 12 Nov. 1977), Article XVIII: (1962–3) ILM 727, and the 1960 Paris Convention on Third Party Liability in the Field of Nuclear Energy, Annex II, (entered into force in 1968): (1961) AJ 1082. The International Convention relating to Intervention on the High Seas in Cases of Oil Pollution Casualties (entered into force 6 May 1975), Article VII: (1970) ILM 25 also leaves open the possibility of an international claim. The 1973 Protocol relating to Intervention on the High Seas in Cases of Marine Pollution by Substances other than Oil (entered into force 30 Mar. 1983): (1974) ILM 605 incorporates this Article by reference. Certain of the bilateral agreements made by the United States to govern the entry of the Nuclear Ship Savannah into foreign ports provide for settlement of claims under international law as an alternative to the main remedy under municipal law. Thus in the agreements with Greece, Norway, and Spain (TIAS 5099, 5576, 5626 respectively) it is provided that the states parties may negotiate a lump sum settlement, each state claiming on behalf of its own nationals and resident aliens. 'In such negotiations, the question of liability and the amount of damage shall be subject to the mutual agreement of the two governments in accordance with the general principles of international law.' Also in the agreement between the United States and Ireland (TIAS 5651), the Government of Ireland expressly reserves the right under international law to settle the claims under generally accepted principles of law and equity. Finally, a few of the many treaties concluded to deal with non-navigational uses of international waterways provide, with little elaboration, for the payment of compensation for damage caused where this is required by international law. See W. M. Bush, 'Compensation and the Utilization of International Rivers and Lakes' (1978), Cambridge (unpublished dissertation), at 164.

71. ILC Yearbooks from 1980.

72. See, for example, I. Brownlie, *System of the Law of Nations: State Responsibility* (1983) 49–50.
73. (1982) ILC Yearbook, i. 224.
74.

SECTION 4

'1. If any activity does give rise to loss or injury, and the rights and obligations of the acting and affected States under the present articles in respect of any such loss or injury have not been specified in an agreement between those States, those rights and obligations shall be determined in accordance with the provisions of this section. The States concerned shall negotiate in good faith to achieve this purpose.

2. Reparation shall be made by the acting State to the affected State in respect of any such loss or injury, unless it is established that the making of reparation for a loss or injury of that kind or character is not in accordance with the shared expectations of those States.

3. The reparation due to the affected State under the preceding article shall be ascertained in accordance with the shared expectations of the States concerned and the principles set out in section 5; and account shall be taken of the reasonableness of the conduct of the parties, having regard to the record of any exchanges or negotiations between them and to the remedial measures taken by the acting State to safeguard the interests of the affected State. Account may also be taken of any relevant factor including those set out in section 6, and guidance may be obtained by reference to any of the matters set out in section 7.

4. In the two preceding articles, 'shared expectations' include shared expectations which:

(*a*) have been expressed in correspondence or other exchanges between the States concerned or, insofar as there are no such expressions,
(*b*) can be implied from common legislative or other standards or patterns of conduct normally observed by the States concerned, or in any regional or other grouping to which they both belong, or in the international community.

SECTION 5

1. The aim and purpose of the present articles is to ensure to acting States as much freedom of choice in relation to activities within their territory or control as is compatible with adequate protection for the interests of affected States.

2. Adequate protection requires measures of prevention that as far as possible avoid a risk of loss or injury and, insofar as that is not possible, measures of reparation; but the standards of adequate protection should be determined with due regard to the importance of the activity and its economic viability.

3. Insofar as may be consistent with the preceding articles, an innocent victim should not be left to bear his loss or injury; the costs of adequate protection should be distributed with due regard to the distribution of the benefits of the activity; and standards of protection should take into account the

means at the disposal of the acting State and the standards applied in the affected State and in regional and international practice.

4. To the extent that an acting State has not made available to an affected State information that is more accessible to the acting State concerning the nature and effects of an activity, and the means of verifying and assessing that information, the affected State shall be allowed a liberal recourse to inferences of fact and circumstantial evidence in order to establish whether the activity does or may give rise to loss or injury.

SECTION 6

Factors which may be relevant to a balancing of interests include:

1. The degree of probability of loss or injury (i.e. how likely is it to happen?);

2. The seriousness of loss or injury (i.e. an assessment of quantum and degree of severity in terms of the consequences);

3. The probable cumulative effect of losses or injuries of the kind in question—in terms of conditions of life and security of the affected State, and more generally—if reliance is placed upon measures to ensure the provision of reparation rather than prevention (i.e. the acceptable mix between prevention and reparation);

4. The existence of means to prevent loss or injury, having regard to the highest known state of the art of carrying on the activity;

5. The feasibility of carrying on the activity by alternative means or in alternative places;

6. The importance of the activity to the acting State (i.e. how necessary is it to continue or undertake the activity, taking account of economic, social, security or other interests?);

7. The economic viability of the activity considered in relation to the cost of possible means of protection;

8. The availability of alternative activities;

9. The physical and technical capacities of the acting State (considered, for example, in relation to its ability to take measures of prevention or make reparation or to undertake alternative activities);

10. The way in which existing standards of protection compare with:
    (*a*) the standards applied by the affected State; and
    (*b*) the standards applied in regional and international practice;

11. The extent to which the acting State:
    (*a*) has effective control over the activity; and
    (*b*) obtains a real benefit from the activity;

12. The extent to which the affected State shares in the benefits of the activity;

13. The extent to which the adverse effects arise from or affect the use of a shared resource;

14. The extent to which the affected State is prepared to contribute to the cost of preventing or making reparation for loss or injury, or of maximizing its benefits from the activity;

15. The extent to which the interests of:

(*a*) the affected State; and
(*b*) the acting State

are compatible with the interests of the general community;

16. The extent to which assistance to the acting State is available from third States or from international organizations;

17. The applicability of relevant principles and rules of international law.

SECTION 7

Matters which may be relevant in negotiations concerning prevention and reparation include:

I Fact-finding and prevention

1. The identification of adverse effects and of material and non-material loss or injury to which they may give rise;
2. The establishment of procedural means for managing the activity and monitoring its effects;
3. The establishment of requirements concerning the structure and operation of the activity;
4. The taking of measures to assist the affected State in minimizing loss or injury.

II Compensation as a means of reparation

1. A decision as to where primary and residual liability should lie, and whether the liability of some actors should be channelled through others;
2. A decision as to whether liability should be unlimited or limited;
3. The choice of a forum in which to determine the existence of liability and the amounts of compensation payable;
4. The establishment of procedures for the presentation of claims;
5. The identification of compensable loss or injury;
6. The test of the measure of compensation for loss or injury;
7. The establishment of forms and modalities for the payment of compensation awarded;
8. Consideration of the circumstances which might increase or diminish liability or provide an exoneration from it.

III Authorities competent to make decisions concerning fact-finding, prevention and compensation.

At different phases of the negotiations of [sic] the States concerned may find it helpful to place in the hands of their national authorities or courts, international organizations or specially constituted commissions, the responsibility for making recommendations or taking decisions as to the matters referred to in I and II.'

75. See, for example, Riphagen at (1982) *ILC Yearbook*, i. 242–3 and Sinclair, ibid., 277.
76. Yankov, ibid., 274.
77. Various writers have suggested that economic efficiency should be the aim of international and national law on the environment. The lack of any helpful international arbitral precedents and the inadequacy of traditional doctrine in this area of the law has led writers to turn to economic theory for guidance as to how to deal with the problem of pollution. But the application of the theories of R. H. Coase (see his seminal work in (1958–61) 3 *Journal of Law and Economics* 1) and his more extreme follower R. Posner (*Economic Analysis of Law* (1972)) to this problem involves difficulties and shows clearly some of the weaknesses of the theories.

To obtain an optimal allocation of resources in this area demands that any activity whose benefit is greater than the costs it causes should be allowed to continue. Whatever mechanisms are employed to control polluting activities should be designed to secure this end. This approach to the problem of pollution has been much criticized and on several different grounds.

First the theory is open to attack as inadequate in terms of economic theory. It has been convincingly argued that Coase and Posner's theory rests on assumptions not realized in fact; the market often fails to achieve an optimal allocation of resources and not only because of the existence of transaction costs. It is not obvious that in the event of market failure the best means to achieve an economically efficient solution is to mimic the market. (Much has been written on this topic. See, for example, A. M. Polinsky (1973–4) *Harvard LR* 1655; A. A. Leff (1974) *Virg. LR* 451; A. Randall (1974) *Natural Resources Journal* 35.) Also, it is well known that where injury is caused to an interest or resource not in anyone's ownership then the operation of the market will not lead to an efficient allocation of resources. Thus on the national level injury to the environment, and on the international level injuries to areas beyond national jurisdiction or to unprotected interests, are not included in the cost of the activity that causes these injuries. As the polluter does not have to pay for all these injuries the market does not operate efficiently, the polluter is not charged with the full costs of his enterprise. A more fundamental problem is that of evaluating any injury to the environment. Any assessment of the costs and benefits of a polluting activity demands a consideration of factors not normally or easily expressed in monetary terms.

Secondly, it may be argued that economic efficiency in the sense of an optimal allocation of resources should not be the overriding consideration in policy making. It ought to be subordinate to the requirements of justice. Or, more fundamentally, it could be argued that economic efficiency is not a value at all, that it is not a standard by which situations are assessed as good or bad. Because of the many uncertainties involved in this area the decision as to which method of pollution control should be employed—to leave it to the market, to try to mimic the market, to introduce regulations imposing liability or standard setting—is ultimately a question of faith. There are great difficulties involved in any attempt to decide which means of control would lead to economic efficiency, and if we abandon economic efficiency as the overriding goal the situation seems even more difficult. It was perhaps this desire for an apparently objective principle by which to assess the acceptability of a particular course of action that constituted the main attraction of economic efficiency as an aim. In fact in their treaties on polluting and ultra-hazardous activities states rely on a combination of these methods—the imposition of liability, prohibition, and standard setting.

The peculiar nature of the problems involved clearly makes it undesirable to rely on judicial remedies alone as a means of dealing with polluting and ultra-hazardous activities. Proof of causation and damage is likely to be difficult, as is any assessment of the extent of the damage. If the imposition of damages is to bring about an economically efficient solution and also to constitute an effective deterrent then it is necessary that the award should include all the costs involved including injury to the public good both on the national and international levels. An accurate calculation of the value to be given to public goods not usually assigned a monetary value is difficult, but if all costs are not included in damages and consistently calculated the deterrent effect will be weakened. The idea that the award of damages will deter, based partly on the theory that it is the aim of the polluter to maximize his profits, may not always be accurate. Sometimes outright prohibition may be necessary. In the area of polluting and ultra-hazardous activities the prevention of harm will often be more important to the victim than any subsequent award of damages.

H. Smets in *The Avoidance and Settlement of International Environmental Disputes* (1974) lists certain other weaknesses of damages as a remedy in this area. He discusses the problem of non-monetary loss, of inextensive loss, of slow procedure, heavy burdens of proof, and the desire of governments to make immediate compromises, to avoid the repetition of polluting activity rather than demand damages.

Bibliography

Abramovsky, A., 'Multilateral Conventions for the Suppression of Unlawful Seizure and Unlawful Interference with Aircraft' (1974) *Col. JTL* 381–405; (1975) *Col. JTL* 451–484.

Akehurst, M., *The Law Governing Employment in International Organizations* (Cambridge, 1967).

Alvarez de Eulate, M. B., 'La restitutio in integrum en la practica y en la jurisprudencia internationales' (1971–2) 29–32 *Revista de ciencia y técnica jurídica* 11.

Amerasinghe, C. F., and D. Bellinger, *Main Points in Decisions of the World Bank Administrative Tribunal* (Washington D. C., 1983).

Amin, S. H., 'Iran–United States Claims Settlement' (1983) *ICLQ* 750–6.

Audretsch, H. A. H., *Supervision in European Community Law* (Amsterdam, 1978).

The Avoidance and Settlement of International Environmental Disputes, Papers Presented at a Conference at Bellagio organized by the American Society of International Law (1974).

Baade, H. W., 'Indonesian Nationalization Measures before Foreign Courts—a Reply' (1960) *AJ* 801–35.

Baxter, R. R., 'Reflection on Codification in Light of the International Law of State Responsibility for Injury to Aliens' (1964–5) *Syracuse LR* 745–61.

Becker, G. L., 'A Short Cruise on the Good Ships TOVALOP AND CRISTAL' (1974) 5 *JMLC* 609–32.

Bissonnette, P. A., *La Satisfaction comme mode de réparation en droit international* (Geneva, 1952).

Blanpain, R. (ed.), *International Encyclopaedia for Labour Law and Industrial Relations* (Deventer, 1977–).

Bloomfield, L. M., and G. Fitzgerald, *Crimes against Internationally Protected Persons: Prevention and Punishment* (New York, 1975).

Bollecker-Stern, B., *Le Préjudice dans la théorie de la responsabilité internationale* (Paris, 1973).

Borchard, E. M., *The Diplomatic Protection of Citizens Abroad* (New York, 1928).

—— *Declaratory Judgments* (Cleveland, 1941).

Boulouis, J., 'La Jurisprudence de la Cour de Justice des Communautés Européennes relative aux relations extérieures des Communautés' (1978) 2 *HR* 335–94.

Bowett, D. W., 'Libyan Nationalisation of American Oil Companies Assets' (1978) *CLJ* 5–8.

—— 'Contemporary Developments in Legal Techniques in the Settlement of Disputes' (1983) 2 *HR* 169–236.

Brierly, J. L., 'The Theory of Implied State Complicity in International Claims' (1928) *BYBIL* 42–9.

Brownlie, I., *International Law and the Use of Force by States* (Oxford, 1963).

—— *Principles of Public International Law* (3rd edn., Oxford, 1979).
—— *System of the Law of Nations: State Responsibility*, Part I (Oxford, 1983).
—— 'The Justiciability of Disputes and Issues in International Relations' (1967) *BYBIL* 123–43.
—— 'International Customary Rules of Environmental Protection' (1973) *Int. Rel.* 240.
Buergenthal, T. 'The Inter-American Court of Human Rights' (1982) *AJ* 231–45.
—— 'The Advisory Practice of the Inter-American Human Rights Court' (1985) *AJ* 1–27.
—— R. Norris, D. Shelton, *Protecting Human Rights in the Americas* (Kehl, 1982).
Busch, J.-D., 'Compensation Awards to International Officials in the Jurisdiction of the UN and ILO Administrative Tribunals' 25 *GYBIL* 433–64.
Bush, W. M., 'Compensation and the Utilization of International Rivers and Lakes' (Cambridge, unpublished dissertation, 1978).
Cabranes, J. A., 'Limitations of Liability in International Air Law' (1966) *ICLQ* 660–89.
Caflisch, L., 'L'Avenir de l'arbitrage intérétatique' (1979) *AFDI* 1–45.
Cahier, P., 'Les Caractéristiques de la nullité en droit international' (1972) *RGDIP* 645–91.
Cambridge Essays in International Law: Essays in Honour of Lord McNair (London, 1965).
Carlston, K. S., *The Process of International Arbitration* (New York, 1946).
Cheng, Bin, *General Principles of Law as Applied by International Courts and Tribunals* (London, 1953).
—— 'The Rationale of Compensation for Expropriation' (1959) *Transactions of the Grotius Society* 267–310.
Christol, C. Q., 'International Liability for Damage Caused by Space Objects' (1980) *AJ* 346–71.
Coase, R. H., 'The Problem of Social Cost' (1958–61) 3 *Journal of Law and Economics* 1–44.
Collins, L., *European Community Law in the United Kingdom* (London, 1984).
Colombos, C. J., *A Treatise on the Law of Prize* (3rd edn. London, 1949).
Darby, W. E., *International Tribunals* (London, 1899; 4th edn. 1904).
David Davies Memorial Institute of International Studies, *International Disputes: The Legal Aspects* (London, 1972).
Delaume, G., 'State Contracts and Transnational Arbitration' (1981) *AJ* 784–819.
De lege pactorum, Essays in Honour of R. R. Wilson (1970).
Dicey, A. V., and J. H. C. Morris, *The Conflict of Laws* (10th edn., London, 1980).
Drucker, A., 'Compensation for Nationalised Property' (1955) *AJ* 477–86.
—— 'Restitution in International Law' (1966) *ICLQ* 263–9.
Dubais, B. A., 'The 1976 London Convention on Civil Liability for Oil Pollution Damage from Offshore Operations' (1977) 9 *JMLC* 61–77.
Dugard, J., 'The Nuclear Tests Cases and the South West Africa Cases—Some Realism about International Judicial Decisions' (1975–6) *Virg. JIL* 463–504.

Dumbauld, E., *Interim Measures of Protection in International Controversies* (The Hague, 1932).
Dunn, F. S., *The Protection of Nationals* (Baltimore, 1932).
Dupuy, P. M., 'Observations sur le crime international de l'état' (1980) *RGDIP* 449–86.
Eagleton, C., 'Measure of Damages in International Law' (1929–30) *Yale LJ* 52–75.
Elkind, J. B., *Interim Protection, a Functional Approach* (The Hague, 1981).
Falk, R. A., and S. H. Mendlovitz (eds.), *The Strategy of World Order* (New York, 1966).
Fatouros, A. A., *Government Guarantees to Foreign Investors* (New York, 1962).
—— 'International Law and the Internationalized Contract' (1980) *AJ* 134–41.
Fawcett, J. E. S., and R. Higgins (eds.), *International Organization* (London, 1974).
Feller, A. H., *The Mexican Claims Commissions* (New York, 1935).
Fischer-Williams, J., 'International Law and Property of Aliens' (1928) *BYBIL* 1–30.
Fitzmaurice, G. G., 'The Case of the I'm Alone' (1936) *BYBIL* 82–111.
—— 'The Juridicial Clauses of the Peace Treaties' (1948) 2 *HR* 259–364.
Gainen, L. F., 'The Application of Article 50 of the European Convention on Human Rights and Fundamental Freedoms' (1974) *NYJILP* 177–89.
Gann, P. B., 'Compensation Standard for Expropriation' (1985) 23 *Col. JTL* 615–53.
Ganshof van der Meersch, W. J. (ed.), *Les Novelles—droit des Communautés Européennes* (Brussels, 1969).
García-Amador, F. V., L. B. Sohn, and R. R. Baxter, *Recent Codification of the Law of State Responsibility for Injuries to Aliens* (Dobbs Ferry, NY, 1974).
Gilmour, D. R., 'The Enforcement of Community Law by the Commission in the Context of State Aids' (1981) *CML Rev.* 63–77.
Goldsworthy, P.J., 'Interim Measures of Protection in the International Court of Justice' (1974) *AJ* 258–77.
Goodrich, L. M., 'Advisory Opinions of the Permanent Court of International Justice' (1938) *AJ* 738–58.
Graefath, B., 'Responsibility and Damages Caused: Relationships between Responsibility and Damages' (1984) 2 *HR* 9–150.
Gray, C. D., 'Interim Measures of Protection in the European Court' (1979) *ELR* 80–102.
—— 'Remedies for Individuals under the European Convention on Human Rights' (1981) *Human Rights Review* 153–73.
—— 'Advisory Opinions and the European Court of Justice' (1983) ELR 24–39.
—— 'Is there an International Law of Remedies?' (1985) *BYBIL* 25.
Greenwood, C., 'State contracts in International Law—the Libyan Oil Arbitrations' (1982) *BYBIL* 27–82.
Gross, L., 'Limitations upon the Judicial Function' (1964) *AJ* 415–31.
Guggenheim, P., *Les Mesures provisoires de procédure internationale et leur influence sur le développement du droit des gens* (Paris, 1931).

Haesler, T., *The Exhaustion of Local Remedies in the Case Law of International Courts and Tribunals* (London, 1968).

Hardy, M., 'Opinion 1/76 of the Court of Justice' (1977) *CML Rev.* 561–600.

Hart, H. L. A., and T. Honoré, *Causation in the Law* (2nd edn., Oxford, 1985).

Hartley, T. C., 'Interim Measures against France in the Lamb War' (1980) *ELR* 363–6.

Hauriou, A., 'Les Dommages indirects dans les arbitrages internationaux' (1924) *RGDIP* 203–31.

Higgins, R., 'The Place of International Law in the Settlement of Disputes by the Security Council' (1970) *AJ* 1–18.

—— 'The Execution of Decisions of Organs under the European Convention on Human Rights' (1978) *Rev. hell. DI* 1.

Hoffman, K. B., 'State Responsibility in International Law and Transboundary Pollution Injuries' (1976) *ICLQ* 509–42.

Jenks, C. W., *The Proper Law of International Organizations* (London, 1962).

—— *The Prospects of International Adjudication* (London, 1964).

Jennings, R. Y., 'State Contracts in International Law' (1961) *BYBIL* 156–82.

—— 'General Course on Principles of Public International Law' (1967) 2 *HR* 323–606.

Jessup, P. C., *Transnational Law* (New Haven, 1956).

—— 'Responsibility of States for Injuries to Individuals' (1946) *Col. LR* 903–28.

Katz, M., *The Relevance of International Adjudication* (Cambridge, Mass., 1968).

Kean, A., 'Strict Liability, Unbreakable Limits and the Warsaw Convention' (1970) *ICLQ* 124–7.

Keith, K. J., *The Extent of the Advisory Jurisdiction of the International Court of Justice* (Leyden, 1971).

Koh, B. C., *The United Nations Administrative Tribunal* (Baton Rouge, 1966).

La Fontaine, H., *Pasicrisie internationale: histoire documentaire des arbitrages internationaux* (Berne, 1902).

Lauterpacht, H., *Private Law Sources and Analogies of International Law* (London, 1927).

—— *The Development of International Law by the International Court* (London, 1958).

Leff, A. A., 'Economic Analysis of Law: Some Realism about Nominalism' (1974) *Virg. LR* 451–92.

Lester, A. P., 'River Pollution in International Law' (1963) *AJ* 828–53.

Lew, J. D. M., *Applicable Law in International Commercial Arbitration* (Dobbs Ferry, NY, 1978).

Lillich, R. B., *International Claims: Their Adjudication by National Commissions* (Syracuse, 1962).

—— *International Claims: Post War British Practice* (Syracuse, 1967).

—— (ed.), *The Valuation of Nationalized Property in International Law* (Charlottesville, 1972–5).

—— (ed.), *International Law of State Responsibility for Injury to Aliens* (Charlottesville, 1983).

—— 'The Rigidity of Barcelona' (1971) *AJ* 522–32.

—— 'Iran–United States Claims Tribunal' (1982) *ASIL* 5–9.

—— and G. A. Christenson, *International Claims: Their Preparation and Presentation* (Syracuse, 1962).

—— and B. H. Weston, *International Claims: Their Settlement by Lump Sum Agreements* (Charlottesville, 1975).

—— *International Claims: Contemporary European Practice* (Charlottesville, 1982).

McGregor, H., *McGregor on Damages* (14th edn. London, 1980).

McNair, A., 'The General Principles of Law Recognized by Civilized Nations' (1957) *BYBIL* 1–19.

McWhinney, E., *The Illegal Diversion of Aircraft and International Law* (Leyden, 1975).

Mankiewicz, R. H., 'The Judicial Diversification of Uniform Private Law Conventions' (1972) *ICLQ* 718–57.

Mann, F. A., *The Legal Aspect of Money* (4th edn., Oxford, 1982).

—— 'The Law Governing State Contracts' (1944) *BYBIL* 11–33.

—— 'Reflections on a Commercial Law of Nations' (1957) *BYBIL* 20–51.

—— 'Money in Public International Law' (1959) 1 *HR* 7–127.

—— 'The Proper Law of Contracts Concluded by International Persons' (1959) *BYBIL* 34–57.

—— 'State Contracts and State Responsibility' (1960) *AJ* 572–91.

—— 'The Theoretical Approach towards the Law Governing Contracts between States and Private Persons' (1975) *Rev. belge DI* 562–94.

—— 'The Consequences of an International Wrong in International and Municipal Law' (1976–7) *BYBIL* 1–65.

—— 'The Aminoil Arbitration' (1983) *BYBIL* 213–21.

Mathy, D., 'Un Juge ad hoc en procédure consultative devant la cour internationale de justice' (1976) *Rev. belge DI* 528–54.

Max Planck Institute for Comparative Public and International Law, *The Judicial Settlement of International Disputes* (Berlin, 1974).

Mehren, R. B. von, and P. N. Kourides, 'International Arbitrations between States and Foreign Private Parties: The Libyan Nationalization Cases' (1981) *AJ* 476–552.

Mendelson, M. H., 'Interim Measures of Protection in Cases of Contested Jurisdiction' (1972–3) *BYBIL* 259–322.

—— 'Compensation for Expropriation: The Case Law' (1985) *AJ* 414–19.

Meron, T., 'The Insurer and the Insured under International Law' (1974) *AJ* 628–47.

—— 'The New Administrative Tribunal of the World Bank' (1981) 14 *NYJILP* 1–27.

Merrills, J. G., 'Interim Measures of Protection and the Substantive Jurisdiction of the International Court' (1977) *CLJ* 86–109.

Morgenstern, F., 'Legality in International Organisations' (1976–7) *BYBIL* 241–58.

Nielsen, F. K. (ed.), *International Law Applied to Reclamations* (Princeton, 1941).

Nishimura, K., 'On Decisions of the US–Japanese, the Anglo-Japanese and the Netherlands–Japanese Property Commissions' (1962) *Jap. AIL* 39–62.

Northedge, F. S., and M. D. Donelan, *International Disputes: The Political Aspects* (London, 1971).

Nussbaum, A., *Money in the Law, National and International* (Brooklyn, 1950).

Ogus, A. I., *The Law of Damages* (London, 1973).

Osieke, E., 'Ultra Vires Acts in International Organizations—the Experience of the International Labour Organization' (1976–7) *BYBIL* 259–80.

Parry, C., *The Sources and Evidences of International Law* (Manchester, 1965).

—— 'Some Considerations upon the Protection of Individuals in International Law' (1956) 2 *HR* 653–725.

Pazarci, H., 'La Responsabilité internationale des états à raison des contrats conclus entre états et personnes privées étrangères' (1975) *RGDIP* 354–421.

Personnaz, J., *La Réparation du préjudice en droit international public* (Paris, 1939).

Pescatore, P., 'Les Communautés et le droit de la responsabilité internationale' (1961) 2 *HR* 1–242.

Polinsky, A. M., 'Economic Analysis as a Potentially Defective Product' (1973–4) *Harvard LR* 1655–81.

Pomerance, M., *The Advisory Function of the International Court in the League and UN Eras* (Baltimore, 1973).

—— 'The Admission of Judges Ad Hoc in Advisory Proceedings' (1973) *AJ* 446–64.

Posner, R., *Economic Analysis of Law* (2nd edn., Boston, 1972).

Pratap, D., *The Advisory Jurisdiction of the International Court of Justice* (Oxford, 1972).

Przetacznik, F., 'La Responsabilité internationale de l'état à raison des préjudices de caractère moral et politique causés à un autre état' (1974) *RGDIP* 919–74.

Rabel, E., *The Conflict of Laws: A Comparative Study* (2nd edn., Ann Arbor, 1958–64).

Ralston, J. H., *The Law and Procedure of International Tribunals* (Stanford University, 1926).

—— *International Arbitration from Athens to Locarno* (Stanford University, 1929).

Rambaud, P., 'Un Arbitrage pétrolier: la sentence Liamco' (1980) *AFDI* 274–92.

Randall, A., 'Coasian Externality Theory in a Policy Context' (1974) *National Resources Journal* 35–54.

Randolph, L. L., *Third Party Settlement of Disputes in Theory and Practice* (New York, 1973).

Raymond, J., 'A Contribution to the Interpretation of Article 13 of the European Convention on Human Rights' (1980–1) *Human Rights Review* 161–75.

Re, E. D., 'Domestic Adjudication and Lump Sum Settlement as an Enforcement Technique' (1964) *ASIL* 39–48.

Reisman, W. M., *Nullity and Revision* (New Haven, 1971).

Reitzer, L., *La Réparation comme conséquence de l'acte illicite en droit international* (Liège, 1938).

Richemont, J. de, *Integration of Community Law within the Legal Systems of the Member States* (Paris, 1978).
Ritter, J. P., 'Subrogation de l'assureur et protection diplomatique' (1961) *RGDIP* 765–802.
—— 'L'Affaire des essais nucléaires et la notion de jugement déclaratoire' (1975) *AFDI* 278–93.
Robertson, A. H., *Human Rights in Europe* (2nd edn., Manchester, 1977).
Robinson, D.R., 'Recent Developments at the Iran–United States Claims Tribunal' (1983) *Int. Lawyer* 661–7.
Rosenne, S., 'On the Non-use of the Advisory Competence of the International Court of Justice' (1963) *BYBIL* 1–53.
Rozakis, C. L., 'Terrorism and Internationally Protected Persons in the Light of the ILC's Draft Articles' (1974) *ICLQ* 32–72.
Rubin, A. P., 'Pollution by Analogy—the Trail Smelter Arbitration' (1970–1) *Oregon LR* 259–82.
Rüster, B., and B. Simma (eds.), *International Protection of the Environment* (New York, 1975).
Ryans, J. K., and J. C. Baker, 'The International Centre for Settlement of Investment Disputes' (1976) *J World TL* 65–9.
Salvioli, G., 'La Responsabilité des états et la fixation des dommages—intérêts par les tribunaux internationaux' (1929) 3 *HR* 235–89.
Sanders, P. (ed.), *International Arbitration: Liber Amicorum for Martin Domke* (The Hague, 1967).
Sandifer, D. V., *Evidence before International Tribunals* (rev. edn., Charlottesville, 1975).
Schachter, O., 'The Quasi-judicial Role of the Security Council and the General Assembly' (1964) *AJ* 960–5.
Schermers, H. G., *International Institutional Law* (Alphen aan den Rijn, 1980).
—— *Judicial Protection in the European Communities* (3rd edn., Deventer, 1983).
Schlesinger, R. B., 'Research on the General Principles of Law Recognized by Civilized Nations' (1957) *AJ* 734–53.
Schreuer, C. C., *Decisions of International Institutions before Domestic Courts* (London, 1981).
—— 'Unjustified Enrichment in International Law' (1974) *AJCL* 281–301.
Schwarzenberger, G., 'The Problem of an International Criminal Law' (1950) *CLP* 263–96.
Schwebel, S. M. (ed.), *The Effectiveness of International Decisions* (Leyden, 1971).
Seidl-Hohenveldern, I., *The Austrian–German Arbitral Tribunal* (Syracuse, 1972).
Selby, J. M., and D. P. Stewart, 'Practical Aspects of Arbitrating Claims before the Iran–United States Claims Tribunal' (1984) *Int. Lawyer* 211–44.
Simmonds, K. R., 'The Evolution of the External Relations Law of the European Economic Community' (1979) *ICLQ* 644–68.
Simpson, J. L., and H. Fox, *International Arbitration* (London, 1959).
Smit, H., and P. E. Herzog, *The Law of the EEC* (New York, 1976).
Stein, T. L., 'Jurisprudence and Jurists' Prudence: The Iranian Forum Clause ' (1984) *AJ* 1–52.

Street, H., *Principles of the Law of Damages* (London, 1962).
Stuyt, A. M., *A Survey of International Arbitrations* (Leiden, 1972).
Subilia, J., 'L'Allocation d'intérêts dans la jurisprudence internationale' (Thesis, Lausanne, 1972).
Summers, L. M., and A. Fraleigh, 'The United States–Japanese Property Commission' (1962) *AJ* 407–32.
Surrey, W. S., 'Problems of the Italian Peace Treaty: Analysis of Claims Provisions and Descriptions of Enforcement' (1951) *Law and Contemporary Problems* 435–47.
Thomas, C. S., and M. J. Kirby, 'The Convention for the Suppression of Unlawful Acts against the Safety of Civil Aviation' (1973) *ICLQ* 163–72.
Tod, M. N., *International Arbitration Amongst the Greeks* (Oxford, 1913).
Trindade, A. A. C., *The Application of the Rule of Exhaustion of Local Remedies in International Law* (Cambridge, 1983).
Tschanz, P.-Y., 'Contributions of the Aminoil Award to the Law of State Contracts' (1984) *Int. Lawyer* 245–81.
Valentine, D. G., *The Court of Justice of the European Communities* (London, 1965).
Varma, A., 'Petroleum Concessions in International Arbitrations' (1979–80) *Col. JTL* 259–88.
Vasarhelyi, I., *Restitution in International Law* (Budapest, 1964).
Venkata Raman, K., (ed.), *Dispute Settlement through the United Nations* (Dobbs Ferry, NY, 1977).
Verzijl, J. H. W., *International Law in Historical Perspective* (Leyden, 1968).
Visscher, C. de, *Theory and Reality in Public International Law* (1957: trans. P. E. Corbett, Princeton, 1968).
Vuyst, B. M. de, *Statutes and Rules of Procedure of International Administrative Tribunals* (Washington DC, 1981).
—— 'The World Bank Administrative Tribunal' (1981–2) *Rev. belge DI* 81–94.
Wainwright, R., 'Article 186 EEC: Interim Measures against Member States' (1977) *ELR* 349–58.
Wallington, P., 'Injunctions and the Right to Demonstrate' (1976) *CLJ* 82–111.
Walters, F. P., *A History of the League of Nations* (London, 1952).
Weston, B. H., *International Claims: Post War French Practice* (Syracuse, 1971).
Wetter, J. G. and S. M. Schwebel, 'Some Little-known Cases on Concessions' (1964) *BYBIL* 183–232.
White, G. M., *Nationalisation of Foreign Property* (London, 1961).
—— *The Use of Experts by International Tribunals* (Syracuse, 1965).
White, R. C. A., 'Expropriation of the Libyan Oil Concessions—Two Conflicting International Arbitrations' (1981) *ICLQ* 1–19.
Whiteman, M., *Damages in International Law* (Washington, 1937–43).
Wilson, R. R., 'Some Aspects of the Jurisprudence of National Claims Commissions' (1942) *AJ* 56–76.
Wolf, K., 'Kostenrecht und Kostenpraxis des Gerichtshofs der Europäischen Gemeinschaften' (1976) *Europarecht* 7–31.
Wood, M. C., 'The Convention on the Prevention and Punishment of Crimes

against Internationally Protected Persons including Diplomatic Agents' (1974) *ICLQ* 791–817.

Wright, Q., 'The Scope of International Criminal Law: A Conceptual Framework' (1974–5) *Virg. JIL* 561–77.

Wyatt, D., 'New Legal Order, or Old?' (1982) *ELR* 147–66.

Young, P. W., *Declaratory Orders* (Sydney, 1975).

Zamir, I., *The Declaratory Judgment* (London, 1962).

Index